DIGITAL APPLICATIONS FOR CULTURAL AND HERITAGE INSTITUTIONS

Digital Applications for Cultural and Heritage Institutions

Edited by
JAMES HEMSLEY, VITO CAPPELLINI AND GERD STANKE

Routledge
Taylor & Francis Group
LONDON AND NEW YORK

First published 2005 by Ashgate Publishing

Published 2016 by Routledge
2 Park Square, Milton Park, Abingdon, Oxon OX14 4RN
711 Third Avenue, New York, NY 10017, USA

Routledge is an imprint of the Taylor & Francis Group, an informa business

British Library Cataloguing in Publication Data
Digital applications for cultural and heritage institutions
    1. Libraries - Data processing - Congresses 2. Museums - Data
    processing - Congresses 3. Museums - Collection management -
    Technological innovations - Congresses 4. Digital libraries
    - Congresses
    I. Hemsley, James
    025'.00285

Library of Congress Cataloging-in-Publication Data
Digital applications for cultural and heritage institutions / edited by James Hemsley.
    p. cm.
    ISBN 0-7546-3359-4
    1. Imaging systems. 2. Digital preservation. 3. Cultural property--Protection.
    4. Information storage and retrieval systems. I. Hemsley, James.

TK8315.D54 2005
306.4'6--dc22

2004051075

ISBN 9780754633594 (hbk)

Contents

Part 3: Recreating and Preserving the Past

Part 4: Digital Archiving

Part 5: Design, Retrieval and Protection

Part 8: Conclusions and Future Trends

List of Figures

List of Editors and Contributors

Editors

James Hemsley   jrhemsley@hotmail.com
EVA Conferences International   www.eva-conferences.com

Vito Cappellini   cappellini@det.unifi.it
University of Florence

Gerd Stanke   stanke@gfai.de
GFaI Gesellschaft zur Förderung angewandter Informatik e.V./Society for the Promotion of Applied Computer Science, Berlin

Strategic Developments

Andrea M. Mulrenin   andrea.mulrenin@salzburgresearch.at
Salzburg Research Forschungsgesellschaft, Austria

J. Taylor   john.taylor@nrc.ca
J.-A. Beraldin
G. Godin
R. Baribeau
L. Cournoyer
P. Boulanger
M. Rioux
J. Domey
National Research Council of Canada

Nadezda V. Brakker   lku@artinfo.ru
Leonid A. Kujbyshev   leonid@evarussia.ru
Centre on the Problems of Informatisation in the Sphere of Culture (Centre PIC),
Moscow

Cooperative Projects

Nuccia Negroni Catacchio   negroni@cilea.it
Dipartimento di Scienze dell'Antichità, sezione di Archeologia, Università degli
Studi di Milano

Laura Guidetti   guidetti@mail.cilea.it
Centro Studi di Preistoria e Archeologia, Milano

Giovanni Meloni   meloni@cilea.it
Maurizio Camnasio   camnasio@cilea.it
Consorzio Interuniversitario Lombardo per la Elaborazione Automatica, Segrate

Anne Griepentrog   *Care of*: geissler@gfai.de
GFaI (Gesellschaft zur Förderung angewandter Informatik e.V/Society for the Promotion of Applied Computer Science, Berlin

Alfred Iwainsky   iwainsky@iief.de
Jan Jordan
IIEF (Institute of Informatics in Design and Manufacturing), Berlin

Romana Krizova   romana@crossczech.cz
Cross Czech, Czech Republic

Recreating and Preserving the Past

Falk Krebs   f.krebs@gestaltung.fh-wiesbaden.de
Edgar Brück   e.brueck@gestaltung.fh-weisbaden.de
Fachhochschule Wiesbaden, Department of Interior Design, University of Applied Sciences

Jana Visnovcova   jana@geod.baug.ethz.ch
Armin Gruen   agruen@geod.baug.ethz.ch
Li Zhang   zhangl@geod.baug.ethz.ch
Institute of Geodesy and Photogrammetry, Swiss Federal Institute of Technology, Zurich

Edvins Snore   edvins@ri.lv
RIDemo, Latvia

Susan Hazan   shazan@imj.org.il
The Israel Museum, Jerusalem

Adam Lowe   alowe@permaprint.demon.co.uk

Digital Archiving

Rudolf Gschwind   rudolf.gschwind@unibas.ch
Lukas Rosenthaler
Roger Schnider
Department of Scientific Photography, Basel University, Switzerland

Franziska Frey
Image Permanence Institute, Rochester NY, USA

Jeanette Frey
Swiss Archive for Monument Conservation, Bern, Switzerland

Wolfgang Mueller   wm@cmb.at
CMB Informationslogistik GmbH, Vienna

Maria Luisa Polichetti   *Care of*: cappellini@det.unifi.it
ICCD Central Institute for Catalogue and Documentation/Instituto Centrale Per Il
    Catalogo e La Documentazione

Design, Retrieval and Protection

Ben Rubinstein   benr@cogapp.com
Cognitive Applications Ltd, Brighton, UK

Holly Witchey   witchey@cma-oh.org
Cleveland Museum of Art

Sigrid Ruby
Ute Verstegen   ute.verstegen@uni-koeln.de
Kunsthistorisches Institut der Universität zu Köln/Institute of Art History, Cologne
    University

Phil Carlisle   philip.carlisle@rchme.co.uk
National Monuments Record Centre, Swindon, UK

John Counsell   John.Counsell@uwe.ac.uk
Faculty of the Built Environment, University of the West of England

Dimitrios K. Tsolis   dkt@hpclab.ceid.upatras.gr
George K. Tsolis   gkt@hpclab.ceid.upatras.gr
Emmanouil G. Karatzas   ekaratzas@hpclab.ceid.upatras.gr
Dimitrios A. Koutsomitropoulos   kotsomit@hpclab.ceid.upatras.gr
Theodore S. Papatheodorou   tsp@hpclab.ceid.upatras.gr
Department of Computer Engineering and Informatics, University of Patras, Greece.

Jean Barda   jean.barda@wanadoo.fr
Netimage, France
Claude Rollin   claude.rollin@sacd.fr
SADC, France

Special Needs

Marcus Weisen marcus.weisen@resource.gov.uk
Learning and Access Team of Resource (Council for Museums, Archives and Libraries), London

Jonathan P. Bowen jonathan.bowen@sbu.ac.uk
London South Bank University

Beate Schulte bschulte@informatik.uni-bremen.de
Ulrike Peter upeter@informatik.uni-bremen.de
Forschungsgruppe Telekommunikation, Universität Bremen

Brigitte Bornemann-Jeske Bornemann-Jeske@t-online.de
BIT Design für Barrierefreie Informationstechnik GmbH, Hamburg

Jochen Scherer j.scherer@kommhelp.de
Kommhelp e.V., Berlin

Interactive Realities and Future Possibilities

Malcolm Ferris Malcolm.ferris@lineone.net
Independent Exhibition Developer and Curator and Leader of the Centre for Research in Electronic Art and Communication, The Faculty of Art and Design, University of Hertfordshire

Alessandro Mecocci alemecoc@tin.it
University of Siena and Etruria Innovazione S.C.p.A.

C. Ciavarella c.ciavarella@cnuce.cnr.it
F. Paternò f.paterno@cnuce.cnr.it
Human Computer Interface Group (HCI Group), CNUCE-CNR, Pisa, Italy

Stephen Brewster Stephen@dcs.gla.ac.uk
Department of Computing Science, University of Glasgow

Anton Nijholt anijholt@cs.utwente.nl
Department of Computer Science, University of Twente, Enschede, The Netherlands

List of Abbreviations and Glossary

This appendix provides information on many of the acronyms and sets of initials used by authors in the chapters, as well as websites for organizations where appropriate. We have used www.http://dictionary.com and http://www.acronymfinder.com/ and recommend their use for any other expressions used in the book.

3D	Three-dimensional
3DML	Three-dimensional mark-up language
3G	3rd generation wireless format: see www.3g-generation.com/ which is the website of UWCC, the Universal Wireless Communication Consortium
ABB	ArcheoBiblioBase, Archives of Russia: see http://www.iisg.nl/~abb/
ADIT	Association on Documentation and Information Technologies, Moscow, Russia (www.adit.ru)
ADSL	Asymmetric digital subscriber line
AIV	Audio, image and video extenders for IBM's BD2
ALM	Archives, libraries and museums
ALT	Alternative text. For browsers that cannot display images, forms or applets, this HTML attribute specifies alternate text: see http://www.w3.org/TR/REC-html40/struct/objects.html#adef-alt
AMR	Association of Museum specialists of Russia: see http://www.amr-museum.ru
Aquarelle	European Commission's Aquarelle project: see: http://vcg.isti.cnr.it/projects/miscellanea/aquarelle/aquarelleinfo.html
BITV	Barrier-free Information Technologies Act: see German language information on http://www.bmwi.de/Redaktion/Inhalte/Downloads/barrierefreie-webangebote,property=pdf.pdf
BMW	Bayerische Motoren Werke (Bavarian Motor Works) German auto manufacturer: see http://www.bmw.com
BRICKS	Building Resources for Integrated Cultural Knowledge Systems: an EC Integrated Project in the Sixth Framework Programme (or FP6)
CAD	Computer-aided design
CAVEAT	Controlling the Authenticity and Versioning of Electronic documents by Accessing a Trusted Third Party
CD-R	Compact disk – Recordable

CEC	Central European Countries
CEC	Commission of the European Communities
Centre PIC	Centre on the Problems of Informatisation in the Sphere of Culture: see www.cpic.ru/Index_e.htm
CHANCE	Cultural Heritage Access through Networked serviCes for Edutainment market: see: http://europa.eu.int/ information_society/programmes/eten/projects/ highlights/docs/H1-chance.html
CHArt	Computers and the History of Art: see http://www.chart.ac.uk/Society,UK
CHIMER	Children's Heritage: Interactive Models for Evolving Repositories (an EC project): see http://www.chimer.org/
CHIN	Canadian Heritage Information Network: see http://www.chin.gc.ca/
CIDOC (ICOM-CIDOC)	The International Committee for Documentation of the International Council of Museums (ICOM-CIDOC): At the time of preparation of this list, see http://www.willpowerinfo.myby.co.uk/cidoc/. A dedicated CIDOC page is planned
CIMEC	The Center for the Cultural Heritage of the Romanian Ministry of Culture: see http://www.cimec.ro/ sitemap_eng.htm
CIMI	Consortium for Interchange of Museum Information: see http://www.cimi.org/
CMS	Content management system
CNC	Computer numerically controlled
CNUCE-CNR	A research institute of the Italian National Research Council. It has been renamed the Scientific and Technology Institute of Information: see http://www.isti.cnr.it/
CSS	Cascading style sheets
CULTIVATE	An EC IST initiative: see http://www.cultivate-europe.org/
DAT	Digital audio tape
DB2	IBM database system
DDA	Disability Discrimination Act
DELOS	The DELOS Network of Excellence on Digital Libraries: see http://delos-noe.iei.pi.cnr.it/
DIG35	Working Group for Metadata Standards for Digital Images: see, for example, http://www.niso.org/ standards/resources/Z39_87_trial_use.pdf
Direct3D	An API (application programming interface) for manipulating and displaying three-dimensional objects. Developed by Microsoft, Direct3D provides programmers with a way to develop 3D programs that can utilize whatever graphics acceleration device is installed in the machine.

	Virtually all 3D accelerator cards for PCs support Direct3D.
DLL	Dynamic link library
DLT	Digital linear tape
DRC	Disability Rights Commission, UK: see http://www.drc-gb.org/
DRM	Digital rights management
DSL	Digital subscriber line
DVD	Digital versatile disc/digital video disc
EAD	Swiss Archive for Monuments: see http://www.kulturgueterschutz.ch/Websitealt/dt/ Publikationen/forumpdf/2002Schuepbach.pdf
EAW	European Archaeology Web: see http://www.xs4all.nl/~mkosian/links.html
EC	European Commission
ECC	Error correction code
ECMS	Electronic copyright management systems
EMN	European Museum Network – one of the pioneering first three EC IST projects in culture and technology
EPOCH	New EC Network of Excellence in the Sixth Framework Programme (2003–2006) on Intelligent Cultural Heritage Systems
ERPANET	Electronic Resource Preservation and Access Network: see http://www.erpanet.org/
ESPRIT	European Strategic Programme for Research and Development in Information Technology: see http://www.cordis.lu/esprit/home.html
ESRC-PACCIT	Economic and Social Research Council (http://www.esrc.ac.uk/) and People at the Centre of Communication and Information Technologies (http://www.paccit.gla.ac.uk/public/start.php)
EU	European Union
EVA	Electronic Imaging and the Visual Arts Conferences: see www.eva-conferences.com
Exabyte	A company and, by extension, a tape format for computer data backup and transfer. The tape is a data quality 8 mm video cassette recorder tape. Exabyte units can store between five and fourteen gigabytes of data per tape. Exabytes are usually attached to Unix workstations.
FINSIEL	The largest software company in Italy, a subsidiary of Telecom Italia: see http://www.finsiel.it/
FTP	File Transfer Protocol
G8	Group of Eight – the countries of Canada, France, Germany, Italy, Japan, Russia, the United Kingdom and the United States. Representatives from these countries meet to discuss economic concerns (G7 in the 1990s before Russia joined)

GIS	Geographic information system
GPRS	General packet radio service
GPS	Global positioning system
GSM	Global system for mobile communications (cellular phone technology)
GUI	Graphical user interface
HATII	Humanities Advanced Technology and Information Institute of the University of Glasgow: see http://www.hatii.arts.gla.ac.uk/
HDTV	High-definition television
HPCN	High performance computing and networking
HTML	Hyper text markup language (and a file extension)
IAMIS	Integrated Automated Museum Information System, a leading Russian system from the Alt-Soft Company, which is concerned with information and communication technologies: see www.evarussia.ru/eva2001/catalog_eng/prod_75.html
IBM	International Business Machines Corporation: see (www.ibm.com)
ICCD	Instituto Centrale Per Il Catalogo e La Documentazione (Central Institute for Catalogue and Documentation): see http://www.iccd.beniculturali.it/
ICHIM	International Cultural Heritage Informatics Meeting: see http://www.ichim.org
ICOM	International Council of Museums: see http://icom.museum/
ICOMOS	International Council On Monuments and Sites: see http://cipa.icomos.org/
ICT	Information and communication technologies
IMPACT	European Commission Technology R&D Programme in the 1990s
IPAQ	Handheld PCs from Hewlett Packard
IPMP	Intellectual property management and protection
IPR	Intellectual property rights
ISDN	Integrated services digital network
IST	Information society technologies
ISTAT	Italian (national) Statistics Institute: see http://www.istat.it/http:
JAWS	JAWS (Job Access With Speech) for Windows from Freedom Scientific (www.freedomscientific.com)
JPEG	Joint Photographic Experts Group (development group for compressed 24 bit colour image storage format; also a file extension): see http://www.jpeg.org/
JPSEC	JPEG 2000 Security
LDAP	Lightweight directory access protocol

LONGDESC	Long description – an HTML IMG (image) attribute
MA	Master of Arts (degree)
Mac	Personal computers manufactured by Apple Computer, Inc.
MAGDA	The Museums and Galleries Disability Association: see www.magda.org.uk
MB	Megabyte
MCN	Museum Computer Network: see http://www.mcn.edu/
MDA	Museum Documentation Association; now termed just mda: see http://www.mda.org.uk/
MIDI	Musical instrument digital interface
MINERVA	EC Network of Excellence: see http://www.minervaeurope.org/
MPEG	Moving Picture Experts Group (International Standards Organisation/International Electrotechnical Commission)
MS	Microsoft
MUVII	Multi-user virtual interactive interface
NARCISSE	Network of Art Research Computer Image SystemS in Europe
NGO	Non-governmental organization
NRC	National Research Council of Canada: see http://www.nrc-cnrc.gc.ca/
OCR	Optical character recognition
ORION	Object Rich Information Network – an EC project on archaeology museums and 3D: see http://www.orion-net.org/
PAW	Project and Analysis Workshops organized and held by ADIT
PC	Personal computer
PDA	Personal digital assistant (electronic handheld information device)
PHP	Hypertext Preprocessor is a script language for creating dynamic web pages
PULMAN	EC IST project on public libraries and new technologies: see http://www.pulmanweb.org
R&D	Research & development
RACE	EC IST R&D programme on telecommunications: see http://www.cordis.lu/ist/ka3/digicult/race.htm
RAPHAEL	Predecessor progamme to Culture 2000
RDBMS	Relational database management system
RFBR	Russian Foundation for Basic Research: see http://www.icsti.su/eng/ois/inforesources/National/russia/rffi.asp
RGAKFD	Russian State Archive for Documentaries and Photos in Krasnogorsk: see http://www.russianarchives.com/rao/archives/rgakfd/textind10.html

RGANTD	Russian State Archive for Scientific and Technical Documentation: see http://www.russianarchives.com/rao/archives/rgantd/
RGB	Red, green and blue
RSL	Russian State Library: see http://www.rsl.ru/defengl.asp
Runet	Russian Internet: see http://www.internet-perm.ru/eng/services/promotion/runet.asp
RUSMarc	Russian communicative format for machine-readable bibliographic record (Russian variant of UNIMARC) developed by the Russian National Library and highly recommended for use in Russian libraries. It is required for support of Z39.50 applications being developed in Russia.
SACD	Société des auteurs et compositeurs dramatiques: see http://www.sacd.fr/index2.asp
SACH	State Administration of Cultural Heritage (China)
SDK	Software development kit
SENDA	Special Education Needs and Disability Act 2001, available from HMSO on-line at www.hmso.gov.uk/acts/acts2001/20010010.htm
SIDAC	Italian multimedia company which was very active in the early 1990s in the cultural heritage sector; subsequently absorbed into FINSIEL, Telecom Italia
SIGEC	Sistema Informativo Generale del Catalogo of the ICDD
SME	Small and medium-sized enterprise
SMS	Short message service
SOCOG	Sydney Organizing Committee for the Olympic Games
Spotnik	A 3DML authoring software package: see spotnik.flatland.com
SQL	Structured query language (database query language)
TACIS	EC programme to assist Russia and the newly independent states: see http://www.tacisinfo.ru/
TAP	Telematics Applications Programme: see http://www.cordis.lu/telematics/home.html
tar	Tape ARchive – Unix's general-purpose archive utility and the file format it uses. Tar was originally intended for use with magnetic tape but, though it has several command line options related to tape, it is now used more often for packaging files together on other media, for example for distribution via the Internet
TEN-Telecom	eTEN is the European Community Programme designed to help the deployment of telecommunication networks based services

	(e-services) with a trans-European dimension: see http://europa.eu.int/information_society/programmes/eten/about/index_en.htm
TIDE	Telematics Initiative for Disabled and Elderly People
TIFF	Tagged image file format
TRADEX	TRial Action for Digital object Exchange, IST-1999-21031, October 2000–April 2002. It was a trial action implemented within the IST programme, focused on the on-line multimedia object transfer. TRADEX considered available copyright marking technologies for solving the illegal copying and proof of ownership problems: see http://lci.det.unifi.it/Projects/projects.html
UDF	User defined functions
UKCLE	UK Centre for Legal Education: see www.ukcle.ac.uk/directions/issue4/senda.html
UML	Universal modelling language
UMTS	Universal mobile telecommunications system
UNESCO	United Nations Educational, Scientific and Cultural Organization: see www.unesco.org
VASARI	Visual Arts System for Archiving and Retrieval of Images: see EC project in culture and ICT, 1989–1991
VIKING	A Raphael educational CD-ROM project on the Vikings
VIRMUS	Virtual Museum – a project supported by FP5, IST Program: see http://www.virmus.com/about_virmus.htm
VISIRE (IST-1999-10756)	VISIRE (Virtual Image-Processing System for Intelligent Reconstruction of 3D Environments) – an EC project: see http://www.inrialpes.fr/movi/euro/
VMC	Virtual Museum of Canada: see http://www.virtual museum.ca/English/index_flash.html
VR	Virtual reality
VRML	Virtual reality mark-up Language
W3C	World Wide Web Consortium: see http://www.w3.org/
WAP	Wireless application protocol
WCAG 1.0	Web Content Accessibility Guideline which was developed by the Website Accessibility Initiative, a working group of the W3C: see http://www.w3.org/TR/WAI-WEBCONTENT/
XML	eXtensible markup language
XSL	eXtensible stylesheet language
XSLT	eXtensible stylesheet language transformations
ZGDV	Zentrum für Graphische Datenverarbeitung (Computer Graphics Center): see http://www.zgdv.de/zgdv
ZKM	Zentrum für Kunst und Medientechnologie Karlsruhe: see www.zkm.de

Acknowledgements

Firstly we would like to thank all the authors of EVA papers since the beginning of the EVA Conferences in 1990. The present collection of papers from EVAs in the early 2000s is just a small selection from some 1,000 papers. Unfortunately many excellent papers have had to be excluded.

Secondly, we acknowledge the efforts of all the host organizations of the EVA Conferences and Symposia around the world in the last 15 years:

- ATC (Athens Technology Center), Greece
- Center PIC, Moscow, Russia
- Czech Technical University, Prague, The Czech Republic
- Dallas Museum of Art, Texas, USA
- GFaI (Gesellschaft zur Förderung angewandter Informatik e.V.), Berlin
- Gifu Prefectural Government, Japan
- Hunterian Museum, The University of Glasgow
- Imperial College, London
- Interactive Institute, Sweden
- International Research and Training Centre, IRTC, Kiev, Ukraine
- The Museum of Modern Art (MoMA), New York, USA
- National Gallery, London
- National Museums of Scotland
- Silesian Technical University, Warsaw, Poland
- Tretyakov Gallery, Moscow
- Tsinghua University, Beijing, China
- University of Florence
- University College, London

In addition, we appreciate the permission of the publishers of the individual EVA proceedings to publish these papers, especially Pigatora Editrice, Bologna.

Thirdly, we thank the European Commission for all its help and investment in the EVA events and its support of the EVA Networking project in 2001 and 2002.

We would like to thank most warmly, Monica and Nicholas Kaayk of EVA Conferences and Jacqui Cornish, Suzie Duke and Jane Read of Ashgate Publishing for their painstaking, patient and valuable work in producing this book.

Finally, many thanks to all the EVA supporters over the years for their continued participation and stimulation and to all those who will do so in the future.

Vito Cappellini, James Hemsley and Gerd Stanke

Dedication

To all those who have participated in Culture and Technology projects internationally.

Chapter 1

Introduction and International Overview

James Hemsley, Vito Cappellini and Gerd Stanke

Aims and Audiences

The first aim of this book is to provide a panorama of leading developments in the field of culture and information and communications technologies (ICT) at the beginning of the new millennium. The second is to show how these constitute a genuine international movement, since although the original basic technology is largely US in origin, its application, further development and refinement is widely diffused with other regions, especially Europe. Increasingly, China, Japan and Russia, for example, are also taking leading roles, due to their rich storehouses of cultural heritage – museums, libraries, archives, archaeological sites and other resources – as well as contemporary cultural creators, including the performing arts. The third is to indicate how the cultural sector itself is becoming recognized as an inspiring technology driver – not just a passive recipient area for the products and services of technological progress. The final key objective is to encourage the growing international cooperation in the intersection of culture and technology, which has been 'pushed' by the European Commission (EC) from the late 1980s. The EC's R&D policies have firmly encouraged cross-border projects across the European Union and other participant countries: since the mid-1990s, broader partnership projects have been fostered, beginning with Canada. National, regional and local governments as well as major charitable organizations and international organizations such as UNESCO and the World Bank have also played an increasingly important role.

Our target readers are, firstly, non-technical professionals and managers in the cultural sector who are engaged in the application of new technologies and, in particular, those who are participating – or considering participating – in project work of such a challenging nature that it is actually leading scientists, engineers and technologists, as well as researchers in other fields such as psychology, to push the technology by inter-disciplinary cooperation. Therefore this book is not a technology guide, the emphasis being rather on trying to present a cross-section of new developments in a form which is readily understandable by non-specialists. However, it is hoped that it will also be of interest to those technical people who are engaged in such work and wish to gain an appreciation of this rapidly developing and changing field as a whole. In particular, we hope that it will be of value to those who, coming from one side or another of the 'great divide' between science and the arts and humanities, have made efforts to become 'bi-cultural'. It has been well recognized for many years that, due to the remarkable growth of knowledge and consequent increasing specialization, the ideal Renaissance reach of Leonardo da Vinci remains far outside that of today's experts. However, there are increasing numbers of those from both sides – represented by the authors of the papers in this work – who, inspired by da Vinci, are trying to at least appreciate the 'other side' and to reach across the divide and help create a kind of human bridge between those in the far reaches of the two worlds. This book recognizes their work and is also aimed at them, to encourage and support their efforts. We also hope that it will prove of interest to policy makers, including government and funding agencies.

The Book's Structure

After this introductory section, Part 1 presents three papers which, from different viewpoints, indicate the strategic value and future potential of the multiplicative relationship: 'culture x technology'. Mulrenin reports on the seminal work of one of the most far-reaching of a series of 'roadmapping' projects, DigiCULT, which was carried out by a pan-European team involving inputs from some 180 top people in the field and supported by the European Commission. This set out perspectives for the field, serving as an aid to subsequent directions and decision making. As a counterpoint, Taylor et al. from Canada show, by means of the story of their scientific work over a decade, how cultural heritage emerged from a 'Cinderella before the ball' position to act as a key driver in their pioneering 3D technology work. Then Brakker and Kujbyshev describe the impressive developments in Russia which, despite the economic problems, are rapidly closing the 'gap' with the West: this paper is in lieu of a series of Russian papers, as the proceedings from the EVA Moscow Conferences are available on the Web (at www.evarussia.ru) and therefore were not included in this book

Cooperative cross-border projects are considered in the Part 2: such initiatives have increasing importance – especially in the European Union – because they also cross sectoral boundaries. Two of the papers describe pan-European projects, both of which include not only the 'old EU' of 15 countries, but also partners from Eastern Europe. Cataccio et al. describe ArchTerra, a cooperation in the archaeological field between a set of typical players in the field. Krizova describes a contrasting project, CHIMER, in which schoolchildren are in the driving user role. The third paper in this group, by Griepentrog et al., shows how two teams in different continents can cooperate, not only in an advanced 3D technical application, but also in mutual stimulation to develop detailed reconstructions – an excellent example of in-depth cross-continental cooperation.

Archaeology and now also increasingly history are taking a major role in the 'culture x technology' scene at the beginning of the 21st century, contrasting sharply with 10 to 15 years earlier when art history and art galleries were the focus of attention; this change reflects the development of 3D technology. Part 3 begins with a paper by Krebs and Brück on a German multi-faith homage to religious architecture and history, both Christian and Jewish. A Swiss team's work on a remarkable 'mountainscape' model is presented next by Visnacova et al. The rich archaeological and technical resources of one of the smaller new EU countries, Latvia, are described in Snore's paper about a virtual open air musuem. Then Suzan

Hazan presents a virtual project at the Israel Museum on its most treasured objects, the Dead Sea Scrolls, and another on an Electronic Art Garden. The final paper in this section deals with both conservation and cultural tourism: Lowe et al. explain work on a high-quality, life-size 3D physical reconstruction (of a very important Egyptian tomb, that of Seti I), which has the dual objective of helping to preserve the original while also providing an attraction for cultural tourists.

Digital archiving is the focus of Part 4, beginning with a useful assessment of the state of the art in 2D digitization at the turn of the millennium by Rudolf Gschwind et al., based on specific practical work at various Swiss museums and libraries. A rare view of developments in the corporate sector is then provided by Wolfgang Mueller, reporting on a comprehensive project carried out for BMW archives. Work at Italy's largest cultural heritage documentation centre, the ICCD in Rome, is now reaching new levels of sophistication with image-based approaches, building on decades of prior ICT work, as described by Maria Luisa Polichetti. This work is also notable for its application of results from a series of EC-supported R&D projects and even one Europe–Japan project.

Design, retrieval and protection is the broad scope of Part 5, which begins with an Anglo-American cooperative project (described by Ben Rubinstein and Holly Witchey) to develop methods and tools for repeated use by museum staff for temporary exhibitions at the Cleveland Museum. Art history university teaching and research has been a key target for image-based systems developers for over 15 years and an ambitious multi-institution German initiative is described by Sigrid Ruby and Ute Verstegen. Databases of monument images offer challenging difficulties in facilitating searching by users and Phil Carlisle's paper provides innovative approaches. Historic gardens and landscapes were a 'Cinderella' area during the first decade of 'culture x technology' and thus John Counsell's interesting paper on work to enable access and help conserve English and French gardens and landscapes is a valuable contribution to showing the wider applicability of imaging technology to our cultural and natural resources. Protection of intellectual property rights is a vexing and longstanding problem area and the two papers by Dimitrios Tsolis et al. and Jean Barda and Claude Rollin provide a picture of the situation in this area in which the problems are certainly not purely technological and financial, but also involve many complex legal and organizational issues.

The special needs of the disabled are the focus of Part 6, although it should be emphasized that making these part of an inclusive approach to accessibility issues in general is a very welcome move. Marcus Weisen first sets out the overall international scene by considering general policy issues and then Jonathan Bowen, the 'father of virtual museums on the Web', addresses the situation with regard to Web systems in particular. The remainder of this section consists of short papers prepared for a special workshop at EVA 2002 Berlin. There are two detailed papers on making the Web more accessible by Beate Schulte and Ulrike Peter and Brigitte Bornemann-Jeske, with a concluding case study on electronic aids for non-speaking people by Jochen Scherer. These kinds of efforts needs to be continued over many years, not just for the European Year of the Disabled (2003), if these disadvantaged sectors of our society are to gain the improved access to our cultural heritage that they deserve.

The last section of selected papers is on 'Interactive Realities and Future

Possibilities', beginning with a paper by Malcolm Ferris on a prize-winning exhibition in which a series of innovative interactive exhibits provided enjoyment and education to many thousands of visitors. The theme of the 'interactive museum' is continued and extended in Alessandro Mecocci's paper describing interactive museum rooms. The third paper, by Ciavarella and Paternò, puts the interactivity into the hands – literally – of the visitors with the use of hand-held devices, a trend which appears likely to continue. Stephen Brewster then describes the application of haptics to provide the sense of touch for users – a new dimension of empowerment, which also has important opportunities for the disabled. Finally, Anton Nijholt brings in another exciting new possibility: musician characters populating scenes with virtual actors, including displaying their emotional reactions.

The final section of the book is a discussion of future opportunities and challenges. As we look back on some twenty years of work on imaging and culture, the temptation to try to look forward another twenty is very strong. Although it is recognized that the only certain thing about such forecasts is that they will be wrong, we nonetheless offer some views on this and hope that this book will contribute to facing the challenges and problems, so helping in the realization of dreams.

The Background to ICT in the Cultural Sector across the European Union

In the UK, the use of information and communications technologies in the cultural sector can be traced back to the 1970s and before, with (in particular) its application for museum collections documentation reflected by the establishment of the precursor of the Museum Documentation Association, now known as the MDA, in Cambridge in the mid-1970s. The field of archaeology was also noted for its use of quantitative analysis and use of computing from an early stage. However, it was only when image capture and processing technologies began to emerge from their special fields of origin, such as the military, that the new technologies succeeded in the 1980s in making a major public as well as 'back-room' impact.

The field of public electronic imaging technology and cultural applications was inaugurated – unsurprisingly in one sense, since it followed previous pioneering efforts a century before the cinema – in France at the opening of the magnificent new Musée d'Orsay in 1986, thanks to visionaries involved in the planning who dared to aim for an image-based visitor information system right from the start. Although sometimes criticized (although just in France itself it seems) for inevitable weaknesses, there can be little doubt that this established the first benchmark and acted as an inspiration for other museums and galleries internationally, with the National Gallery in London setting the next such benchmark with their 'Microgallery' in 1991. This 'second-generation' visitor information system, developed by a small innovative British multimedia company Cognitive Applications, was then taken up in the US, firstly by the San Diego Gallery of Art and then the National Gallery in Washington. Rapid diffusion of such systems then followed across the world, until their present ubiquitous nature.

In parallel with the first French visitor system developments, other work of a more academic nature was also taking off in various countries, as indicated for example by the formation of CHArt (Computers and the History of Art) in the mid-1980s under the leadership of Professor William Vaughan at Birkbeck College, London University, who also created the first MA course in Art History and Computing. In addition R&D projects were being conceived by mixed-sector academia, museum and industrial teams in various European countries, with three such project consortia winning funding from the European Commission:

● European Museum Network, EMN, working to develop systems for pan-European access to museum object images and information – well before the Web and even suitable telecommunication systems were available, but pointing the way for subsequent efforts.
● NARCISSE, aimed primarily at CD-ROM development for conservation purposes, rather than public access, but also carrying out new digitization system development work.
● VASARI, Visual Arts System for Archiving and Retrieval of Images (the acronym devised by Dr David Saunders of the National Gallery, London, as a clear homage to the famous Italian 'Father of Art History'), for ultra-high-quality imaging direct from paintings

These three consortia, involving different sectors from a number of European countries including Italy and Spain, were led respectively by German, French and British organizations. Curiously they were funded by three different units at the EC, the two for Computing (ESPRIT) and Telecoms (RACE) operating from Brussels, and one from Luxemburg (IMPACT) for market-oriented applications. All three units operated within the second five-year European R&D Framework Programme and were later amalgamated in the 1990s, reflecting 'convergence'. These three pioneering projects were funded by the EC despite a lack of recognition at that time of the cultural sector being an appropriate one for information and communications technologies R&D.

Thanks to strong EC interest as well as demand and political, media and professional public interest, these three projects were followed by hundreds more pan-European ones in the 1990s, involving not only R&D, but also by the EC's RAPHAEL and Culture 2000 programmes of the Cultural and Education Directorates (also merged during the decade). There have been a considerable number involving the use of technology, such as the VIKING project, which produced a CD-ROM distributed free to schools in the partner countries, and was carried out by the National Museum of Denmark, the National Museum of Ireland and the National Museums of Scotland, the coordinating partner. For a helpful complete list of the partners and coordinators of the most recent IST projects see www.cordis.lu.

In the R&D area special mention should be made of the Telematics Applications Programme, TAP, which supported over 100 projects involving the development and experimental application of innovative technology for the library field. Of note was the absence of a similar special programme for museums or other areas such as archives: a more general cultural heritage R&D technology programme had been considered in the early 1990s, but was not followed through at the time due in part to concerns that this might lead to a 'ghetto' effect. Indeed it was judged by some observers that, by thus permitting museums (in particular) a free rein to participate in technology projects across the whole range of technologies in which R&D was being carried out, the museum community received a comparable amount of both EC Framework Programme funding and R&D effort in the early and mid-1990s as the libraries – not a normal budget division. The range of projects supported in the period up to 1997 by the European Commission was shown in two compendia, produced as part of the EVA Cluster projects (1996 and 1998), now unfortunately out of print, which provided summaries of some 100 EC projects across a variety of different programme areas which had been gradually coalescing during the mid-1990s. It is the nature of high-tech R&D to be risky and so inevitably many of these were not as successful as had been hoped — for example, as the Internet and the Web burst onto the scene, work on other approaches was rendered obsolete. However, it is noteworthy that the cross-European team working relationships formed in them tended to be quite persistent and helped in subsequent successful projects: in others the research lines opened up by the more successful ones (such as the VASARI project) have been continued and applied by the resulting VASARI lab/centres in London, Florence and Munich as well as by other project partners, notably the Centre de recherche et restauration des musées de France (C2RMF).

The mid-1990s were also characterized by ambitious European and international efforts to encourage the application of ICT to the cultural heritage sector; unfortunately neither the Memorandum of Understanding nor the G7 initiatives had the desired impact, due in large part to the difficulties of mobilizing effective coordinated action at the European and international levels respectively. However, it is noteworthy that such initiatives seem to reappear in different incarnations and the current efforts by, for example, UNESCO and the EC itself with the 'New Instruments' of the Sixth Framework Programme appear to have more than a passing similarity with these *fin de siècle* attempts to produce major global engagement between the cultural heritage sector and the ICT industry. The latter was itself in the throes of massive restructuring, with the efforts of Europe to protect and build up its own computer industries in particular failing in the face of strong US and Japanese competition. In hindsight it may well prove to be the case that the lower-profile but patient and persistent work of such international groups as ICOM/CIDOC and their national counterparts made a greater contribution in the standards arena through the 1990s than the high-profile initiatives.

In 1998, at the beginning of the EC's Fifth Framework (1998–2002) R&D Programme in the Information Society technology area, the pressure to establish a specific action line for cultural heritage proved unstoppable. Thus a dedicated unit under Bernard Smith was set up in Luxemburg, profiting from the previous work, including that of special programmes such as IMPACT. With a budget of some 70 million euros, this unit funded over 100 projects ranging from cutting-edge technology R&D such as ARCHEOGUIDE (Reality-based Cultural Heritage On-site Guide) and ARCO (Augmented Representation of Cultural Objects) (both of which were driven by museums and archaeologists) to application and demonstration projects like VIRMUS, the first EC-supported IST trial project from Latvia. The steadily increasing role of the New Accession States was a notable feature in recent years and this issue is given particular attention in the concluding chapter. Importantly, this unit also supported 'transition' projects from the Fifth to Sixth Framework (2003–2006) Programme, with some, such as DELOS for Digital Libraries and MINERVA for national ministry cooperation, actually spanning both, thus providing continuity of efforts. There were others such as eCultureNet for a very broad approach, ERPANET on conservation, and ORION for archaeology, museums and 3D, all of which involved the building of 'networks of excellence' and preparation of research roadmaps. An important victory was the inclusion of cultural heritage in the new Framework Programme despite an overall reduction in the number of topics covered: there was also a strong organizational link with 'technology-enhanced learning'. At the time of writing, preparations are in full swing for the Sixth Framework Programme and the first wave of projects in the cultural heritage area are already launched including BRICKS (a large 'integrated project' on cultural heritage systems) and EPOCH (the network of Excellence for Intelligent Cultural Heritage systems). A comprehensive overview of EC IST initiatives, including the linkage of national efforts, is provided in Smith (2003).[1]

Thanks to the EC's web-based information system, news is available on all these projects, as well as those from other EC initiatives such as TEN-Telecom, and many previous ones are available, especially on www.cordis.lu. It should be emphasized, however, that the presence of EC support has been much more pervasive since many cultural institutions have participated in technology R&D projects from other parts of the IST programmes, so that the danger of a 'cultural ghetto' has been averted. Moreover, there has been considerable technology-based work included in the Culture 2000 Programme of the EC's Directorate for Culture and Education, although its main thrust has been 'content', showing how cultural and educational content have become increasingly intertwined. A notable feature in the EC-funded projects has been the participation of different sectors including academia, industry and government as well as the cultural sector itself, plus much cooperative input from different countries (including increasingly from outside the European Union since the mid-1990s).

Significantly, however, it is still impossible to speak of a 'single European market' in cultural technology since, apart from the major American and Japanese companies, the market is divided by national or linguistic/cultural barriers. As one dynamic but small Italian multimedia company's marketing director (anonymously) said in 1992: 'We are too large for Italy but too small for Europe'. That situation on the supply side does not seem to have altered significantly since then.

National Scenes in Europe and International Comparisons

The situation across Europe and the world is characterized by remarkable diversity. To indicate this we shall here restrict attention to providing thumbnail sketches of five countries (Italy, China, Japan, Scotland and Ukraine) to illustrate some of the principal developments, with the case of Russia also being described in much more depth in the Brakker and Kujbyshev paper. For greater understanding of different national scenes across Europe the valuable survey carried out by the EC's MINERVA project, *Coordinating Digitisation in Europe* (2003), is most useful, as are the survey and reference lists developed prior to and in the course of the eCultureNet project by Kim Veltman et al. (www.eculturenet.org). In addition, of course, the variety of the different national backgrounds of the contributing authors to this book provides indications of the richly diverse scene.

North America

The scene here is, of course, much more accessible, thanks to the Web, to conferences and to publications as well as the high-profile activities of leading museums and galleries and companies such as IBM: see for example the publications of museums on the Web and ICHIM (www.ichim.org/), which also provide much information on the overall international scene. Naturally there have been many important developments in the US, but it is striking that in the early 1990s the National Gallery in Washington and the San Diego Art Gallery both chose Cognitive Applications, a small British multimedia company, to design their new image-based visitor information sytems. The Getty Museum was extremely active and influential in the 1990s until strategic changes led to a reduction in its efforts, which since have been renewed. In Canada there were many pioneering developments with CHIN, the Canadian Heritage Information Network, taking an especially important role.

Italy

In the late 1980s and early 1990s Italy was regarded by the Italians themselves as somewhat behind other countries as regards the combination of culture and technology, despite the efforts of academic centres, such those as in Florence and Pisa, and pioneering initiatives from the government field, such as Rome's ICCD led by Maria Luisa Polichetti. The country's latent culture and technology power was, of course, recognized by many – including national multimedia companies such as SIDAC (later absorbed into FINSIEL, belonging to Telecom Italia), international companies such as IBM (which worked with the Vatican) and major Japanese company initiatives (with the Uffizi in particular). Preceding text-based work such as that from Pisa provided one basis, as did the Signal Processing R&D, focusing increasingly on image processing, in particular, from the University of Florence and the National Research Council: such work then diffused to other universities and research centres. A striking, but little commented aspect was the impact of the 'Peace Dividend' following the fall of the Berlin Wall, the collapse of the USSR and the consequent reduction of military R&D expenditures: this led to a number of experienced and knowledgeable researchers looking to the cultural heritage sector, among other things, as a promising field in terms of jobs, self-actualization and achievement. The role of the government at city, regional and national levels became an increasingly proactive one with, in particular, the Florence and Tuscany governments (followed by others) trying to capitalize not only on the enormous cultural heritage assets, but also their strong high-tech industries. At the national level, the creation of the Italian national programme PARNASO[2] was fundamental, including specific attention to accentuating positive linkages with European R&D projects: this approach has been termed the 'Italian Model', leading not only to stronger national efforts but also greater participation by Italian organizations in the European projects – a 'virtuous cycle'. Another positive factor has been the particular situation of Italian banks, which are legally obliged to contribute certain amounts of financial support to the cultural sector: this therefore includes technology applications, for example in conservation, restoration and access. Positive 'knock-on' effects were to be seen in the related areas of cultural tourism and education, the latter being an acknowledged area of Italian strength as regards learning resources (MINERVA report, 2003, page xix). The result, at the beginning of the 21st century, is that Italy now has the most active combination of players in the field, including not only the cultural heritage sector, universities and government, but also a considerable number of companies, ranging from small innovative recent start-ups such as CENTRICA in Florence, to very large ones such as Engineering, the prime contractor in the new EC-integrated project, BRICKS. Another notable entrant is ELSAG-Finmeccanica, the leader of the Pistoia project, a major comprehensive digital archiving and access project for this gem of a Tuscan town close to Florence. However, the journey has not been without its 'false dawns' and disappointments, ranging from the dashed hopes of one Italian businessman to become 'the Bill Gates of the Cultural CD-ROM business' in the early 1990s to the fate of a number of cultural heritage dot.coms, such disappointments of course not being unique to Italy. Nonetheless, there has been a clear change in Italy's position since the mid-1980s; in particular Tuscany, has taken its rightful position as the leader in the new 'Digital Rinascimento' (Renaissance).

Scotland

Scotland, in the European north, arguably has as much, if not more, in common with its Scandinavian neighbours across the North Sea than with England across the land border. Scotland's journey towards devolution from London political control and closer moves towards 'Europe' have formed an important contextual factor in the 'culture and technology' situation over the last 15 years. In the early 1990s, for example, Scotland was not even 'on the map' in a London briefing on new academic telecommunications networks and museums. This was reflected in the lack of Scottish multimedia companies at the time, so that the National Museums of Scotland were obliged to look southwards as far as Italy as well as to the rest of Britain and westwards to California for help in planning the new multimedia systems to form an integral part of the new Museum of Scotland targeted for 1998, an important symbol of progress in this journey. Opened on time and to budget, this last major new museum of the 20th century in Europe reflected not only an 'object-led' design concept in the purpose-built museum building, but also the creation of a strong in-house technical capability, Now dubbed The Multimedia Team or TMT, and led by Michael Spearman (also an archaeologist), this has since spun off into an Irish–Scottish commercial company, Kestrel 3D, also using Canadian technology (see Taylor et al.'s paper). The National Museums of Scotland were thus also in a position to lead the creation of the Scottish Cultural Resource Access Network, SCRAN, recognized as one of the leaders in the new generation of organizations bridging the space between the cultural heritage sector and users (in this case the educational sector in particular) with innovative user-licensing models as well as

Internet and Web-based technologies. SCRAN, led by its first director, Bruce Royan, mobilized by a project-based approach the efforts and talents of several hundred heritage organizations and technical partners across the whole of Scotland with significant skills development resulting – an important by-product of this large public investment from the UK's National Lottery. Developments were thus by no means restricted to the capital and in particular its larger sister, Glasgow, also made great strides in the 1990s including, for example, a set of innovative student projects each year at the University of Glasgow between its Hunterian Museum and the Computer Science Department – termed by American admirers 'the Glasgow Model' for such cooperation – and the HATII (Humanities Advanced Technology and Information Institute) initiative. In addition, the Colleges of Art in both Edinburgh and Glasgow were making important contributions, as well as other colleges and universities across Scotland and museums and libraries as far north as the Shetland Isles. The result at the beginning of this century was that Scotland had, like Italy, moved dramatically up the 'relative capability' curve as regards culture and technology, as indicated by a number of Scottish organizations, including SCRAN, taking a very active role in European projects: for example, the National Museums of Scotland led the ORION project on Archaeology, Museums and 3D, and Scottish companies such as 55 Degrees from Glasgow won projects in London – a 'levelling of the playing field'.

Ukraine

We have selected this country rather than one of the 'New European' states such as the Czech Republic or Poland (both venues of EVAs in 2001 and 2002 respectively) precisely because it is so little known, even in Western Europe. This historically important nation of nearly 50 million people lies strategically between the new European Union and Russia and, as expected by many, will probably eventually join the EU, perhaps as early as 2010. Its capital, Kiev, contains in its centre a wonderful UNESCO world heritage site, Pechersk Lavra, a magnificent religious complex. Less known are the Ukraine's very strong science and technology capabilities, whose leading works during and since the Soviet times are only recently being appreciated in Western Europe and internationally. The proceedings of EVA 2002 Kiev are available on the Web at www.dlab.Kiev.va/eva/, so only a few of the paper titles are provided here to encourage readers to explore Ukrainian work in the field and, ideally, make contact with the authors:

• 'The ways of solution of the problem of a long-time storage of information', written in digital form, by V. Petrov, A. Kryuchin, C. Shanojlo, I. Kossko and V. Kravets: Institute for Information Registration Problems, Kiev, Ukraine
• 'Creating 3D models of objects by their stereo images for virtual museums', D. Rjabokon: International Research and Training Center, UNESCO, Kiev, Ukraine
• 'Directions for development of technologies for creating the electronic library's information resources in Ukraine', O. Barkova: Vernadsky National Library of Ukraine, Kiev, Ukraine
• 'Computer information system of Lviv State Natural History Museum',

P. Zhezhnich, A. Vovchina: National University 'Lvivska Politehnika', Lviv, Ukraine
- 'The CD "Treasures of Kiev-Pechersk Lavra"', T. Mozharovskaja: Kiev-Pechersk National Historical & Cultural Reserve, Kiev, Ukraine
- 'Pedagogy oriented web-design for the distance learning web-books', A. Zhuravliov, I. Zhuravliova: Distance Learning Center, Ukrainian Academy of State Government of the President of Ukraine, Kiev, Ukraine
- '3D reconstructions of ancient settlements and buildings from Ukraine', M.M. Videyko: Research Institute for Cultural Heritage Preservation, Ukrainian Ministry of Culture and Arts
- 'Virtual expositions on the web-site of the State Library of Ukraine for Children', I. Torlin: State Library of Ukraine for Children, Kiev, Ukraine.

In addition to these Ukrainian and other papers from Russia, Sweden and the UK, there were several cooperative German-Ukrainian papers showing how they are effective in bilateral cooperation and they are keen to extend such cooperation. See also *Ukraine – A Key Future Partner* (Hemsley, 2002).[3]

Japan

As in so many ways, Japan from the first followed a completely different trajectory from the Western countries in the 'culture x technology' field. In the early 1990s, for example, the Japanese pursued the 'Hi-Vision' route in museums, reflecting the enormous multi-billion dollar investment efforts being made then into high-definition television in both Japan and Europe. In particular, the Gifu Prefecture, strategically located between Tokyo and Osaka, took a pioneering role in introducing these systems into museums – notable aspects included the use of these high-quality analogue systems and the introduction of multi-viewer systems rather than the single-user systems prevalent in the West. Unfortunately for the major European and Japanese companies involved in this field, the US digital versions out-flanked these analogue efforts and this also led eventually to Japanese efforts in culture and technology adopting a similar approach to those in the West. In this Japan had a strong asset: powerful computer manufacturers, telecom companies, advertising and printing companies took a strong interest in this promising field, with particular interest in European and Chinese cultural treasures as well as, of course, in Japan's own rich cultural heritage. This pent-up interest in the field of 'culture x (digital) technology' was shown dramatically at the first EVA conference in Gifu in 1998, attended by 1,000 people – to this day, still the largest single event internationally in the field. The situation as of the beginning of the 21st century may be seen from papers at the third biennial EVA Gifu in 2002. For example, the first Japanese paper was by Toshuro Kamuchi from Hitachi on digital image system technology and its applications to digital archives where

> the main focus of our development is to preserve the aesthetic quality as well as the historical significance of cultural heritages, and to make them accessible by people anywhere around the world.

Applications were presented on the picture rolls of Genji, wall paintings from a Japanese castle and the digital Silk Road project. Other 'big company' papers included ones from NTT Data and Dentsu, and also an interesting closure of the circle on digital high-definition television, including 3D graphics, from Seiji Kunishige of the Japan Broadcasting Corporation. Another particular feature has been the very active role of regional governments, shown by papers from Ishikawa Prefecture as well as papers on this issue by university speakers.

China

The remarkable cultural history of China presents a fertile field for technology: concomitantly with China's economic growth this developed rapidly in the late 1990s and early 2000s, as shown at the first EVA Beijing in 2002.[4] Papers such as that by Hu Jiang of the Shanghai Museum were on a par with those of their peers in the West. Of particular appeal has been the work of Ling Chen and her colleagues and students of Tsinghua University, the 'MIT of China', with charming combinations of poetry, history, the performing and visual arts and, more recently, sports and folk medicine in work directed at the Beijing Olympics (2003). Three examples drawn from EVA 2002 Beijing indicate the nature of Chinese efforts at the beginning of the new millennium – drawing on the thousands of years of China's cultural heritage:

- In 'Digital Dunhuang – The Digital Technique Practice of Cultural Relics Protection', Liu Gang of the Conservation Institute of Dunhuang Academy describes the history and the current and planned digitization work at the Mogao Grottoes – 'the greatest repository of Buddhist art in the world' – with 492 well preserved caves, frescoes covering 45,000 square metres and over 2,000 painted sculptures, the whole site lying strategically on the Silk Road. Liu Gang indicates the dispersed worldwide Dunhuang documentation resources, from ancient manuscripts to the first photographic records by British, French and Russian visitors a century ago, through various replicas to the latest 3D digitization efforts. Current aims include not only providing scholars internationally with access to the whole corpus, but also contributing to conservation and restoration, including the creation of virtual caves for tourists so that the 'travel boom' does not destroy the very objects that tourists come to see – a theme addressed in the Lowe et al. paper on Egypt.
- 'On Digitization for Large-scale Chinese Ancient Classics: Theory and Practice' by Zhang Zhoucai and Wang Ledong provides an overview of digization work for 'e-SiKuQuanShu' on the largest collection of Chinese classics in the Royal Library and 'e-SiBuCongkan', the most frequently researched Chinese classics series. Use of the ISO/IEC 10646 standard as well as new OCR techniques and multilingual approaches indicate a well-thought-through and implemented set of approaches which have been integrated into a software package for digital libraries. The paper closes with a call for the creation of a 'unified textual heritage data center' on the Internet. With the weight of the world's largest population and the long history of China, it should not be surprising that the Chinese take a major role in such initiatives.

● 'Digital Archive of Chinese Traditional Art – Shadow Theatre' by a group of students from the Printing University of Beijing under a group name – 'The First Multimedia Work Studio' – provided an enchanting presentation of a prize-winning CD of this folk-art, including the history of the form, combining 'rich colors, pleasant music and simple and elegant pictures with Chinese characteristics'. Specific attention was given to both effective navigation techniques for easy-to-use interaction and a convenient printing facility – all sufficiently simple for subsequent exhibition at EVA London.

Judging by these and the many other works presented at EVA 2002 Beijing, including in particular an environmental protection piece combining good design, powerful message and humour from a Tsinghua University student team, there can be little doubt that the Chinese will be making a sizeable impact in the 'culture x technology' world.

These vignettes only hint at the diversity and richness of developments around the world and recourse may be made to the Web to discover more. This book provides insight into many international projects and will, we hope, attract readers to participate in EVAs, to meet leading people in the field and to exchange information and share ideas.

Because of the transitory nature of websites not all of the corresponding references in the book will lead to successful location over the book's lifetime. In this case we suggest firstly that the interested reader tries to search for a possible replacement site and then contact the corresponding author(s) if necessary.

Notes

1. Smith, Bernard (2003) 'Activities and Research for Cultural Heritage in the European Union', EVA 2003 Moscow, Proceedings, see http://evarussia.ru/eva2003/english/index.html.
2. PARNASO: Patrimonio Artistico Ricerca e Nueve Tecnologie Applicate allo Svilluppo e alla Occupazione: www.murst.it/Ricerca/Parnaso/protocollo.html.
3. Hemsley, James R. (2002) *Ukraine – A Key Future Partner*, EVA 2002 London Proceedings, VASARI, now available from EVA Conferences, London.
4. The Chinese papers may be found in the Summary Proceedings of EVA 2002 Beijing produced under the direction of Associate Professor Ling Chen of Tsinghua University (lingc@tsinghua.edu.cn).

PART 1
STRATEGIC DEVELOPMENTS

Chapter 2

DigiCULT: Unlocking the Value of Europe's Cultural Heritage Sector

Andrea M. Mulrenin

Abstract

The strategic study 'Technological Landscapes for Tomorrow's Cultural Economy (DigiCULT)' aimed at providing European archives, libraries and museums with a roadmap of the technological, organizational and political challenges they need to face in the period 2002 to 2006. Based on the overall objective of increasing the value of digital cultural heritage resources by making them more easily accessible to a broader audience with the use of ICT, the study, with the help of 180 international experts in the cultural heritage sector, identified the most pressing issues and challenges in this process and provided recommendations for the relevant stakeholders. In this paper, a selection of four key issues (that is, sustainability of e-services, technical interoperability as a basic requirement for cross-sector search, the threat of a technology gap, and human capital as a key factor of cultural heritage organizations) are discussed in more detail.

Technological Landscapes for Tomorrow's Cultural Economy: The DigiCULT Study

Archives, libraries and museums (ALMs) all over Europe face similar challenges as they try to take advantage of information technologies in the emerging digital cultural economy. While the conversion of all sorts of contents into bits and bytes opens up totally new opportunities for interoperability and information exchange between the formally separated 'memory institutions' and other sectors, it also causes challenging problems and difficulties that are not only of technological but also of an organizational and political nature.

To provide memory institutions with better information on how to face these challenges, the European Commission, DG Information Society, Cultural Heritage Applications D2, in July 2000 issued a Call for Tender for a strategic study on 'Technological Landscapes for Tomorrow's Cultural Economy', DigiCULT in short. The DigiCULT study aimed to provide the cultural heritage sector, and particularly archives, libraries and museums, with a technological, organizational and political roadmap to be prepared for future development within the next five years, pointing out and describing the new tools they would need in the future cultural economy.

At the end of January 2001, the DigiCULT study was launched, its objectives being to:

- provide an in-depth analysis of the state-of-the-art technologies, content, cultural services and applications as well as (user) demand in the sector of European digital archives, libraries and museums (ALMs)
- highlight the surrounding framework and its necessary evolution, as there are organizational issues, financial aspects and legal implications with regard to intellectual property rights
- give a detailed account of national policies and initiatives as they provide a strong impulse for a positive development of the cultural heritage sector
- finally and most importantly to draw conclusions and formulate recommendations, both for players in the ALM industry and policy makers at the national and EU levels, on measures to be taken in order to exploit the opportunities and to overcome current technological impediments.

Focusing on four topical areas – technology, national policies and initiatives, organizational and financial issues, as well as exploitation and services and demand – the study tried to identify the essential issues that will govern future development and, as such, are crucial for strategic organizational, technological and political planning.

Over a six-month period, international experts from the cultural heritage sector participated in the DigiCULT study in 24 interviews, six expert round tables and two on-line Delphi surveys and shared with the team their opinions and views on the key issues that are most likely to influence future trends and, thus, future planning. Overall, over 180 international experts of the cultural heritage sector have been engaged in the study.

This paper provides some of the key findings of the DigiCULT study.

A Paradigmatic Shift: From Building Collections to Providing Access

Being digital for European cultural institutions is not an option but a reality. Despite the fact that only a small amount of the digital data produced daily is of long-term value and subject to the attention of archives, libraries and museums, it creates a major challenge to our memory institutions. Today, cultural institutions are confronted with a virtual explosion of digital cultural information of all types and formats, including digital images, audio and video recordings, electronic text, interactive and multimedia applications, as well as geographic information.

As a result, many archives, libraries and museums have turned into hybrid institutions that take care of both analogue and digital cultural collections. Besides dealing with the traditional analogue materials like books, sculptures, paintings and official records, they collect, manage, store and provide access to a variety of digital cultural artefacts, including digitized legacy resources, digital data about cultural resources, and born-digital cultural resources.

While dealing with digital information has been daily practice within European archives, libraries and museums for quite some time, institutions still find themselves struggling to understand the full implications of new technologies on their institutions, their clients and the public.

The initial enthusiasm about digital information and its promise to both rescue and permanently preserve our endangered cultural heritage, while opening up the gates to a 'library without walls', has worn off. Instead, cultural institutions have started to realize that the organizational and financial problems related to managing ICT-based cultural resources are greater than expected, and that the technological solutions for capturing, storing, searching and retrieving digital cultural information are far from being foolproof.

What is emerging slowly, however, is awareness within the cultural community about the real strengths of digital information. Above all, the advent of the Internet has opened up and brought into the limelight one particular function of memory institutions in a so-far unknown dimension and quality: providing access. Through the networked and distributed nature of the World Wide Web (WWW) and ICT-based end-user devices such as mobile phones or PDAs, archives, libraries and museums have now the potential to reach and be reachable for completely new audiences worldwide. Over the networks, users of cultural information can potentially search and retrieve innumerable resources, without the limitation of geographical, institutional or sectoral borders.

The general view of the experts suggests that providing access to the rich European cultural heritage resources has become a new focus for European memory institutions. They stipulate that cultural collections and holdings kept in archives, libraries and museums all over Europe are at their best when used. As a result, what we can observe within the community of European heritage institutions is a paradigmatic shift from building collections to providing access.

Yet providing access is not sufficient to truly unlock the value of cultural heritage institutions. It is actually only the basis of a process that also involves other stakeholders to bring cultural heritage resources and the knowledge resting within cultural heritage institutions to the attention of a broader public.

Thus, the question remains: *How can we make better use of the immense cultural heritage resources and bring them to the attention of a broader public?*

Unlocking the Value of Cultural Heritage: A Four-Layer Model

Providing access is only the first step in a four-layer model for fully unleashing the value of the cultural heritage sector. However, given changing patterns and modes of cultural consumption in the Information Society that will centre around communicating over computer and wireless networks, cultural heritage resources will only be valuable in the future if they are easily available in digital form. Thus, a basic requirement is to integrate cultural objects into the digital domain through digitization.

At the beginning of 2000, European member states took different approaches in formulating cultural heritage policies, yet despite their difference they all have the same objectives: to digitize cultural heritage resources, make them accessible for a broader audience and thus increase their value. Nevertheless, as with providing access, digitization does not guarantee that cultural heritage resources are used more broadly. Instead, what we found is that these digital resources actually remain within a very limited user group, namely the scholarly community.

Today, it is mainly researchers and scientists who use their knowledge and expertise to generate new content by contextualizing cultural heritage resources.

The results of this process are usually scholarly articles printed in journals or published electronically in e-journals. These publications are, again, the material that memory institutions pick up and integrate into their pool of cultural resources. Thus, new knowledge based on cultural resources is created, yet this knowledge largely remains within a particular user community, that is, universities and scholars. To increase the value of digital cultural resources, all stakeholders in the cultural heritage sector should seek *to break out of this cycle of knowledge generation* by building or supporting contextualized presentations for new target groups, based on the expert knowledge that resides within memory institutions.

Yet another step forward in unlocking the value of cultural heritage resources is the extension of the concept of creating narratives and contexts for users of digital cultural heritage resources. When future users are put into the position of building their own environments and/or actively contributing and participating in this process of establishing knowledge communities, they will be able to establish a sense of ownership they could not otherwise develop.

This process of unlocking the value of cultural heritage resources can be expressed in a four-layer model, as shown in Figure 2.1.

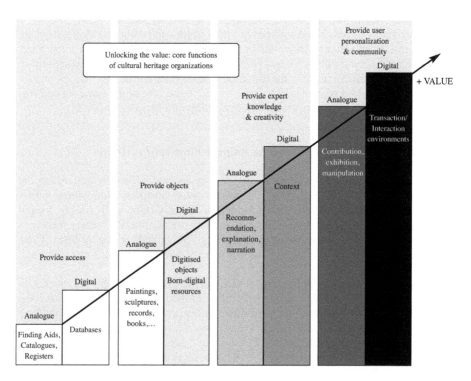

Figure 2.1   Unlocking the value of cultural heritage resources; the DigiCULT four-layer model

Within the four layers of increasing the value potential of cultural heritage resources – providing access to information, retrieving digital objects, providing expert knowledge and creativity, and finally, user and community personalization – libraries, archives and museums play different roles according to their core functions. While libraries and archives primarily work in the two bottom layers, providing access to information and retrieval of digitized objects (and long-term preservation), museums operate also on the third level when creating contextualized presentations based on expert knowledge.

Yet to follow through these stages and thus substantially increase the value of cultural heritage resources demands both entirely new organizational structures and skill sets that only a few cultural heritage institutions possess today, as well as new policies and legal frameworks. Here are some of the issues which the experts participating in the DigiCULT study have highlighted.

Unlocking the Value through Political Action

Sustainability is the key for bringing cultural heritage to the attention of a broader audience.

There is a growing expectation by national governments that (digital) cultural resources can be commercially exploited, up to the level at which cultural heritage institutions are, to a certain degree, self-sustainable. According to estimates of experts, however, only about 5% of the cultural heritage resources that archives, libraries and museums take care of are commercially exploitable. In addition, as current examples show, building up exploitable services requires a considerable amount of initial investment that most cultural institutions do not have at their disposal. Unlike the United States, where other financing sources such as donations, sponsorship or public–private partnership are more readily available, European institutions will probably not receive more than 10% of their revenue from these sources. As a consequence, with some exceptions, in the future cultural heritage institutions will receive 85–90 % of their financing out of public funds.

If not self-sustainability, what can be expected, however, is that cultural heritage institutions will try to increase the overall margin by increasing usage of cultural heritage resources. Thus memory institutions will be able to benefit from economy of scale with regard to digitization and resource management costs. The initial investment for digitizing and making accessible cultural heritage resources will be leveraged through intensive use. The cost for storage, maintenance and delivery of digital cultural resources can be justified more easily by the higher number of actual users.

Recommendations   National governments need to express a clear commitment to future sustainability of cultural e-services that make use of digital objects, without expecting cultural heritage institutions to be self-sustainable. Governments should be clear about this; after all, what the public purse will pay for is the intellectual value, not the commercial value of cultural heritage resources.

Unlocking the Value through Technology

With regard to increasing the value of cultural heritage resources, archives, libraries and museums today are largely concerned with solving the problems related to providing access; that is, the issues of standards which enable technical and semantic interoperability for cross-sectoral search and retrieval.

Historically each of the three sectors has over the centuries developed different data structures to best fit its needs. Although considerable progress has been made within some sectors, for example within the library community, cross-sectoral and international database searches still cause technological problems. These technological issues are well known among domain experts.

Today's biggest obstacles to providing seamless access to heterogeneous databases are:

● the different, sector-specific information exchange standards (data structure standards)
● a variety of cataloguing rules (data content standards)
● lack of authority files and thesauri
● multilingualism.

Standard compliance is crucial in the effort to provide seamless access. Yet, as standards evolve constantly, one of the major challenges for memory institutions is how to keep track of the rapid development without jumping on the wrong technological 'bandwagon'. Many different international bodies and standard consortia are involved in defining and issuing standards, but none has the final authority. Thus, the question remains for ALMs as to whom they can trust, especially for small institutions that:

● are still unaware of the implications of adopting inappropriate or proprietary standards
● do not have access to the relevant material, as many of the guidelines are either unknown or not available in native languages.

Current research projects in this field focus on overcoming the 'standards jungle' by establishing technological gateways that can work with the varying standards used in cultural heritage institutions. This is achieved by strictly separating data structure and presentation format. The technological basis is the XML-standard. Despite the progress made in this area, there are general concerns as to whether the data structures that developed over the centuries are adequate to meet the needs of the Information Society.

With regard to authority files and (multilingual) thesauri, the challenge is not so much a technological as an organizational one. Success in this area depends on the ability of cultural heritage institutions to agree across sectors, on a limited set of requirements.

In addition, the issue of semantic interoperability (that is, the fact that similar cultural objects are described differently, with different meanings) has not yet been solved. Also the problem of multilingualism still remains a challenge for future research.

Recommendations   The European Commission, special interest non-governmental organizations (NGOs), international standard consortia and ALMs will need to cooperate to establish sector standards. Experts visualize different stakeholders for standards synchronization: these include a central EU standards authority, NGOs, national bodies and international consortia. Therefore, a first step is to establish consensus about an international standards authority and its tasks. To do this, all relevant stakeholders need to be involved to develop a viable model on how to best reach agreement on sector standards and dissemination of results.

National governments as primary funders should actively promote the use of announced or open standards by making standards compliance a requirement for future funding of cultural heritage projects.

National governments also need to establish mechanisms for successful dissemination of standard guidelines to regional cultural heritage organizations to avoid the danger that these organizations are disconnected from the general development. Two viable models of how this might be done are:

- Setting up a central helpdesk, say within one of the large national cultural heritage institutions.
- Establishing national cultural R&D centres. These centres should be members of the all-important standards consortia, participate in test beds and, finally, translate results and existing guidelines to make them widely available also to regional cultural heritage institutions. In addition, these R&D institutes would monitor and test new technologies in order to issue recommendations and provide support on technological questions to small archives, libraries and museums.

The European Commission as a primary funding body should actively promote the use of announced or open standards by making standard compliance a requirement for future funding for proposers of cultural heritage projects.

Closing the Technology Gap

This is the basic requirement for avoiding a technological divide within the cultural heritage sector.

Archives, libraries and museums, which have already become hybrid institutions, have developed a fairly good understanding of the technological challenges of the digital domain. Although they still struggle to solve the problems involved, they at least have entered the value chain of making cultural heritage resources more readily accessible. Experts estimate, however, that perhaps only 25% of all cultural heritage institutions in Europe are actually in the position to participate in the digital era. Yet a large majority of memory institutions – the local museum focusing on the history of a village, the community or church library or the highly specialized historic archive – do not even possess the resources, human, financial and technological, to accomplish the most basic things, such as digitally cataloguing their holdings.

In fact, with research and development efforts focused exclusively on technological innovation, the threat is growing that technology will become the essential separator between those cultural institutions that are publicly visible and those that are not. This would widen the gap even further between those institutions working with technologies and those which do not.

Recommendations   Future EC R&D programmes in the cultural heritage sector should leave room for initiatives that focus on consolidation and sustainability rather than on technological innovation.

Similar to those programmes supporting small and medium-sized enterprises (SMEs), the European Commission should launch take-up measures particularly targeted at small cultural heritage institutions to enable them to catch up on technology. Teaming up with organizations who already have great experience and using them as centres of excellence could be one way of approaching the widening technology gap between cultural heritage institutions.

Unlocking the Value through Organizational Measures

Human capital is a key resource of cultural heritage institutions.
Cultural heritage institutions need to constantly train their staff and invest in their 'human capital' to increase the knowledge, competency and skills of management and personnel. It must be clear that the essential intellectual capacity of cultural heritage institutions in the knowledge society lies in the value they add to 'born-digital' or digitized cultural resources. This value lies mainly in the knowledge and expertise they bring to digital objects, not in the digital objects themselves; that is, the descriptions, contextualization, explanation, interpretation and stories that really involve potential users. In addition, even if they do not understand themselves as commercial organizations, they need to develop business skills to better address the needs of their future audiences.

Cultural heritage institutions must be oriented towards future challenges and must therefore constantly monitor, develop, incorporate and share new competencies they need in the digital environment. It is essential for them in this environment to develop and implement new ways of incorporating the real value of the institution (that is, knowledge and expertise) into the technological infrastructures themselves (for example, by being able to recommend information sources or to contextualize cultural heritage objects on-line).

Recommendations   Cultural heritage institutions should constantly monitor and incorporate new competencies they need in the digital environment, particularly in order to develop new concepts, services and products for the knowledge society.

To guarantee sustainability, national governments need to provide the 'training facilities' for cultural heritage institutions to develop in particular their project management skills and the basic know-how to participate in the digital domain.

Reference

European Commission (2002), *The DigiCULT Report: Technological Landscapes for Tomorrow's Cultural Economy – Unlocking the Value of Cultural Heritage*. Full report

January 2002, ISBN 92-828-5189-3. The English full report and the executive summaries (available in English, German, French and Italian) may be downloaded at http://www.digicult. info/pages/report2002/dc_fullreport_230602_screen.pdf.

Chapter 3

Culture as a Driving Force for Research and Technology Development: A Decade's Experience of Canada's NRC 3D Technology

J. Taylor, J.-A. Beraldin, G. Godin, R. Baribeau,
L. Cournoyer, P. Boulanger, F. Blais, M. Picard,
M. Rioux and J. Domey

Abstract

In 1981, the National Research Council of Canada (NRC) commenced research on the development of 3D laser scanner imaging technology. Initially it was thought that development would be driven primarily by industrial applications. However, in the past decade, the cultural sector has become one of the main driving forces. The purpose of this paper is to present an overview of some of the cultural applications developed during the past decade that have helped drive the development of the technology.

Introduction

The idea that led to the invention of NRC's 3D digital imaging technology started as a result of scientific curiosity. It was triggered by a little device called a 'lateral effect photodiode' (Figure 3.1). It is a small photosensor which converts the position of an incident light beam to an electrical signal. Marc Rioux initially bought it around 1980 for its functionality.

> It combined my three main scientific interests, physics, light and geometry: the physics of the photoelectric effect that converts photon to electron; the use of light – especially the laser light to produce an extremely small focused beam; and the geometry associated with its function of giving the beam position on its surface. The device was not used for at least a year, but I knew that it would be useful someday.[1]

A year later, in 1981, he thought of the idea of using it as the sensor in a 3D camera for robot vision applications. Subsequently, with his colleagues at the National Research Council, he designed, patented and developed NRC's first laser scanner.

In the early stages of development in the mid-1980s, although the museum sector

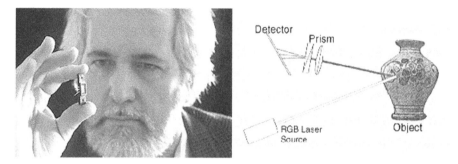

Figure 3.1   Marc Rioux, inventor of the first laser scanner, and the basic concept

was identified as one of several areas of potential application, it was thought that the development of the technology would primarily be driven by industrial applications. These applications included robot vision systems, inspection, and rapid prototyping as well as medical and anthropometrical applications.

Figure 3.1 (right) illustrates the principle of the 3D technology. An RGB (red, green and blue) laser source projects a small 50-micron white light laser spot on the object. The light beam reflected back to the camera is separated into its red, green and blue components and converted into an electronic signal by the detector. The position on the detector is a function of the position (x, y and z measurements) of the spot on the object. Significantly, the shape and colour measurement are recorded simultaneously. The complete object is recorded by scanning the spot over the entire object.

However, following presentations at several international conferences in the early 1990s, including EVA '92 in London,[2] our attention became increasingly drawn to cultural applications. We at the NRC started to receive application inquiries not only from Canadian institutions but also from international museums and cultural organizations in the UK, France, Italy, USA, Israel, China and South Africa. In addition to scanning traditional museum objects, these inquiries included ones about scanning archaeological sites, paintings, sculptures, architectural elements, replication as well as VR (virtual reality) theatre and web display applications. Very seldom were two inquiries the same.

Significantly, each inquiry brought with it not only a new application, but also the requirement to develop and test a new aspect of the technology. For documenting features such as brush-stroke details on paintings or tool-mark details on sculpture, a high-resolution system was needed. A portable system was needed for archaeological and architectural site recording. A large volume camera was required for large sculptures. The ability to measure surface reflectance along with the shape of an object opened new possibilities in condition monitoring. New and improved software programs were needed for each scanning application as well as for new display technologies including interactive/immersive 3D VR theatres and web productions. As time went on and the inquiries kept coming in, we recognized that the cultural applications were driving the development of the technology.

Up to 2001, ten Canadian companies had licensed various segments of the technology and it is used for a wide range of applications – not only in the cultural sector, but also for industrial, space, modelling and display applications. The purpose of this paper is to present a summary of some of the more significant cultural applications which have driven the development of the technology. Several of these have been reported in more detail in papers at various EVA Conferences as well as in other forums.

NRC 3D Imaging Technology

Three high-resolution 3D imaging systems, the High Resolution Laser Scanner, the Biris 3D Laser Camera and the Large Volume Laser Scanner (Figure 3.2), each designed for different imaging applications, have been applied to a variety of cultural recording projects.[3–6]

The High Resolution Laser Scanner simultaneously digitizes the 3D shape and colour of traditional museum objects and provides a maximum depth resolution of 10 microns.[7–10] In Figure 3.2 (left) it is shown scanning a ceramic figurine.

The Biris system is a portable 3D monochrome imaging system and is ideally suited for field recording applications.[11–13] It provides an accuracy of 80 microns at a range of 0.3 m. The Biris camera (middle) can be mounted either on a conventional tripod or on a linear translation stage for scanning.

The Large Volume Scanner is a research prototype system for high-resolution monochrome 3D digitization of large structures at a standoff distance from 50 cm to 10 m.[14–15] At a standoff of 50 cm, it provides a resolution of 70 microns. The scanner (right) can be mounted on a telescoping tripod and raised to a height of 10 m to scan large objects such as outdoor sculpture.

These systems use a low-power non-damaging laser light to digitize sequential overlapping images from multiple points of view over the surface of an object or site. Once scanned, data modelling and display software is used to integrate the multiple view datasets into a seamless archival quality high-resolution 3D digital model of the object.[16,17] The software also enables the data to be used for a variety of heritage applications.

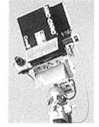

Figure 3.2   The High Resolution Laser Scanner (left), the Biris 3D Laser Camera (middle) and the Large Volume Laser Scanner (right)

Cultural Applications

During the research and development phase of the technology, as noted above, we have collaborated on a number of projects to test and demonstrate the cultural applications with several Canadian and international museums and cultural agencies. The following is a summary of some of these projects for interactive display, archival recording and replication applications.

Interactive Display Applications

A unique feature of this technology is that the scanner digitizes details of objects at high resolution and in perfect registration. This enables the rendering of very accurate 'high-fidelity' 3D models for interactive display on high-end information kiosks or in 3D VR theatres within a museum or at a remote site connected with high-speed communications systems. One of the primary 'driving force' applications has been unique interactive displays for museum exhibitions as well as for web-based virtual museums. For example, high-resolution 3D digital models of museum objects can be transmitted to remote locations using modern communication systems for interactive manipulation in information kiosks and home computers. Similarly, archaeological sites can be digitized and interactively displayed in 3D VR theatres. In addition, compact 3D models, which retain excellent model-to-object fidelity, can be used for interactive web exhibitions.

Remote interactive 3D display   In the 1997 exhibition *The 3rd Dimension: A New Way of Seeing in Cyberspace*, at the Canadian Museum of Civilization, one of NRC's industrial partners, Hymarc, developed a Colorscan system (Figure 3.3) for digitizing objects from the Museum's collection.[18] Two interactive display stations were used for stereo image display – one at the Museum (Figure 3.3, left) and the second at a 'remote site' at the Royal British Columbia Museum in Victoria (Figure 3.3, right). Visitors could select an object from a menu, examine it and access associated text information. Stereo viewing glasses were provided for viewing the images in stereo. In addition to rotating the object, visitors could zoom in and examine specific details of interest.

Figure 3.3   The Hymarc Colorscan system

Interactive 3D virtualized reality   Interactive 3D virtualized reality systems are increasingly being used for museum display and heritage site interpretation applications. In a virtualized reality display, the simulation models are created from 3D imaging data recorded directly from the site or object.[19] The systems provide a real-time interaction with the models in a display that gives the user 3D immersion in the model world and direct manipulation of objects. These systems offer the potential of accurate 'digital reconstruction' of archaeological and historic sites as well as 'digital repatriation' of models of artefacts, which have been removed to distant museums, back into the virtualized model of the original site.

In May 1998, the exhibition *Mysteries of Egypt* opened at the Canadian Museum of Civilization in conjunction with the world première of the IMAX movie *Mysteries of Egypt*. With an attendance of nearly 700,000, it was the most popular exhibition presented by the Museum and the second all-time highest attendance generator for a temporary exhibition in Canada.

As a new feature, the Museum collaborated with NRC and several industrial partners on the construction of a virtual reality 3D theatre and on the production of a VR tour of the tomb of Tutankhamun.[20] The latter featured a virtual visit into the burial chamber. Visitors to the actual tomb can enter only the first undecorated antechamber; a railing prevents entry into the burial chamber. The 3D model of the tomb (Figure 3.4) was prepared from survey data provided by the Theban Mapping Project using a CAD program called ArchiCAD. Texture maps of the paintings in the burial chamber were mapped on the 3D model using detailed colour slides provided by the Getty Conservation Institute. Permission to use the survey data and slides was granted by the Supreme Council of Antiquities in Egypt.

To illustrate the concept of 'digital repatriation', a 3D model of a replica of Tutankhamun's funeral mask was integrated into the 3D model of the tomb. The replica was scanned using the Colorscan system. The mask model was placed inside the sarcophagus where it was found and was introduced into the display at the conclusion of the tour to demonstrate how models of objects, which are originally associated with a site, can be reintegrated into a digital reconstruction.

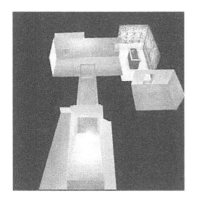 

Figure 3.4   3D models for the tour of Tutankhamun's tomb

Interactive web display   In April 2001, the Canadian Heritage Information Network (CHIN) launched the new Virtual Museum of Canada (VMC).[21] During the planning stages for the VMC, CHIN conducted a survey of focus groups with an interest in museums and culture across Canada.[22] One of the results noted in the report was:

> In each session, a portion of the participants had clear expectations of a three-dimensional tour of one or many museums. Some of these participants clearly explained how the website user would be able to control their path through a museum, allowing them to pivot and view any section of the museum and objects in the museum in 3D.

To meet this objective, NRC collaborated with the Canadian Museum of Civilization on the production of *Inuit 3D*, one of six inaugural VMC exhibitions. *Inuit 3D* is an interactive exhibition in which visitors navigate through three exhibition halls and interactively examine twelve 3D models of Inuit objects from the Museum's collection.[23]

Within the constraints of a web exhibition, a primary objective was the display of 3D models of the objects which represented the shape, subtle colour variations, material characteristics (ivory, bone, stone, metal) and features such as tool-mark details as closely as possible to the actual object. In short, the *fidelity* of the 3D models to the actual objects was a priority.

As noted above, the High Resolution Laser Scanner records high-resolution models of objects that can be used for the display of accurate '*high-fidelity*' 3D on high-end information kiosks. For *Inuit 3D*, the PolyWorks™[24] software suite was used to prepare lower-resolution models, which retained excellent object–model fidelity for web display. In compressing the high-resolution models, the software computes a texture-mapped compressed triangular mesh. The algorithm for the automatic generation of the texture map is coupled to the mesh vertex removal compression. When the tessellated texture map is applied to the compressed model, it generates a 3D appearance that approximates the appearance of the full resolution coloured model (Figure 3.5).

The upper and lower images of the flying bear on the left of Figure 3.5 illustrate the high-resolution model while those on the right illustrate the compressed model used in *Inuit 3D*. The high-resolution model contains 443,628 polygons of shape information (lower left) in an 11.8 megabyte file. This model is the archival quality model. The compressed model contains 1,000 polygons of shape detail (lower right) in a 1.2 kilobyte file. When a 512 x 512 texture map is applied to the compressed model (top right), it generates a 3D appearance that approximates the appearance of the full resolution coloured model (top left). Thus a close approximation to the fidelity of the high-resolution model is retained in the 3D models used for web applications such as *Inuit 3D*.

Archival Recording

Another major driving force has been the application of the technology to provide archival quality records or '3D digital models' of important museum objects, architectural elements and heritage sites for cultural institutions. Once the object or

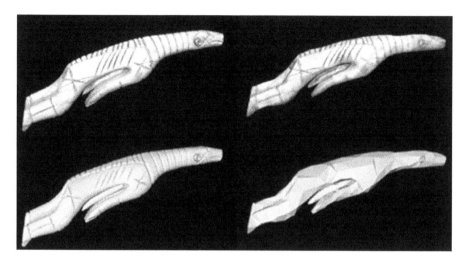

Figure 3.5   *Inuit 3D* **flying bear models**

site is recorded, the data provides an archival record, which can then be used for a wide variety of applications – including display, research, conservation and replication – without the need to re-digitize the object for each application. The following are some examples.

Archaeological sites   As a result of the construction of a hydroelectric dam on the Yangtze River, in the Three Gorges area of China, an estimated 800–1,000 heritage sites will be flooded and lost by 2009. The recording of these sites represents a significant and high priority challenge for the State Administration of Cultural Heritage (SACH). In September 1999, NRC collaborated with the Canadian Foundation for the Preservation of Chinese Cultural and Historical Treasures and Innovision 3D – one of our industrial partners – in a pilot project to demonstrate the application of Biris 3D technology for recording some of these sites.

For the pilot project, a laboratory research prototype system was taken to China and used to scan a rock-carving niche at the 9th-century Bei Shan site near Dazu (Figure 3.6). Subsequently, working with ShapeGrabber Inc.,[25] another NRC industrial partner, Innovision, designed and built a portable 3D imaging system for use by SACH in recording the sites. Innovision is currently continuing collaboration with Chinese officials on this project.

Figure 3.6 shows the Biris system set up on scaffolding at niche no.147 at Bei Shan (left and middle): the archival 3D model recorded by the system is shown on the right.

Sculpture and architectural building elements   Projects have also been undertaken to demonstrate the applications of 3D scanning systems for archival recording of sculpture and architectural building elements.

Figure 3.6   Portable 3D imaging system at Bei Shan, China

To demonstrate the application for recording large outdoor sculpture, the Large Volume System was used to digitize the sculpture *Mythic Messengers* by the artist Bill Reid at the Canadian Museum of Civilization. The sculpture measures 9 m long x 1.2 m wide and is mounted 4 m above ground level on an exterior wall at the Museum (see Figure 3.7, left). The objective was to prepare an accurate archival 3D digital record of the sculpture, which could be used to prepare an accurate scale replica of the sculpture.

To scan *Mythic Messengers*, the camera, attached to a remote controlled pan-and-tilt unit, was mounted on a custom-designed telescopic tripod, which enabled it to be raised to a height of 10 m (Figure 3.7, left). Scans of over 100 different views of the sculpture were recorded at a resolution in the order of 1 mm to produce a colour-coded image (Figure 3.7, middle right). The multiple view scans were then merged into a single 3D digital model (Figure 3.7, lower right). This was used to prepare a 2 cm x 10 cm scale replica.

In 1998, in collaboration with the University of Ferrara in Italy, the Biris system was used to digitize a number of architectural building elements on the façade of the 8th-century Abbey of Pomposa, near Ferrara (Figure 3.8). The building elements included scans of a rosone, a peacock and a column as well as a large 2 m x 6 m area of the façade. For heritage preservation applications, the image data documents the surface condition of features at the time it was digitized. The Biris camera is shown mounted on a conventional tripod (left) scanning the rosone (middle). The

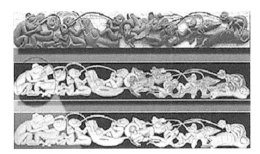

Figure 3.7   3D scanning of a large outdoor sculpture, *Mythic Messages*, in Canada

Figure 3.8   3D imaging of façades, Abbey of Pomposa, Italy

archival digital model (right) records the surface shape and condition of the object after 1,100 years' exposure to the elements. Additional details on this project can be found in references 11, 12 and 26.

Replication Applications

In the museum community, there is substantial economic interest and activity in the replication and sale of objects. The 3D image data can be transferred into CAD models for fabricating accurate 1:1 or scale replicas using modern replication technologies such as stereo lithography. There are four important advantages to this approach for museum and heritage applications:

● Unlike direct casting, the object is not touched or damaged during scanning.
● Scale replicas made using the 3D model data are much closer or truer representations of the shape of the original object than those copied by hand.
● The data can be formatted to machine the replica directly (positive mode) or to make a mould (negative or inverse image).
● Similar to print making, the artist or museum owning rights to the object can make scale replicas of works for sale as limited edition replicas.

As an example, during the exhibition *Mysteries of Egypt*, the Canadian Museum of Civilization used the Large Volume Laser Scanner to scan a large model of a sphinx in order to prepare smaller replicas for sale in the Museum shop during the exhibition (Figure 3.9). The original sphinx measured 2 m in length while the scale replicas were 28 cm and 11 cm in length. (This exercise provided a revenue stream both for the Museum and NRC.)

Beyond the fabrication of replicas, the same technologies can provide important assistance in restoration after severe damage. A three-dimensional model could be used to enable reconstruction of an item with a controllable level of fidelity to the original.

Figure 3.9   Making sphinx replicas for museum shop sale at the Canadian Museum of Civilization

Conclusions

As noted in the introduction, cultural sector applications have become one of the main driving forces in the development of NRC's 3D technology. These applications require high quality digitizing systems to record a wide range of sizes, shapes and materials as well as a variety of data processing and display systems to utilize the data for different goals.

The involvement of members of the cultural sector in the early steps of the research on 3D imaging and modelling at NRC proved beneficial to both parties: the researchers obtained valuable feedback on the technology, and new research impetus; museum and curatorial staff were exposed very early to an emerging technology, and were able to steer aspects of its development towards the solution of important problems.

Research that was aimed at heritage applications led to new developments and applications of the technology that was relevant in other sectors, as well as to new business opportunities for our industrial partners.

Notes

1   Marc Rioux, Project Leader, 3D Sensors, Visual Information Technology, Institute for Information Technology, National Research Council of Canada, Ottawa, Canada, K1A 0M8 (marc.rioux@nrc.ca).
2   Baribeau, R., Rioux, M., Cournoyer, L. and Godin, G. (1992), 'Applications of colour and range sensing for the recording and study of museum objects', EVA '92, London, Electronic Imaging and the Visual Arts, 31st July 1992, *Proceedings*, ISBN 0 9519980 3 X.
3   Taylor, J.M. and Beraldin, J.-A. (2001) 'Heritage recording applications of high resolution 3D imaging', EVA 2001, Florence, Electronic Imaging and the Visual Arts, 26th–30th March 2001, *Proceedings*, pp. 40–5.
4   Godin, G., Cournoyer, L., Domey, J. and Taylor, J., 'Three-dimensional recording of objects and sites using laser range imaging', Quaderni 10, Centro di Ricerche Informatiche per i Beni Culturali, X 2000, ISSN 1126-6090, pp. 139–50.

5 Beraldin, J.-A., Blais, F., Boulanger, P., Cournoyer, L., Domey, J., El-Hakim, S.F., Godin, G., Rioux, M. and Taylor, J. (2000) 'Real world modelling through high resolution digital 3D imaging of objects and structures', *ISPRS Journal of Photogrammetry and Remote Sensing*, 55, pp. 230–50.

6 Additional information on NRC 3D technology and on the museum and heritage applications can be found on our web site at: http://www.vit.iit.nrc.ca/.

7 Baribeau, R., Cournoyer, L., Godin, G.and Rioux, M. (1996) 'Colour three-dimensional modelling of museum objects', *Imaging the Past, Electronic Imaging and Computer Graphics in Museum and Archaeology*, British Museum Occasional Paper Number 114, London, pp. 199–209.

8 Baribeau, R., Rioux, M. and Godin, G. (1992) 'Recent advances in the use of a laser scanner in the examination of paintings', Restoration '92, Amsterdam, *Proceedings*, pp. 69–73.

9 Baribeau, R., Rioux M. and Godin G. (1992) 'Colour reflectance modelling using a polychromatic laser range sensor', *IEEE Transactions on Pattern Analysis and Machine Intelligence*, vol. 14, no. 2, pp. 263–9.

10 NRC has licensed this technology to Arius3D (http://www.arius3d.com).

11 Beraldin, J.-A., Blais, F., Cournoyer, L., Rioux, M., Bernier, F., and Harrison, N. (1998) 'Portable digital 3-D imaging system for remote sites', 3D Data Modelling and Imaging – The 1998 IEEE International Symposium On Circuit and Systems, Monterey, CA, USA, 31st May–3rd June, pp. 326–33.

12 See: *Imaging for Rapid Response on Remote Sites* on our website at http://www.vit.iit.nrc.ca/.

13 NRC has licensed this technology to the ShapeGrabber Corporation (http://www.shapegrabber.com/). Innovision 3D provides a commercial scanning service using this scanner (http://www.innovision3d.com).

14 Rioux, M., Beraldin, J.-A., Blais, F., Godin, G. and Cournoyer, L. (1997) 'High resolution digital 3-D imaging of large structures', Three-Dimensional Image Capture, *SPIE Proceedings*, vol. 3023, 11th February 1997, San Jose, CA, pp. 109–118.

15 See: *Demonstration of Heritage 3-D Imaging Applications in Israel* on our website http://www.vit.iit.nrc.ca/.

16 Soucy, M., Godin, G., Baribeau, R., Blais, F. and Rioux, M. (1996) 'Sensors and algorithms for the construction of digital 3-D colour models of real objects', *ICIP-96 Proceedings*, 1996 IEEE International Conference on Image Processing, Lausanne, Switzerland, vol. II of III, 16th–19th September 1996, pp. 409–12.

17 The suite of PolyWorks™ software 3D modelling tools is available from InnovMetric Software Inc. (http://www.innovmetric.com), an NRC licensee.

18 Livingstone, F., Evans, K., Taylor, J., Rioux, M., and Arsenault-Desfossés, H. (1997) 'The 3rd dimension: a new way of seeing in cyberspace', EVA '97 Paris, Musée du Louvre, Electronic Imaging and the Visual Arts, 2nd September 1997, *Conference Proceedings*, 10.1–10.13.

19 Boulanger, P., Taylor, J., El-Hakim, S. and Rioux, M. (1998) 'How to virtualize reality: an application to the re-creation of world heritage sites', VSMM98, International Society on Virtual Systems and Multimedia, 18th–20th November 1998, Gifu, Japan, *Conference Proceedings*, 39–45.

20 MacDonald, G., Corcoran, F., Taylor, J., Boulanger, P. and Rioux, M., (1999) 'CMC's 3D Virtual Reality Theatre: VR tours of two tombs during the *Mysteries of Egypt* Exhibition', MMM99, Multimedia Modeling, Ottawa, Canada, 4th–6th October 1999, *Conference Proceedings*, edited by A. Karmouch, pp. 167–177.

21 http://www.virtualmuseum.ca/

22 Nadeau, R. (2000) *Concept Testing of The Virtual Museum of Canada, Summary Focus Group Report*, Decima Research Inc., prepared for the Canadian Heritage Information Network (http://www.chin.gc.ca/Vmc/e_report.html).

23   Corcoran, F., Demaine, J., Picard, M., Dicaire, L.-G. and Taylor. J. (2002), 'Inuit 3D: An Interactive Virtual 3D Web Exhibition', Museums and the Web 2002, Boston, 17th–20th April 2002, CD of Proceedings.
24   PolyWorks™ (www.innovmetric.com)
25   http://www.shapegrabber.com
26   Addison, A.C. and Gaiani, M. (2000) 'Virtualized architectural heritage: new tools and techniques', *IEEE MultiMedia*, April–June 2000, vol. 7, no. 2, pp. 26–31

Chapter 4

The Information Society and Technology (IST) in Russian Culture: Strategic Review and New Initiatives

Nadezda V.Brakker and Leonid A. Kujbyshev

Abstract

The paper presents recent trends in state information policy in the Russian cultural sphere and reviews legislation supporting the Information Society. It looks at the best examples of IST in Russian museums, galleries, libraries, archives, non-movable heritage and the performing arts. New perspectives in international cooperation are welcomed.

The Face of the Russian Internet

Different sources show different figures for the number of Internet users in Russia. For example, according to the Ministry for Economic Development and Trade Data, now (as at the end of 2003) 8.5 million users have access to the Internet, 35% of them use the Internet at home, 45% in their offices, 20% via public access points. In 2005–2006 the number of Internet users in Russia should grow by a factor of 2.3 times and will become 20 million.

According to the Web-Vector project, the Russian Internet audience grows 10–12% every quarter. If in the beginning of 2003 5.1 million people used the Internet every month (3.6 million of them living in large cities) then in the first quarter of 2004 the monthly audience would be about 5.7 million, including 4.2 million living in large and medium cities. Among the Internet users living in the cities, 47% use the Internet every day and 21% once a week.

Most of the increase in users of the Russian Internet (shortened to Runet) was due to so-called irregular users who visited the Internet more than once. This means that the Internet is still needed for work and education and that the effort of organizing common access Internet points in libraries, museums, clubs and educational institutions is not wasted and brings new Internet users. This reinforces the idea that for Russia, with its vast territory and poor population, the possibility of Internet access in places of common use in libraries, in the universities or at school is very important.

Of Russian Internet users, 79% are younger than 45. Stable growth of Internet users among managers (20%) and students (30%) is registered. Some 35% of the

Runet audience use the Internet at home and 73% of them have a monthly income below $100 per person.

The majority of Internet users are still from Moscow (38%) and Saint Petersburg (9%); they are well educated (78% are university graduates or students).

At the beginning of March 2002 the largest search engine in Runet, Yandex, estimated Russian Internet volume at 1 terabyte (2^{40} bytes). In 2000 the Russian Internet became much 'wider', that is, many new sites with just a few pages appeared. This was because in 2000 several large hosting portals (like narod.ru) were opened. They gave to anyone free space for sites, 3rd level domain addresses (like xxx.narod.ru) and easy tools to create web pages without special training. By contrast, in 2001 there was a process of growing 'in depth', and sites grew larger. The overall volume of Runet more than doubled whilst the number of new sites was less than in the previous year. The median volume of a site (server) became larger then in the 'pre-hosting' period and is now 2.5 megabytes. (http://www.yandex.ru/chisla.html).

Cultural resources on Runet, according to Spylog analysis (http://www.spylog.ru) comprise 17.6% of the sites visited. The number of cultural Internet projects is constantly growing (by approximately 20% a year). The most speedily growing fields are photography (29%), theatre (23%), art (22%) and cinema (22%).

Russian Government Policy and the Internet

Federal bodies started to pay serious attention to the Internet and to the Information Society after President Putin signed the Okinawa Charter on Global Information Society, which was then adopted by G8 in July 2000.

Russian state Information Society policy is becoming more and more specific. On 10th January 2002 President Putin signed a federal law on electronic signatures, the main idea of which is that an electronic signature is legally equivalent to a graphic signature and a document signed electronically has all traditional functions. A law on electronic business was discussed in the State Duma and passed the first reading.

A Federal Programme, 'Electronic Russia 2002–2010' has been adopted. It states that development of information and communication technologies (ICT) is a global trend in world development. Modern ICTs play a decisive role in economic competitiveness and integration into the world economic system and improve effectiveness on all levels in state and private sectors. ICTs give a technological basis for the development of civil society as they give open and prompt access to information through the global Internet. The Programme will enable maximum use of intellectual potential, provide a way to enter the world post-industrial economy on a basis of cooperation and open information, overcome the 'digital divide' and protect human rights, including the right of free access to information and the right to protect private information (http://www.netoscope.ru/docs/2766.html). It is a pity that the Ministry of Culture is not an official partner of the Programme but cultural heritage projects can be supported on a project-by-project basis.

The government decree on Internet connections in post offices all over Russia aims to provide Internet access to people lacking facilities and skills. The plan is to organize centres of collective Internet access in 1,860 regional post offices. In March 2003 the KiberPost@ Net had 2,600 Internet points. Currently [2004] the Ministry of Communication is developing a project ('Ciberpress') for electronic delivery of newspapers and other periodicals: the list now includes 84 titles. This helps significantly reduce the delay in periodicals supply to faraway Russian regions.

In 2001 the Ministry of Education of Russia, in cooperation with regional authorities, completed a programme of computerization of country schools, supplying hardware and software to schools and providing training to teachers in 97% of schools (http://ccs.mto.ru/results.html). In 2002–2003 the Ministry of Education supplied computers to orphanages and schools for orphans and to school libraries and continued the programme of the Internet access improvement in schools.

Several projects involving training courses for school teachers are managed by the Federation of Internet Education (www.fio.ru). One of the projects ('Generation.ru') is supported by an oil company, YUKOS. The goal of 'Generation.ru' is to overcome a serious gap between Russia and other countries in ICT skills and equipment in educational institutions. The project will run for five years and organize Education Internet Centres in 50 regions where more than 250,000 school teachers will learn how to use the Internet for education. These teachers will be able to teach more than 10 million pupils. By now 41 Centres are open in Russian regions. From 21st March 2000 to 3rd March 2004, 95,185 school teachers were trained under the project.

The Federal Programme 'Electronic Government' is very successful: official Internet sites have been opened for the President, the Security Council, the Russian Government, (http://www.gov.ru/, http://www.government.ru/), the State Duma, and for all Ministers of regional administrations (http://www.egovernment.ru/).

IST in the Russian Cultural Sector

General

The Ministry of Culture also has an Internet site (http://www.mincultrf.ru/), which is becoming more important for cultural sector management. The site keeps information on the Ministry structure and staff, a reference list of federal and regional cultural institutions, documents, plans and programmes, laws on museums, libraries, etc., news and other useful information.

Some Internet servers of regional administrations have pages on culture with lists of institutions, news and events, art galleries, etc. For example, the Vologda region Internet site (www.vologda-oblast.ru) is in Russian, English and German; the Karelia Republic official site (www.gov.karelia.ru) is Russian, English and Finnish and has a culture and tourism section; Evenkia (http://www.krasu.ru/evenkia_e/ex1/index.html) has English pages with information on nature, tourism, traditions, rituals, a list of artists and an art gallery.

Culture of Russia (www.RussianCulture.ru) is an official portal of the Ministry of Culture of the Russian Federation. The project was started in 2000. The idea of the portal is to present Russian culture and to serve as an educational resource for a wide audience. The pilot version has a news and events section and three ways in: topic entry (fine art, literature, architecture, theatre, cinema, music, applied arts), type entry (people, works, stories, events, sites, cultural institutions guide and board) and a timescale. The pilot version contains 1,515 objects, 252 people, 484 works, 557 images, 557 organizations, 16 articles, 2,457 links between the objects and 60,684 words in the searching guide. It will be bilingual but now only menus and the front page are in English. The portal has an attractive design and is going to be a good encyclopaedia of Russian culture, with its own rich information resource and some links to other cultural information resources. Culture of Russia does not create its own catalogue of Internet resources but links to portals and servers with rich catalogues of cultural resources. Because of lack of financing the portal is still in a pilot version.

Libraries

Libraries are ahead of other cultural sectors in IST. In many libraries of Moscow and Saint Petersburg (for example, the Kievskaya library system www.libnet.ru) and in all large state regional libraries there are *mediathekas* or Internet halls with free Internet access. Many libraries provide their catalogues on the Internet. The list of available library catalogues can be found at the site of the Russian Library Association (www.rba.ru) which plays an important role in the process of library informatization. The Library Department of the Ministry of Culture organizes and actively supports IST processes in libraries. One of the main efforts was the development of the Russian UNIMARK version, officially adopted in 2002. Since 1997 the Department has led a specialized programme called LIBNET (Library Net) (www.ruslibnet.ru) or 'Development of All-Russia Information Library Computer Net'. One of the LIBNET programme projects is a National Information Library Centre (www.nilc.ru).

The first stage of the project (2001–2003) is to create a specialized net for the united electronic catalogue of Russian libraries. The catalogue will play a very important role and will make it possible to obtain information on the stocks of all the largest libraries of Russia, to organize intelligent document delivery to users all over Russia, to coordinate the development of library stocks and to organize shared cataloguing for the majority of Russian libraries. Currently the National Information Library Centre keeps catalogues of new books of the Russian State Library (Moscow) and the Russian National Library (Saint Petersburg) and a mechanism for downloading catalogue descriptions which can be used by any subscribing library.

At the end of 1998 an 18-month project under TACIS (Creating an Information System for the Russian State Library) was started: this was the Russian State Library (RSL) Information Project. It aimed to support the modernization of the Russian State Library from a traditional to a digital library, introducing new information technology to meet the growing information needs of the Russian market and to bring to life the vast resources of the national library. The TACIS project was successfully finished in 2000 with the conference 'Digital Future of the Libraries'. On 12th March 2002 the Russian State Library announced a new international project funded by the Andrew W. Mellon Foundation, 'Development of digital services system for RSL users'.

In 2003 the Library Department of the Ministry of Culture started the project 'National Digital Library', aimed at digitizing and making accessible full texts of books. The first stage of the project is the digitization of the dissertation theses deposited in the Russian State Library.

The Russian Information Library Consortium (RILC) is a consortium created by the partners of the project 'Russian libraries in the third millennium'. The project is funded by the European Commission, under the aegis of the 'Key Institutions' of the IBPP or Institutions Building Partnership Programme. This built on the results of the TACIS TELRUS 9705 Project (1998–2000), which introduced a fully integrated library system to the Russian State Library in Moscow. RILC pursues different and broader objectives, involving a partnership of five important Russian libraries, which are working towards the goal of developing and implementing a joint web gateway to their bibliographic and full text electronic resources, utilizing the Z39.50 protocol and gateway software with advanced searching capabilities. The partnership includes the Russian State Library, the Russian National Library, the Russian State Library for Foreign Literature, the Parliamentary Library and the Moscow State University Academic Library.

Museums

Museums are some way behind libraries in IST. Electronic catalogues of Russian museums contain no more than 10.8% of Russian museum holdings and these catalogues are without images in the main. There are practically no museum catalogues on open access though there are some leaders. For example, the State Hermitage Internet site (http://www.hermitagemuseum.org), designed with IBM support, is considered to be the best and was awarded the National Internet Prize in 2001 and 2002. In 2001 the first museum on-line shop, with all necessary components of e-commerce, opened at the State Hermitage site (http://shop. hermitagemuseum.org/index.html). The State Rybinsk architecture and art museum-reserve was the first museum in Russia to open its full collection catalogue on the Internet (http://rmuseum.orbis.spb.ru) with good search facilities. The catalogue is based on the specialized software for museum collection management, IAMIS2000, designed by ALTSOFT (Saint Petersburg).

Though there is no specific IST programme for museums in the framework of the federal programme 'Culture of Russia (2001–2005)', the Museum Department of the Ministry of Culture initiated a project to develop the United Museum Catalogue. The project is currently at the stage of software testing and thesaurus development.

The portal 'Museums of Russia' (www.museum.ru) plays the leading role in presenting museum information on the Internet. Since 1996 this portal has been developed by the non-commercial institution Russian Cultural Heritage Net. Since 1996 the portal has been improved several times to answer growing user needs and has won more than 30 awards, the National Internet Prize being one of them. Among cultural sites the portal is the leader in number of citations and in number of visitors. The portal is important both for professionals and for the public and includes:

● all-Russia Museum Register of 3,000 museums, redesigned in 2001

- all-Russian museums news: 500 articles a month, 5 magazines, 7,000 subscribers, republication by largest Internet portals
- discussion forum in electronic conferences and on-line chat
- annotated catalogue of about 700 museum sites (Russia and internationally) and net services
- a section for professionals with news, publications, contacts, exhibition exchange, professional sites list, museum institutions, Internet lecture hall
- e-mail service for Russian museums giving an e-mail address for each museum
- 'visiting cards' of 4,500 museum specialists.

The portal plans to add a children's section, cultural tourism section, Internet shop and a gallery.

The (museum) Association on Documentation and Information Technologies or ADIT (www.adit.ru) plays a major role in museum IST activities. Since 1997 ADIT has organized annual conferences, such as 'Museums and Information Space: informatization and cultural heritage', in different cities. The 7th ADIT conference was in the Pushkin Museum (Pskov region) 15th–18th April 2003. ADIT was the Russian organizer of the annual CIDOC conference in Saint Petersburg, 1st–5th September 2003 with the topic 'Electronic Museums in Modern Society: Challenges and Contradictions'. ADIT was a partner in the EU 'Open Heritage' project, aiming to present the Karelia region in the open European net. Another project (Russian Dimension) was born as a consequence of ADIT participation in Open Heritage. The project develops models for applying new technologies to Russian regional memory institutions. The aim of the project is twofold. On one hand it provides services for the museum, ranging from network and facility management to promotion. On the other hand it presents the museum as a part of the cultural heritage of a region, thus strengthening the profile of the region and enhancing its attractiveness towards the cultural tourist.

The most proactive education techniques are used at 'Project and Analysis Workshops' (PAW), organized and held by ADIT jointly with its partner, the Future Museum group. The key topics of PAW are information management in the cultural sphere, information technology and the cultural heritage. The workshops are targeted at administrators of culture departments and organizations and the staff of museums and libraries. A workshop of this kind is aimed primarily at generating ideas and developing them into projects. Participants of a PAW are not divided into trainers and students. Every workshop has participants, experts, coordinators and a facilitator who enables communication in the sessions. PAWs are collective efforts at which problems are first identified and then ideas are generated and formed into projects. Activities include group work, masterclasses, lectures, presentations, expert consultations and plenary sessions. In just fifteen months, over 300 heads of culture departments and museum and library staff came from various Russian regions to be trained at PAW. A follow-up on the workshops is the education manual on information technology and the cultural heritage now available at http://www.future.museum.ru, the web page of the Future Museum.

Other professional museum associations also play an important role in the museum sector; for example, the Association of Museum Specialists of Russia or AMR, http://www.amr-museum.ru). The AMR Resource Centre is a coordination and management body of AMR with the following goals:

- development of the AMR information collecting function, consulting service and publication of an AMR members' reference book
- improving museum communications through IST and integration with other communities
- publication of the magazine *World and Museum*
- web studio for museum sites development
- creation of a research library, digital library and *mediatheka* for museum specialists;
- organization of seminars, conferences, workshops, training courses and competitions.

Archives

Archives are the most 'closed' part of the Russian cultural heritage, though IST is bringing about considerable changes in this sector. The Federal Archive Service of Russia has an Internet site (http://www.rusarchives.ru) with information on the archive sector, legislation, a catalogue of federal and regional archives, documents, a list of archiving institutions, thematic databases, archive education information, a list of reference books and other publications, news and other useful information. A catalogue of the Moscow and Saint Petersburg Archives in Russian and English (http://www.openweb.ru/rusarch/index.htm) is based on a specialized database called ArcheoBiblioBase (ABB). This was designed as a result of a Russian–US joint project with the Russian Federal Archive Service, the State Historical Public Library and the Saint Petersburg branch of the Russian Academy of Science Archive.

'Personal Photodocuments Internet-catalogue of the Central State Archive of cinema and photo documents of Saint-Petersburg' (www.photoarchive.spb.ru) is a good example of an on-line catalogue. Currently it provides access to 12,280 document descriptions and 1,734 personalia automatically generated from the archive database. The access mechanism is based on intranet-Internet technologies and has a good search engine with effective searches on headings, key words and context. The importance of the on-line catalogue will grow, since the full archive collection has 500,000 unique photo documents. The database is managed by archive specialists with technology and software developed by ALTSOFT (Saint Petersburg).

A new project started in 2000 is the Russian Archives Online (RAO), the main objective of which is the creation and launching on the Internet of large volume databases containing descriptions of audio and visual materials from Russian archival collections. It aims to provide access to archival documents for numerous users in Russia and worldwide. Although Russian archival collections are well organized on the basis of traditional, 'pre-computer' methods, one can use their materials only after tiresome research efforts on site, having looked through cards of paper catalogues written either manually or with the help of a typewriter. Even in Russia there are few people who are aware of the rich audio and visual archival collections. Making on-line educational resources (in particular, connected with the history of Russia) based on archival collections constitutes a top priority activity within the framework of the project.

The project also foresees e-commerce; that is, licensing archival audio and visual materials selected from specially created databases. The proceeds will be used for collection preservation. This has already begun. The project is supported by a number of international organizations – the US Agency for International Development, Internews, the Open Society Institute, UNESCO, as well as the Russian Foundation for Basic Research (RFBR). Apart from archive employees, the Keldysh Institute of Applied Mathematics, the Russian Academy of Sciences, Moscow and Texas Universities and the Abamedia Company (USA) contribute to the development of the project.

The actual work began as far back as 1996 when a decision was made to create an electronic catalogue of the Russian State Archive for Documentaries and Photos in Krasnogorsk (RGAKFD). This archive possesses the largest collection of documentaries and stills that reflect the history of Russia and the Soviet republics. The Krasnogorsk Archive has in its stock more than 215,000 reels of documentaries and more than 38,000 titles, of which more than 1,000 date back to before the Revolution. The Archive stores more than one million photos and negatives, as well as unique albums of the last Tsar's family. The Krasnogorsk collection, representing an illustrated history of Russia from the middle of the nineteenth century, not only arouses the interest of non-fiction filmmakers and mass media all over the world, but also constitutes a major source of documentary materials for scientific and especially historical research. The archival collection plays an even more important role for the whole range of activities connected with education, both in Russia itself and beyond.

At present the database for the electronic catalogue of the Krasnogorsk Archive contains descriptions of the larger part of its collection of films (40,500 descriptions). The catalogue can be accessed on-line (http://rgakfd.internews.ru/catalogue.htm) and is distributed on CDs. Cataloguing continues and in a year the database will have descriptions of the whole film collection. This year an English version of the electronic catalogue has been started. A methodology has been developed and tested to use Systran Professional machine translation, with the subsequent editing of the texts entered into the electronic catalogue database containing English descriptions of films from the RGAKFD collection. Some 3,000 descriptions have been translated and launched on-line (http://rgakfd.internews.ru/ecatalogue.htm). As the analysis of the results gained shows, this methodology used for translating a large volume database into English gives a result that is quite acceptable from the point of view of quality at relatively low cost. The Krasnogorsk electronic catalogue will be wholly translated into English on the basis of this approach. Completing the Krasnogorsk Archive catalogue and its translation into English are financed by the Open Society Institute. Apart from the Krasnogorsk Archive catalogue, two other catalogues that represent the collection of the Russian State Archive for Scientific and Technical Documentation (RGANTD) have been made and launched on-line. This archive stores a large number of unique photos and films about the history and development of astronautics, missiles and spaceships. Within the framework of the project, a catalogue was made that includes 3,000 photos of the greatest interest and their descriptions from the Archive collection. Space photos cataloguing was sponsored by UNESCO. The catalogue was launched on-line and its CD version has already been prepared.

Non-Movable Heritage

The portal 'Architecture of Russia' (www.archi.ru) has been on the net since July 1999 and deals with the history of Russian architecture, modern design and construction projects. It is addressed to architects, art critics and those, who are interested in Russian culture. It covers the history of the architecture of Russia and the non-movable heritage of history and culture and includes news, publications, competitions, problems of restoration, educational institutions, bibliography and links, a catalogue of monuments (now 370 monuments, 940 photos) and a catalogue of new buildings (in development). It is available in English and Russian.

The catalogue has one record for each architectural monument. It consists of one photo, brief textual information and the plan or graphic reconstruction of the original view of the monument. There is the section 'More' for most of the records, with detailed texts and additional illustrations. In the upper part of this page it is possible to choose how to search the catalogue (by alphabet, by chronology, by place, by architect, by style). According to the user's choice, a specified table of contents appears on the left to help to define the choice more precisely; for example, monument types (bridge, cathedral, church, chamber, commercial court etc.).

The alphabetical list is subdivided according to the general names of buildings (cathedral, church, mansion, etc). Within these main sections objects are organized alphabetically according to their conventional names. Churches are disposed by dedication (Trinity, Assumption, etc.), other edifices by the best known appellation (Sheremetiev Palace, Demidov Palace, etc.). The chronological list is divided according to the main periods of the development of Russian architecture. Inside this section objects are placed in chronological sequence.

'Architecture of Russia' was awarded the Grand Prix in the Art and Museums section of the Intel Internet Prize contest in 2000.

'History and Cultural Monuments of Pskov and Pskov region' (www.opskove.ru) is the full Internet catalogue of a region's non-movable heritage and is the first of its type in Russia. This is an Internet presentation of an image database developed and maintained by Pskov Research and Application Centre on History and Culture Monuments Preservation. The catalogue includes more than 400 full and well-structured architectural and historical descriptions of the most valuable monuments of Pskov and its region, with more than 1,000 images and plans, 350 personalia and 100 historical events. The project is run by ALTSOFT (Saint Petersburg) http://www.altsoft.spb.ru .[5]

EVA Moscow and its Strategic Role

Since 1998 the annual international conference EVA Moscow (www.evarussia.ru) has played an important role in the Russian 'culture x technology' sector. Centre PIC is the main EVA Moscow organizer in cooperation with the State Tretyakov Gallery and VASARI Enterprises UK (now EVA Conferences International).

The themes of EVA Moscow are actually wider than electronic imaging and the visual arts and cover all aspects of new technologies in cultural heritage. Though EVA Moscow is mostly oriented to the heritage institutions, it includes a strong

R&D aspect as well. EVA Moscow has a strong international aspect and is the only conference in Russia where specialists from different sectors of the cultural area (museums, galleries, libraries, archives, non-movable cultural heritage institutions) gather to discuss common problems of new information and communication technologies implementation in cultural heritage area. The government, research and technological sectors are also involved.

Conclusions and Future Perspectives

At the beginning of the 1990s, Russia was well behind Europe and North America in the field of 'culture x technology' – by some estimates five to six years. This gap has since been closed substantially and this is exemplified at EVA Moscow and the major annual Libraries Conference in the Crimea (which has over 1,000 participants).

Russia's great cultural heritage and now very lively cultural scene, allied with strong technological skills, indicate that Russia will make continuing progress – ideally with strong international partnerships as already shown by Russian participation in the CULTIVATE Russia, EVA Networking and MUVII projects. In July 2002 two more EU projects with Russian participation start; these are E-Culture Net and PULMAN XT. In the Sixth Framework Programme (or FP6), Russia participates in MINERVA PLUS, CALIMERA and BRICKS. It is hoped that Russia will play a key role in the Sixth Framework Programme, including working with EU partners to help other countries in the newly independent states (such as Ukraine and the new Central Asia States) to become very involved in European-wide and international work in information society technologies in culture.

Notes

1   Khan-Magomedov, J. (2003) RUnet and virtualisation of culture', *Proceedings of EVA 2003 Moscow*, Russian nonprofit center for internet technologies, Moscow, www.evarussia.ru.
2   Kniazeva, N. (2001) 'Project initiatives of ADIT', *Proceedings of EVA 2001 Moscow*, Moscow, 2001, p. 53, http://www.evarussia.ru/eva2001/english/index.html.
3   Noll, L. and Lebedev, Alexey (2001) 'ADIT in the Continuous Education System', *Proceedings of EVA 2001 Moscow*, Moscow, 2001, pp. 49–50, http://www.evarussia.ru/eva2001/english/index.html.
4   Petrov, L. and Grinfeld, Petr (2001) 'Internet-intranet catalogue of the Saint-Petersburg central state cinema & photo archive', *Proceedings of EVA 2001 Moscow*, Moscow, 2001, pp. 9~2~1 (in Russian), http://www.evarussia.ru/eva2001/russian/index.html
5   Grinfeld, P. (2001) 'Internet presentation of Pskov & its region's architectural, historical and cultural monuments data base as a core for cultural tourism information supply', *Proceedings of EVA 2001 Moscow*, Moscow, 2001, pp. 8~3~1 (in Russian), http://www.evarussia.ru/eva2001/russian/index.html.

PART 2
COOPERATIVE PROJECTS

Chapter 5

ArchTerra: An EU Project to Promote Cultural Cooperation among Eastern and Western European Archaeological Communities

Nuccia Negroni Catacchio, Laura Guidetti, Giovanni Meloni and Maurizio Camnasio

Abstract

ArchTerra had as its principal aims the networking and internationalization of existing academic resources and historical and cultural achievements between Eastern and Western Europe. The partners of the project joined in a consortium, with the purpose of establishing the technical infrastructure and software tools needed by IT researchers in archaeology to provide both practical demonstration of the transnational nature and urgency of archaeological research and management, and the benefits and efficiencies of Internet use. They aimed also to strengthen the existing scientific relations between the EU and the CEC and to promote long-term joint initiatives.

Introduction

The networking and internationalization of existing academic resources and historical and cultural achievements, as well as the research efforts of the academic community in the field of archaeology using computer, information and communication technologies, is a recent trend with a rapidly growing impact on archaeological research, management and education. Although the countries of Eastern Europe have an important place in the historical and cultural development of Europe, many cultural institutions there could not participate substantially in this process of intensifying information exchange, due to their past isolation and current economic problems. There is thus the spectre of an ever-widening *information gap* between the affluent countries of Western Europe and those countries struggling at the margins.

The Copernicus project INCO 977054 was named ArchTerra (http://archterra.cilea.it)[1] and was one of the first to help redress the imbalances in access to European networking facilities for professional archaeologists from Bulgaria, Romania and Poland, and to provide the impetus for an active expansion of archaeological Internet communication and information services, both within the CEC (the Central European Countries) and between the EU and the CEC. The project, whose logo is shown in Figure 5.1, was implemented as a research network, bringing together computer scientists and archaeologists from five EU and three CEC countries (Bulgaria, Romania and Poland). It encompasses tasks and objectives in four areas:

- technical installation (computer hardware and software, networking infrastructure)
- transfer of expertise (technical workshops, extended visits, discussion lists)
- creation of new content (Web database and exhibitions) and tools for its management
- dissemination (international conferences, printed guides, www hosts).

The Consortium for the ArchTerra project comprised the following partners:

- Groningen Institute of Archaeology of the Rijks Universiteit Groningen (Holland) – RUG
- Consorzio Interuniversitario Lombardo per la Elaborazione Automatica (Italy) – CILEA (in collaboration with the University of Milan, Department of Antiquity Sciences, Archaeology Section)
- Institute for Information Investigations of the New Bulgarian University (Bulgaria) – III NBU AIM
- Institutul de Memorie Culturala (Romania) – CIMEC
- Muzeum Archaeologizne w Poznaniu (Poland) – MAP.

The main goals of ArchTerra were to:

1. Establish the technical infrastructure and software tools needed to allow IT researchers in archaeology from CEC to join the EAW (European Archaeology Web), as national Web hosts of the ArchWeb network in the three participating CEC countries. These hosts were to be located at the main research organizations responsible for archiving, maintenance and supply of information in these countries.

Figure 5.1   The ArchTerra project logo

2. Provide practical demonstration of the transnational nature and urgency of archaeological research and management, and the benefits and efficiencies of Internet use, to professional and general users alike. End-users were to be able to access both the presently available on-line electronic resources and a core set of demonstration resources from CEC (including web pages, museum databases, live presentations and virtual tours).
3. Strengthen existing scientific relations between EU and CEC and to promote long-term joint initiatives for collaboration, demonstrating the richness and fragility of the European archaeological heritage, by gathering partners and collections from across Europe. For this purpose, solutions to specific hurdles for international collaboration (translation schemes for languages with different alphabets, multilanguage and multicultural thesauri of terms and articles, international heritage legislation) were to be explored.

Services Provided

Glossaries and Thesauri

One of the core objectives of the ArchTerra project has been breaking down existing language barriers to the communication of archaeological information and resources. Therefore a Multilingual Interfaces Workshop was held at the joint Computer Applications in Archaeology session of the Union Internationale des Sciences Prehistoriques et Protohistoriques Commission IV (CAA/UISPP) conference in April 2000.

The main goal of the multilingual glossary for Eastern European Archaeology is to create an easier access to the products created within the ArchTerra project for users belonging to different countries. The main language of the glossary is English, followed then by the native languages of the participants: Bulgarian, Polish, Italian and Romanian.

Mediolanvm

This is an easy-to-use website for information exchange between those who offer and search for fieldwork opportunities (Figure 5.2 shows its home page). An on-line database allows students and researchers to find out about, and take part in, archaeological fieldwork projects conducted all over Europe; conversely, it allows European universities and other organizations planning archaeological fieldwork to post detailed information directly on the Internet, without any intermediary.

Its main goal is to facilitate information exchange and cooperation between the European universities and bodies involved in archaeological fieldwork and cultural heritage conservation.

The name Mediolanvm[2] expresses both its location in Milan and its mediating role in promoting archaeological fieldwork throughout Europe.

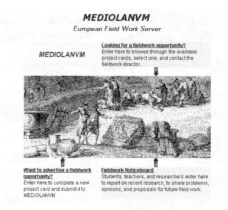

Figure 5.2   Mediolanvm home page

The ArchWebs Nodes

ArchWebs are national nodes for access to archaeological web resources. Though no formal organization exists, ArchWebs have been created and maintained in some Western European countries, and the ArchTerra project has set out the implementation of similar nodes for Romanian, Polish and Bulgarian archaeology.

The tools developed can be adapted to the needs of further ArchWebs and other archaeological websites which are to be developed throughout Eastern Europe, and will be made available by the Consortium partners on request.

ArchWeb Bulgaria   ArchWeb-BG follows the structural guidelines of the Consortium. It presents contemporary archaeological thematic investigations in Bulgaria and gives a concise overview of the major interdisciplinary domains and achievements. Its structure is subordinated to the archaeological periodization schemes used in Bulgarian archaeology. Its aim is to summarize the main development stages of Bulgarian archaeology as a profession. All the approximately 100 pages of text are richly illustrated (see Figure 5.3 for an example) and are hyperlinked throughout in order to allow fast *vertical* and *horizontal* switches within the frame of the presentation of Bulgarian archaeological issues.

ArchWeb Poland   ArchWeb-PL was also developed according to the guidelines for national archaeology gateways set out by the Consortium.

The on-line database of Polish archaeologists and archaeological institutions uses a specially designed textual data format with inserted HTML tags in order to improve data retrieval. Queries are entered from a web page using a form with a JavaScript-driven system of menus where the user can restrict the query by institution type and/or administrative district. The request is sent to a Perl script which searches the data according to criteria defined by the user and gives back a Web document with a list of entries found. Every item on the list shows the name

Figure 5.3   The largest of all golden proto-Bulgarian belt-trims, found near the village of Vetren, Silistra district

of either an archaeologist or an institution (depending on the type of search) with all the relevant information. In the case of individuals, the data displayed include her/his e-mail address and the name of the institution where she/he is employed.

ArchWeb Romania   ArchWeb-RO was based on the pre-existing website of CIMEC, the Center for the Cultural Heritage of the Romanian Ministry of Culture. As suggested by the Consortium guidelines, it has sections providing access to Romanian institutions, publications, legislation and indexes of journals, and also presentations of important archaeological sites, such as Targul de Floci, Histria and Targsor. The CIMEC databases of archaeological sites and of archaeological excavations in Romania from 1983 to 2000 can also be accessed from ArchWeb-RO.

The wealth of archaeology in present-day Romania is a reflection of its position

Figure 5.4   Scene CXXXVIII of Trajan's Column showing the capture of Dacians' treasure

as a site of constant ebb and flow of conquest, settlement and migration over the millenia. The legacy of Roman conquest, for example, is recorded on Trajan's Column in Rome.

Museum Information System

Eastern European archaeological museums, like most of their western counterparts, are small and poorly staffed. The staff is often unaware of the possible migration of its records to a digital Museum Information System. Such migration is an indispensable condition to be able to share information about its holdings over intranets and the Internet.

One of the core objectives of the ArchTerra project has therefore been to supply a model information system for archaeological museums according to existing international standards which could then be adapted to the needs of each museum and could be implemented at a relatively low cost.

The data model developed under the project was initiated as an implementation of the CIDOC model of Information groups and Information categories.[3, 4] During the course of the work it was essentially enhanced according to the CIDOC Object-oriented data model recommendations as well as existing practice at the Archaeological Museum in Sofia,[5, 6, 7] so as to fully match current practice. The result is a set of three models which are fully CIDOC compliant and can be used for implementation of a broad range of museum information systems in Archaeology and other fields of cultural heritage:

• object-oriented museum data model. This is developed in a standard subset of Universal Modelling Language (UML)[8] and can be used for implementing either an object-relational or a standard relational database with museum information;
• procedural data processing model. This is developed in a standard subset of a highly intuitive visual flowchart language and can be used as a technical reference specification for developing desktop, client/server and Internet/intranet information systems;
• set covering user profile. This is developed as a list of overlapping role sets with attached functions and can be used for implementing flexible database access discipline and for database administration of types of information systems.

From this model two different databases have been generated: an object-relational database for Oracle 8 RDBMS, and a standard relational database for Oracle/MS SQL Server RDBMS. In addition to these databases, three separated client/server development tools have been experimented with for the actual implementation of the museum information system:

• Oracle Developer for implementation of both client/server and Internet/intranet information systems using Oracle Designer generated Forms/PL/SQL code;
• Oracle Jdeveloper for implementation of both client/server and Internet/Intranet information systems using visually programmed Java code;

- Oracle WebDB for implementation of a simple Internet/intranet information systems using visual templates.[9]

The musem Site template developed under ArchTerra consists of two parts:

- Museum Database. This part of the template is entirely independent from the database in use, since it relies on features found in any standard relational database, including Oracle, Informix, Microsoft, Sybase and public domain databases like mySQL;
- Museum Information System. This template, although designed using specific Oracle client modules for interaction with the database (Forms and PL/SQL), is relatively universal; it can be directly implemented by other clients, such as Microsoft Visual Basic, and adapted for any public domain tools such as Java.

The most important activities which can be registered with the museum information system entirely characterized in term of tables and relationships are:

- collection of artefacts
- acquisition of man-made entities and artefacts
- transfer of custody for museum objects
- organizing exhibitions
- moving and temporary de-accessing of museum objects
- disposal and de-registering of destroyed and/or lost objects, etc.

Conclusions

The project reached its aim to demonstrate the transnational nature and urgency of archaeological research and management necessities even among countries with very different historical, political and economical backgrounds. It also allowed to prove that the benefits and efficiencies of Internet use, both for professional and general users, are much more apparent within those countries having a different level of access to economic and technical resources than the so-called Western countries.

The interaction with Eastern European partners allowed also to design some very useful tools to share information and background among researchers throughout countries with different languages and even different alphabets, which have been kept apart for decades not just by the geographical boundaries. Glossaries and thesauri have been studied in order to break down the existing language barriers to the communication of archaeological information and resources; a new upgrade to ARGE (Archaeological Resource Guide of Europe) has also been implemented and to facilitate international cooperation in planning and execution of archaeological fieldwork throughout Europe, Mediolanvm Fieldwork Service have been completely restructured and redesigned.

Notes

1   Negroni Catacchio, N., Guidetti, L., Meloni, G., Camnasio, M., and Van Leusen, M. (2001) 'ArchTerra: An EU project for enhancing the cultural co-operation between archaeological communities of East and West Europe', *CILEA Bulletin*, April 2001, no. 77, pp. 4–9 (http://cdl.cilea.it/routing.asp?ISSN=11202440).

2   Negroni Catacchio, N., Guidetti, L, Camnasio, M., Ferrari, R. and Van Leusen, M. (2000) 'Mediolanum, European fieldwork server', in *CILEA Bulletin*, June 2000 n. 73, pp. 7–12, June 2000 (http://cdl.cilea.it/routing.asp?ISSN=11202440). The project has also been presented at the CAA Conference held at Ljubljana in April 2000: Negroni Catacchio, N., Guidetti, L., Camnasio, M., Ferrari, R. and Van Leusen, M. 'ARCHEO-EXPLORER, European fieldwork server'.

3   International Documentation Committee of the International Council of Museums (1993) *The CIDOC Information Categories. ICOM/CIDOC Data Modeling Working Group, International Guidelines for Museum Object Information* (http://www.cidoc.icom.org/guide/guide.htm).

4   International Documentation Committee of the International Council of Museums (1995) *ICOM/CIDOC Data Modelling Working Group, CIDOC Conceptual Reference Model Recommendations* (http://www.ville-ge.ch/musinfo/cidoc/oomodel/index.htm).

5   Vassilev, V., Stoev, I., Gaydarska, B., Alexandrov, S., Nehrizov, G. and Vaklinov, M. (1999) 'CIDOC data model implementation in the ArchTerra project – Museum Information Systems', *CILEA Bulletin*, no. 69, pp. 15–30 September 1999, (http://cdl.cilea.it/routing.asp?ISSN=11202440).

6   Vassilev, V., Korladinov, E., Alexandrov, S., Gyadarsk, B. and Vaklinov., M. (1996) 'Entering museum treasures through the windows', Information Technologies in Social Sciences and Humanities International Summer School, Burgas Free University, 1996.

7   Vassilev, V. (1997) *Information Systems for Processing Archaeological Data – The Human Behind the Finds*, Sofia.

8   Dorsey, P. and Hudicka, J. (1999) *Oracle8 Design Using UML Object Modeling*, Berkeley, CA: McGraw-Hill.

9   Vassil Vassilev, V., and Gaydarska, B. (2000) 'Reducing the complexity of CIDOC object-oriented model through ontological minimization', CAA 2000, Durham, University of Durham, 19th–20th February 2000.

Chapter 6

CHIMER – A Cultural Heritage Application for 3G Environment Developed by European Children

Romana Krizova

Abstract

CHIMER is one of the Heritage for All projects from the Sixth Call of the IST Programme. It sets out to capitalize on the natural enthusiasm and interests of children in developing new approaches to the use of evolving technologies for documenting items of cultural interest in their local communities. The project combines not only partners from many different countries (Czech Republic, Finland, Germany, Holland, Lithuania and Spain) but also partners with very different expertise. It brings technical experts into co-operation with researchers from museums and teachers from elementary schools.

Introduction

The charm and importance of this project lies in its focus on working with children who are main project content providers. The project aims to establish the European Cultural Heritage Archive. The content of this archive will be based on local heritage from the six partners' countries. The scientific and general information provided by museologists and teachers will be complemented by the children's interpretation: CHIMER is supporting the natural creativity and investigation skills of children by encouraging them to explore new tools for creating digital content. Twelve-year-olds in five countries of Europe will follow the guidance of museologists and teachers in building digital maps combining geographical coordinates: these are detected using GPS devices with the creative use of mobile technologies and digital cameras. In this way, children will combine drawings and photographic images with their own comments on items of interest. Little by little, they will participate fully in creating a digital archive of their own towns, villages and surrounding communities which should enhance interest in their regions, not only for children but for other age groups. All these aims correspond to CHIMER official objectives:

- establishing an open international network of schools, children and public institutions (see Figure 6.1)
- introducing eLearning by developing an innovative paperless direct 'touch-

Name of the partner	Contact person	E-mail
Bedrijfsregio (coordinator)	John Spee	j.spee@bedrijfsregio.nl
Cross Czech	Romana Krizova	romana@crossczech.cz
Ciberespacio (technical coordinator)	Daniel Weiss	dweiss@wanadoo.es
ZGDV	Stefan Hassinger	hasinger@rostock.zgdv.de
IMI	Nerute Kligiene	nerute@ktl.mii.lt
Vilnius Minties School	Rima Markuniene	rastine@delfi.lt
Okresni Muzeum v Klatovech	Lubos Smolik	muzeum.klatovy@tiscali.cz
Zakladni Skola v Chanovicich	Bozena Legatova	chanovice@ms1.ipnet.cz
Groene Poolster	Anton Grolle	groenepolster@planet.nl
Municipality of Mazaricos	Jose Romero Maneiro	mdm@mudima.org
CRA	Rosa Barreiro	cra@craescuela.net
ABO Akademi	Bill Anckar	christer.carlsson@abo.fi
Bad Doberan	Werner Basedow	w.basedow@mitrax.de
Fraunhofer	Bodo Urban	bodo.urban@rostock.igd.fhg.de

Figure 6.1   List of CHIMER partners

and-learn' cognitive learning method based on a combination of the use of technology and content management
● involving children in developing the new generation of platforms and tools
● combining available Internet, GPS and GIS technologies in order to develop interfacing and user access tools adapted to evolving 3G networked multimedia technology.

The work on CHIMER dated from 1st March 2002 and it was completed in August 2004. During this period CHIMER had to deliver its five main components: the Digital Heritage Archive, eMap, eGuide, mGuide and cognitive methodology. These components are closely linked.

The CHIMER Digital Heritage Archive

This is an open platform for storing the geo-heritage content in different formats. It is now set up and ready to be enriched with new information by any user who joins the established network of individuals, schools, teachers, cultural institutions, municipalities, etc. It is a combination of multiple databases (that is, an existing proven platform), which will contain digital information in many different formats (existing or evolving). This ensures full compatibility with evolving UMTS technology. In order to ensure the replicability of the system of databases CHIMER uses a simple system of access databases which are widely available and are affordable for any school in Europe. Its management can be handled by any teacher of computing.

Museologists, in co-operation with children and teachers, have selected the local cultural repositories to be digitized and developed in the project, such as castles, manor houses, museums and their collections, churches, monasteries, towers, bridges, local environmental resources and the most interesting and inspiring social history associated with each. These items will be in details documented both by children and cultural institutions developing a two-layer information structure – information by children and information by scientists. The information provided by museologists is more detailed and is also provided in a form of texts. On the other hand information produced by children is rather more visual and creative. Children are producing photos, making drawings, taking short video shots, making sound commentaries, singing songs, etc. All this data is then post-produced by children using Photoshop, VideoStudio, Sound Forge, etc. In this way CHIMER is trying to catch children's creativity and their view of their local world of cultural heritage. This aspect is a heritage on its own and can later be seen as a point of view of the generation born at the turn of the millennium and at the gate of the wireless age.

eMap

This is a platform which gives added value to the content from the Digital Heritage Archive. Together they form a high-quality background for retrieving focused geo-cultural information through digital and mobile devices. The vector eMap is the only possible type of digital map to be used with both the Internet and WAP, GPRS and UMTS technologies.

eMap is a vector map of each Chimer local territory: together they form the common Chimer virtual territory. In most cases these maps were provided by local municipalities. Children, teachers and museologists are selecting places of interest, which are included in the project. Together with creating information for the Digital Heritage Archive they are collecting geographic information data using a GPS device. At the same time, children track and record points of the route along the way between places of interest, as shown in Figure 6.2. All this data, together with icons of monuments drawn by children, will then be downloaded and merged with vector maps of the selected territory (see Figure 6.3). The data itself is stored in access databases which are linked to vector maps in a simple way. Different types of monuments or objects appear in different layers and can be viewable on the map according to the request of the end-user. CHIMER vector maps are being adapted and modified in ArcView software. This software is, though, a bit complicated for children. As a lighter version CHIMER uses OziExplorer to teach children how to calibrate a bitmap map, how to vectorize it and the purpose of doing it.

eGuide

The electronic guide is a multilingual multimedia Internet tool operating on a platform of geo-heritage information retrieved from the content stored in the Digital Heritage Archive linked to the eMap. Most digital guides are based on an interactive map, which is a scanned image with interactive points. CHIMER's eGuide works

**Figure 6.2   Children collecting and creating information about local heritage
and gathering coordinates with GPS**
Museo Digital de Mazaricos

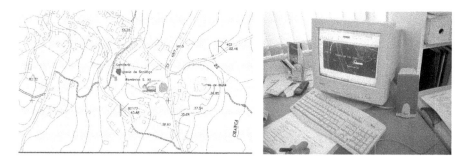

Figure 6.3   Cadastral map with children's icons and the digitized map
Museo Digital de Mazaricos

with real geographic information stored in vector mode and as such it is much more
precise and exploitable, which allows it to provide location-based services such as
proximity services, geocoding and routing.

In this way end-users will be able to choose if they want to see the information
produced by museologists or by children or both. The children's version is rather
more multimedia and creative. Users will be able to choose an area and get all the
information available about this area, such as information about particular objects
and how to reach them on foot or by car or train.

The eGuide is based on the information produced by all the participating schools
and cultural institutions. As shown in Figure 6.4, it is an English web portal linked
to local portals in local languages.

Figure 6.4   CHIMER Internet portal

mGuide

The mobile guide is the second multilingual multimedia tool operating on a platform of geo-heritage information retrieved from the content stored in the Digital Heritage Archive linked to the eMap. It is a wireless, personal, multimedia system for accessing information services focused on geo-heritage and retrievable through mobile devices. The mobile terminal, such as a mobile phone or PDA or pocket PC is associated with a person rather than a place and the network knows the current location of the particular terminal. These are the powerful features of the multimedia environment of 3G.

We can really only apply the term 'multimedia tool' to mobile devices operating under UMTS. Both GPRS and WAP are still limited. mGuide will, however, operate under all three technologies. CHIMER carried out the work on this application between September 2003 and February 2004.

Association of a terminal with a person also creates the opportunity for messaging services amongst closed user groups or specific communities of interest. The dramatic growth in short message service (SMS) traffic in GSM networks illustrates the demand for such messaging capabilities. The always-on characteristic of 3G networks will enable instant messaging capability, and the high data rates available will add image and video capability to create a fully operating multimedia messaging service.

The mGuide aims at being a fully multimedia application providing a highly personalized interface. This is one of the key problems of present applications on the market. The technology exists, the infrastructure is built up, the content is digitized and stored in databases but what is still missing is a personalized interface which will enable end-users to get the information they want at any time and place in a way which they can understand and within a short time. CHIMER works with children and that is why personalization and visualization is one of the most important issues. The Finnish partner, Abo Akademi, is developing the application which will be downloadable to the mobile phone. This application will contain a personal guide for the end-user. This guide will speak to the end-users and will tell them all they want to know about a chosen area or object (as shown in Figure 6.5). So children will be able to see a chapel which will move and talk to them about its own history.

The mGuide, in combination with other deliverables, can serve as a model for other institutions that decide to make similar content open and available. Over time, if other museums or schools adopt this model, a vast collection of educational resources will develop and facilitate widespread exchange of ideas about innovative ways to use those resources in teaching and learning.

The mGuide will serve as a common channel of intellectual activity that can stimulate educational innovation and cross-disciplinary educational ventures.

The CHIMER Methodology

This style of working with children is based on cognitive principles. The methodology used encourages children to learn how to obtain information, how to pass this information on to other children and how to process it in a way which will be both usable and appealing to the others; that is, processing this data in a digital format. Each country will bring its own input in general project methodology by developing it in its own way in its own region, taking into account national character, skills of teachers and children, technical equipment and creativity of children.

The aim of CHIMER methodology is not to teach children how to use digital instruments and tools. There are already existing methodologies and many manuals. The methodology of CHIMER focuses on explaining to children what the maps are, what types of formats and scale they have, why we need GPS and how it can be related to physical maps and physical objects and to its digital interpretation. The aim of CHIMER is to make children realize that we can share all this heritage which is local at the first level. This heritage can be shared on networks, both wired and wireless, and so it becomes an integral part of the common European and world

Figure 6.5   Expected type of mGuide interface where the child communicates and guides others

heritage (see Figure 6.6). The other focus point of CHIMER is to make children overcome possible barriers of working with digital instruments and to consider them modern creative tools on the same level as pen and paper.

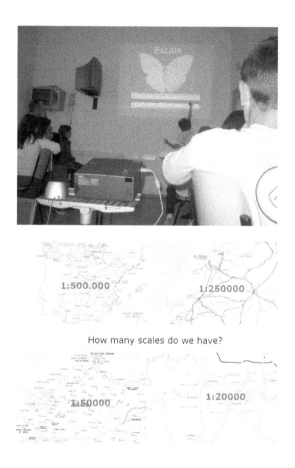

Figure 6.6   Spanish teacher explaining the concept of scale to children
Museo Digital de Mazaricos

Note

www.chimer.org/ provides a comprehensive description and presentation of the entire results of the completed project. However, the paper was kept mainly as originally written in order to provide the freshness and idealism of the 'in-process' project description. [Eds]

Results and Future Developments

During the project the work in progress could be clearly seen by visiting the consortium's website, www.chimer.org and now all the principal results may be seen there. There is a completed Didactical Unit with a complete description of the cognitive method used during the project, a didactic model for the implementation of a web-based geo-heritage information system and a manual for using the 3G mobile technology for retrieving the heritage information anywhere at anytime by anyone. The website offers a possibility to explore CHIMER territory via the Internet application eGuide. It is possible to search through partner's local sites and to find information about the mGuide application developed for handheld devices.

The results have been used by the consortium's schools, as shown in Figure 6.6, and their availability on the web has enabled others to use them freely. As mobile technology becomes increasingly available we believe that this kind of approach will become even more relevant. In particular, we hope that the role of children in a central position in a technology R&D project will be followed in other projects. Currently several of them are being prepared on both national and international levels.

Chapter 7

The German–Japanese Project for Virtual Reconstruction of Two Valuable Destroyed Buildings

Anne Griepentrog, Alfred Iwainsky and Jan Jordan

Abstract

The paper describes a German–Japanese project from the first idea to the final success. The goal of this project was the virtual reconstruction of two valuable destroyed buildings by means of a new, intercontinental cooperation between Japan and Germany. The corresponding teams in the cooperating institutions in Gifu and Berlin had the opportunity to learn much about the architecture of the other culture by the reconstruction of Berlin City Castle (Germany) and Nobunaga's Residence in Gifu (Japan) respectively. Furthermore the 3D models of both buildings had to be integrated into more complex presentations. For example, the model of Berlin Castle became a part of a bigger project, the Virtual Reality World of Berlin.

The paper starts with an introduction to the origin of the project and a summary of the involved institutions. Then it reports on the preparatory work – the study of sources and digitizing of documents. It continues with the process of data transfer between Gifu and Berlin and the successful 3D modelling of the two historical buildings. The conclusion contains the presentation of project results.

Introduction

Computer-based 3D modelling and visualization offer a new approach to the reconstruction of destroyed cultural buildings and provide opportunities to produce photo realistic images or walkthroughs quickly and at low cost. Details, colours (texture maps) and views can be accurately replicated. Of course, this applies to not only the outer parts of a building, but the interior too. Once this has been achieved, any view, colour or detail may be easily modified to meet new or other requirements. An animated walkthrough is the best and most impressive way to support the imagination – it is possible to look at the destroyed building as it was.[1-4] Moreover, the virtual reconstruction offers opportunities to combine images of the former environment of the destroyed building with synthetic images derived from the 3D model of the building.[5,6]

Considering the various advantages, we believe that three-dimensional modelling, and especially virtual reconstruction, are replacing artists' drawings or physical models as the means of presenting reconstructions of destroyed buildings.

At EVA'98 in Gifu, Alfred Iwainsky presented a paper on these advantages of virtual reconstruction of buildings and demonstrated some examples for the visualization of valuable damaged buildings, like the reconstruction of the famous Great Altar of Pergamon.[7] The specified examples showed that valuable damaged or destroyed buildings can be virtually reconstructed with a high degree of authenticity and a low budget in comparison with a physical rebuilding.

At the end of this conference, Professor Iwainsky expressed the idea of starting cooperation between Berlin and the prefecture of Gifu with an intercultural project – the virtual reconstruction of important but destroyed buildings in Japan and Germany. The German team would carry out the virtual reconstruction of a Japanese building and become acquainted with Japanese architecture and civilization. A Japanese team would reconstruct a German building. This idea attracted attention, but was not pursued immediately.

After the visit of the vice-governor of Gifu Prefecture, Mr Tsuneo Morimoto, to Berlin's WISTA Science Park the project proposal was developed further. In the autumn of 1998, the governor of Gifu Prefecture, Mr Taku Kajiwara, wrote to the Governing Mayor of Berlin, Mr Eberhard Diepgen, saying that Gifu Prefecture would like to promote and sponsor development of the ideas of Professor Iwainsky. In the winter of 1998/1999, the Berlin Senate made three important decisions:

1. That Berlin would participate in this project, too.
2. That the German building for the virtual reconstruction would be Berlin City Castle.
3. That the 3D model of Berlin City Castle had to be integrated into the Virtual Reality World of Berlin, 'Virtuelles Berlin', developed and managed by Artemedia Productions GmbH. This vast VR environment would generate a visual response in real time. Therefore the model had to be sufficiently simplified.

In April 1999 the Berlin Senate gave the corresponding order to the IIEF and one month later Gifu Prefecture decided on the virtual reconstruction of the destroyed residence of Oda Nobunaga in Gifu. Now the actual work could begin.

The following institutes worked together in the project:

*   VR TECHNO CENTER Inc., Gifu
*   Softopia Japan
*   Institute of Informatics in Design and Manufacturing (IIEF) at Berlin
*   Society for the Promotion of Applied Computer Science (GFaI), Berlin.

The 3D modelling of Berlin Castle was carried out in the VR TECHNO CENTER Inc. and in the Institute of Informatics in Design and Manufacturing (IIEF) at Berlin. The Society for the Promotion of Applied Computer Science (GFaI) was responsible for modelling Nobunaga's Residence. Softopia Japan was responsible for colour information processing for Nobunaga's Residence.

Investigation, Source Analysis and Digitizing of Documents

Berlin City Castle had a dynamic history. The foundation stone was laid in the 15th century. The castle was often reshaped and it was largely destroyed during the Second World War. The ruins were blasted in 1950.[8,9] Since the beginning of the last decade there has been a discussion about whether the castle should be physically reconstructed again.

Immediately at the beginning of the actual project work the manifold sources for the reconstruction of Berlin Castle had to be investigated. Many experts and institutions supported us in this task. The material collection became very extensive because of the large dimensions and the complex structure of the castle. But the extent of the material collection was not the main problem. The most important question was, rather, how it would be possible to present the vast amount of information in a form easily understandable by people working on the other cultural construction.

Therefore the goal of the first working phase was to generate a complete and familiar base without contradictions for the virtual reconstruction of Berlin Castle for the Japanese team. Modern computer technology offers excellent tools for solving this problem. At first the team in Berlin digitized the relevant material that was found in books, photo and map collections and other sources.

In order to represent the relationships of the individual objects to each other, the team at the IIEF created a series of schematic graphics of the castle. These schematic drawings were integrated into an HTML presentation with the following elements:

- schematic surveys of the building with expressive symbols representing links to further elements of the presentation (Figure 7.1)
- explanatory texts
- black and white photos of the castle
- coloured photos of existing buildings that were built with similar materials (Figure 7.2)
- maps
- ground, roof and floor plans (Figure 7.1)
- drawings of the front of the castle.

Altogether the HTML presentation consisted of 400 digital components on 32 pages. Finally the whole HTML presentation was stored on a CD-ROM and sent to VR TECHNO Center Inc.

This presentation form proved to be very instructive. For instance, clicking with the mouse on a camera symbol triggers the visualization of a photo corresponding to the chosen camera position and direction. In a similar manner the Berlin team produced the references to the front and section drawings and to the ground plan and the maps of the roof area. It was very important for the VR-specialists not only to receive a lot of good material, but additionally an ergonomic and efficient structure of the knowledge behind it.

The initial material for the modelling of the Nobunaga Residence consisted of building maps in the correct scale prepared by the Japanese team. Moreover the Japanese team made available detail views (Figure 7.3) by reference to buildings existing today. The photos were necessary for the production of digital textures on the surfaces of certain elements of the residence.

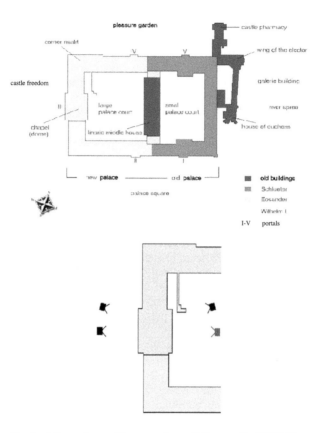

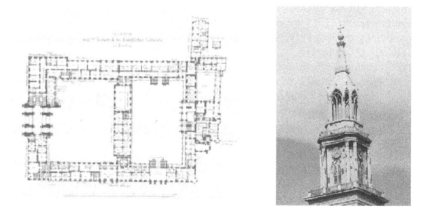

Figure 7.1   Part of the schematic overview of the castle (HTML presentation)

Figure 7.2   Examples of sources for the reconstruction of Berlin City Castle

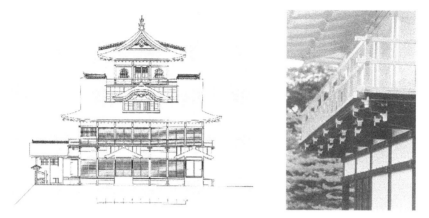

Figure 7.3   Examples of sources for the reconstruction of Nobunaga's Residence

But these data were not sufficient for the modelling of a residence of another, distant cultural complex. Many questions, for example, on the pillar and roof constructions remained open. From which material was the roof of the palace made? Was it covered with brick, straw or reed? This and other questions could be answered only by an intensive study of the Japanese architecture.

The Virtual Reconstruction

After the allocation of the necessary material the actual modelling process could start. Because of the high complexity of Berlin Castle, the Berlin team also modelled sections, for example the famous 'Schlüterhof'. The software tool 3D Studio Max, supporting the technology of solid modelling, was used for the virtual reconstruction of both buildings.

At first the lines in the three-dimensional space representing the edges of the buildings were drawn. Single components of the buildings, like walls, columns or rafters, were built up from standards, modified by Boolean operations or connected in groups. Frequently recurring objects were replaced by references on the original. However pure line graphics, so-called wire frame representations, are not suitable to mediate a spatial impression of three-dimensional objects. If all edges of such an object are visualized by lines, whether they are visible from a given view direction or not, then it is impossible to perceive the geometrical properties of the building (see Figures 7.4 and 7.5).

With the inclusion of material characteristics, lighting conditions and corresponding colours into the modelling process, so-called photo-realistic computer graphics could be provided. They deliver good impressions of the objects, as can be seen from Figure 7.5.

Because of the need to generate realistic views of the electronic model (Figure 7.6) in real time, the number of polygons of Berlin Castle had to be reduced to only

Figure 7.4   3D wire frame representation of Nobunaga's Residence

**Figure 7.5   Window enclosure: digital picture (left), 3D wire frame
representation (2nd from left), 3D representation with simply
shaded object surfaces (3rd from left) and 3D model with texture
(right)**

50,000. For presentation purposes, not subject to real-time requirement, a more
detailed model with a higher geometric solution was developed. This model was
simplified later: in order to provide a good optical impression, two-dimensional
textures and/or patterns were mapped on the surfaces of the solids. Amongst other
things these patterns represented three-dimensional elements of the building. In this
manner large parts of the front of the castle could be modelled by only one planar
area.

The generated model of the castle could now be observed from any position, any
view direction and in practically any lighting conditions. It was also possible to

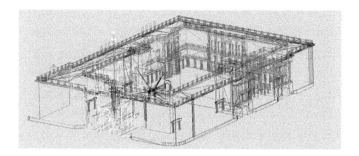

Figure 7.6   3D wire frame representation of Berlin Castle (simplified model)

generate computer animations – so-called walkthroughs – that simulate the movements of a visitor around and through the building.

Project Experiences and Results

An important human result of this project was that the members of the German team enjoyed the study of historical and architectural aspects of Japanese culture. They worked with great enthusiasm.

At the beginning of the project, there were no agreements about technical tools or forms of the intercontinental communication. However, soon the Internet proved to be an excellent basis for administrative and technical cooperation. Nearly everything was exchanged in digital form. It was not necessary to make even one phone call.

One of the most astonishing project results was the following: only based on the digitized material and without any further inquiry, the Japanese specialists developed a part of the castle model that fitted exactly into the whole model developed in Berlin. This included both geometry and colour/texture. Figure 7.7 shows a view of the western part of Berlin Castle modelled by the team in Gifu Prefecture.

A photo-realistic view of Nobunaga's Residence is shown in Figure 7.8.

The results of the German–Japanese project were presented for the first time in the framework of the Asian-Pacific Weeks in Berlin in September 1999 with much response in the media.[10] Therefore we decided to provide a CD-ROM, 'The Berlin City Castle – History and Virtual Resurrection' at the end of 1999. In addition to the results of the virtual reconstruction of both buildings, this electronic publication contains an excursion into the history of Berlin Castle and a short representation of the project story. This CD has found wide interest, certainly because the discussion on the future of Berlin Castle and the Castle Place has intensified in the last few years.

Figure 7.7   The virtual reconstruction of the western part of the castle, carried out in the VR Techno Center in Gifu Prefecture

Figure 7.8   The virtual reconstruction of Nobunaga's Residence

Acknowledgements

We thank the following persons for supporting the German–Japanese Virtual Reality Project: Michihiro Inagaki, Tsuneo Morimoto, Shinichi Ohno, Prof. Dr Jörg Albertz, Wilhelm von Boddien, Ullrich Gellermann, Helga Rönsch, Albert Wiedemann.

Notes

1   Iwainsky, A., Jordan, J., Griepentrog, A. and Takeuchi, A. (1999) 'Interkulturelle digitale Rekonstruktion eines umstrittenen Bauwerkes'. INFO '99 Telekommunikation,

Electronic Commerce, Digitales Büro, Anwendungen für Wirtschaft und Verwaltung, Potsdam, 29th–30th October 1999.

2   Iwainsky, A. and Schulze, J. (1994) 'Modelling and visualization of large cultural objects', *Proceedings of the 5th Eurographics Workshop on Visualization and Scientific Computing*, Rostock, Germany, 30th May–1st July 1994.

3   Iwainsky, A. and Schulze, J. (1995) 'Virtual reconstruction of cultural objects', *Information Services and Use*, no. 15, IOS Press, 1995, pp. 303–16.

4   Iwainsky, A. (1998) 'Virtuelle Rekonstruktion von Bauwerken', *CADplus*, no. 1, 1998.

5   Griepentrog, A., Pocher, M. and Sieck, J. (1995) *Präsentation von Produkten und Dienstleistungen kleiner und mittelständischer Unternehmen mit Hilfe multimedialer, in die betriebliche Infrastruktur integrierter Systeme*, Abschlussbericht des AIF – Projektes 9063B, GFaI e.V., Berlin.

6   Pocher, M. and Sieck, J. (1995) 'MUSY: a multimedia planning and design system', EVA '95, London, Electronic Imaging and the Visual Arts, 24th–29th July 1995, pp. 61–4.

7   Iwainsky, A. (1998) 'Virtual reconstruction of buildings and other structures', *Conference Proceedings*, 8th–9th April 1998, Gifu City, Gifu Prefecture, Japan.

8   Peschken, G. and Klünner, H.W. 1998 *Das Berliner Schloss*, Propyläen Verlag, 4th edition, 1998.

9   Geyer, A. (1993) *Geschichte des Schlosses zu Berlin. Vom Königsschloss zum Schloss des Kaisers (1698–1918)*, Nicolaische Verlagsbuchhandlung Beuermann GmbH, Berlin, 2nd edition.

10 *Der Tagesspiegel*, 'Im Sinkflug über das Stadtschloss', Berlin, 30th September 1999.

PART 3
RECREATING AND
PRESERVING THE PAST

Chapter 8

German Historical Buildings in 3D: From Cathedral to Synagogue and Jewish Quarter

Falk Krebs and Edgar Brück

Abstract

The visualization of the architectural design of historic German religious buildings, both as regards interiors and exteriors, is addressed in this paper with regard to three case studies:

- *Wetzlar Cathedral, which dates back 1,100 years*
- *the virtual reconstruction of a destroyed synagogue*
- *the virtual reconstruction of the Jewish quarter in Regensburg, destroyed in the Middle Ages.*

The technical work carried out by student teams supervised by faculty members is described for the whole of each project. The results bring to life a series of important historical buildings and remind us of their stormy past.

Introduction

Students at the University of Applied Sciences in Wiesbaden have been using 3D computer technology for visualization of their architectural designs for several years. In combination with the field of heritage preservation, the university has created many excellent animations, winning important international awards. The paper gives an overview of the whole workflow, starting from the first lesson for beginners and ending with the projection of the newest research projects. It will be a journey through time and space and it will explain the concept of education.

The following case studies are described in the paper:

- Wetzlar Cathedral – the visualization of 1,100 years of building history
- memo38 – the virtual rebuilding of a destroyed synagogue
- the Jewish quarter in Regensburg – the visualization of the Jewish district destroyed in the Middle Ages.

Wetzlar Cathedral

The Project and its Aims

The visualization of changes over 1,100 years in the design of Wetzlar Cathedral focused on the following key features: its Carolinian foundation, the Romanesque basilica, Gothic churches, the hypothetical realization of Gothic concepts and the schematic representation of individual stages of construction during the years 1230 to 1860. The research was carried out in two phases, as described below.

Investigation of Historical Building Data

The information obtained from the excavation of the cathedral was insufficient for the reconstruction of the initial architecture. Since neither ground plans nor descriptions existed, the investigation primarily used comparative studies of religious buildings of the same period. Measurements were taken of the various available fragments of the cathedral and then compared with the reconstructed data of the Einhards-Basilica (Carolinian Style) in Steinbach and of the late-Romanesque pre-monastery church in Ilbenstadt. Further information was found in the thesis of Eduard Sebald (1989) and in further special articles on the subject.

Data processing

Due to the complexity of the cathedral's individual style, various detailed 3D CAD computer models and animations of the geometry and appearance had to be developed. Examples of these are shown in Figures 8.1 and 8.2. The Carolinian foundation required some 180,000 polygons; the late Romanic phase 270,000, and for the 'Gothic Vision' (Figure 8.3) of the cathedral 2.5 million polygons had to be computed and edited. Great importance was attached to a detailed compilation of

Figure 8.1   Carolinian building AD 897

Figure 8.2   Romanesque building AD 1280

Figure 8.3   Part of the 'Gothic vision' of the cathedral

geometric aspects, a representation of the materials and their surfaces, which gives a most realistic impression.

memo38

The project

In March 1998 interior design students began a 'memo38' group to work on the computer reconstruction of the destroyed Synagogue of Wiesbaden (see Figures 8.4 and 8.5). The project was divided into two parts: in November 1998 the exterior was reconstructed, then in November 1999 the interior of the synagogue was presented in a computer animated film. The name 'memo38' evokes memory, memorial, commemoration and 'not forgetting'.The project's logo was suitably simple yet dignified (Figure 8.6).

Research

Since the construction files with plans and drawings have been lost completely, the 'memo38' group's research depended on collecting photographs gathered from local townspeople and information provided by historical institutions and archives. First we searched in Wiesbaden but soon we learned that these photographs were not sufficient for the reconstruction of the interior. Some photos had gone abroad with emigrants and fortunately were discovered by personal communication. One turned up at the Jewish Museum in Paris; it was most valuable because it had been taken

Figure 8.4   Destruction of the Wiesbaden Synagogue (1939)

Figure 8.5   The site of the Wiesbaden Synagogue (1995)

Figure 8.6   The logo for the memo38 project

before a redecoration of the interior around 1904. The ornaments shown matched the few sketches by Phillip Hoffmann that survived in the architect's family and are now part of the historical collection of the Wiesbaden Museum. Since these drawings and watercolours are the only information of the colour scheme which the architect designed, they could then be the basis of our texture colours. Some questions we could not answer from the documents found in Wiesbaden, so we tried to solve them by studying similar buildings. We looked, for example, at the Berlin Synagogue that was built just three years earlier in the same style. In contrast to Wiesbaden, there were still good drawings in existence. Also very important was our consultation with members of the local Jewish community, both of the former congregation and that of today. Their recollections helped us with more accurate colouring of the tiles and other details. Being told by someone who actually still remembers the original synagogue was very important. Thus we learned about the passing of time. Now is the very last chance to collect authentic information from personal recollections.

The most moving moments occurred when visitors who had prayed and sung in the beautiful sanctuary came to see our work in progress. Marthel Hirsch who played the organ from 1936 to 1938 opened her photo album for us, providing the only inside view of the dome.

Reconstruction

Paulgerd Jesberg, a teacher at the university, had prepared geometrical studies that sharpened our understanding of the building's proportions. By combining his information with a close analysis of the photographs, we were able to determine scales and measurements. Next we divided the building into separate segments. Each student was assigned a different part for editing. An intensive analysis of each element and its ornamentation was carried out. Figures 8.7 and 8.8 show two of the very detailed and successful results.

Purpose

The content of our project is not an abstract architectural object. This film is a visible, virtual and enduring memorial to the congregation and community of the Wiesbaden Synagogue, as well as a resource for anyone interested in architectural and social history. The richness of the results can be seen in Figure 8.9, which shows the interior. What began solely as an undertaking of computer reconstruction broadened into a significant historical and sociological research project. It is of immense value not only for us as the creators of the project but also for anyone who learns about our work. Computer technology and the Internet may prove to be an effective tool in communicating and commemorating historical events, buildings and artefacts. Out of the shards of history this CAD animation revives and recreates memory.

Figure 8.7   Reconstruction of the interior

Figure 8.8   View of the synagogue from the south-east

Figure 8.9   Inside the synagogue

Results

The end product took more than 12,000 hours of work. A number of Jews from Wiesbaden and their families had the opportunity to see the film. They appreciated young people in Wiesbaden spending so much energy and time on this project. The film was displayed on a large screen directly at the site several times, for the 9th November (Kristallnacht) commemoration. Afterwards a construction container was used as a temporary exhibition space. It also received press and radio coverage. In 2000, an exhibition was designed and shown in the Active Museum of German Jewish History, Wiesbaden. This innovative approach to a topic of Jewish tradition caught the interest of scholars and of archaeologists and experts in heritage protection. We were invited to conferences and presentations at various universities and research institutes. The quality of the film design and the use of music were acknowledged by the 'animago 3D' Awards 1999 and 2000. By applying CAD to the topic of German Jewish history we confronted the visitors of technological fairs with the theme of commemoration.

The Jewish Quarter in Regensburg

Virtual reconstruction and visualization of the Jewish district destroyed by pogroms during the Middle Ages is the topic of this case study, drawing on both history and archaeology. During road works in the Neupfarrplatz in Regensburg, workers stumbled upon parts of old cellars and foundations. In subsequent excavations important parts of the old Jewish quarter were gradually brought to light. The discovery of parts of the Gothic synagogue, built on Roman foundations, was classified as a historic sensation. The Jewish quarter in Regensburg is known as the oldest one in southern Germany, with over 700 years of history. Some idea of its character and atmosphere can be seen in Figure 8.10.

Figure 8.10   A corner of the Jewish Quarter in Regensburg

Investigations

Parts of the uncovered cellars within the old Jewish quarter were restored by the city of Regensburg and transformed into an underground museum – the so-called 'document Neupfarrplatz'. The idea was to elaborate the history of the Neupfarrplatz into a virtual reconstruction and to present this visualization in the museum. It was the Fachhochschule Wiesbaden, University of Applied Sciences, Department of Interior Design, which was given the task by the city of Regensburg to work out and realize this virtual presentation. The financing of this project is sponsored, in cooperation with the Jewish Museums in Prague and Vienna, by the European Union Programme 'RAPHAEL – Maintenance of European Culture'.

General Preparations

The reconstruction works of the synagogue are mainly based on the only two preserved plans of the interior parts of the synagogue. The analysis of these two copperplates (by Albrecht Altdorfer) had been undertaken by a group of students from the Technical University of Darmstadt. Together with curators and scientists in Regensburg, a series of streets (streetscape) of the Middle Ages had been reconstructed in a two-dimensional design, which was then transformed by computer (using a 3D CAD system) to visualization stage. Very helpful in some parts for the visualization was the data collected by ArcTron during the excavations. Besides experiences and material from the archives of the city of Regensburg, references and publications of the synagogues in Prague, Speyer and Worms turned out to provide a very helpful basis for further reconstruction works on the synagogue in Regensburg.

The Results

The result of the medial reconstruction shows a 3D presentation of the Gothic synagogue (Figure 8.11), old streets and interior and outside views of Jewish houses – all easy to understand, even for non-professionals. Nevertheless, one always has to consider that a virtual reconstruction can only be an attempt to represent the original situation of the buildings within the former Jewish quarter.

Conclusions

Taken together, these three joint student–faculty case studies illustrate, firstly, the usefulness of 3D technology in visualizing both destroyed and still existent important buildings for educational purposes. Significantly however, they also indicate the impact on the wider community of understanding and confronting the past.

Figure 8.11   Interior of the Gothic synagogue AD 1519

Reference

Sebald, Eduard (1989), 'Die Baugeschichte der Stiftskirche St. Maria in Wetzlar', Ph.D. thesis, Johann Wolfgang Goethe University.

Chapter 9

Image-Based Object Reconstruction and Visualization for Inventory of Cultural Heritage

Jana Visnovcova, Armin Gruen and Li Zhang

Abstract

The paper reports on two projects producing photo-realistic 3D models using modern techniques of analytical and digital photogrammetry. The first project aims at documentation of the oldest preserved large relief model of Switzerland: this requires a high-quality object reconstruction. The second application presents modelling and visualization of one of the complex towers of the famous Bayon temple of the ancient city of Angkor Thom in Cambodia, based on the use of small-format tourist-type photography. The manual, semi-automated and automated photogrammetric procedures described include photo-triangulation, digital surface model generation and techniques of texture mapping.

Introduction

The preservation and inventory of cultural heritage has become a task of great concern nowadays. In a rapidly developing world a need arises for the documentation of the present state of historical artefacts. Object reconstruction based on terrestrial and aerial imagery has been widely adopted in the recording of architectural monuments, historical urban centres and archaeological sites. However, in the field of museum inventory, these procedures still have a high level of undiscovered and under-utilized potential. Photogrammetric approaches to modelling and visualization of cultural heritage offer accurate methods for 3D object reconstruction, including quantitative evaluation of the results. Acquired datasets can be integrated into cultural heritage information systems with the possibility of spatial analyses and future update.

We present two applications for image-based modelling and visualization of cultural heritage items: the evaluation of a historical relief model of Central Switzerland and the reconstruction of a Buddhist tower of the Bayon Temple of Angkor Thom, Cambodia. The first application is a contribution to the use of new information technologies for historical cartography. The second one aims at a low-cost image-based procedure for the modelling of large irregular objects and, as such, it represents an interesting alternative to laser scanning.

Pfyffer's Relief

At the Gletschergarten Museum in Lucerne, Switzerland, the oldest preserved large relief model of the country has been on display since 1873. Constructed between 1762 and 1786 by Franz Ludwig Pfyffer von Wyher, the 6.7 x 3.9 m^2 relief shows Lake Lucerne and neighbouring areas. At a scale of about 1:11,500 it represents an area of 4,100 km^2 about one-tenth of Switzerland (Figure 9.1). The model is constructed from pieces of timber, bricks, charcoal and cardboard with a mixture of gypsum, sand and beeswax as a top layer. The relief's topography is based on field measurements performed by Pfyffer, after his discharge from the French army services by King Louis XV with the rank of lieutenant general. The relief model of Franz Ludwig Pfyffer served as a basis of several printed maps issued at the end of the century.

The cultural-historical masterpiece of Franz Ludwig Pfyffer is nowadays a subject of scientific evaluation concerned with two main goals:

● image-based 3D reconstruction of the relief for the documentation of cultural heritage
● comparison of the 'virtual' Pfyffer relief with current map information for the purpose of research in the history of cartography and investigation of Pfyffer's surveying procedures.

This paper reports on the generation of the texture-mapped 3D model of the historical relief. The development of procedures for the analysis of the relief's accuracy is not within the scope of this paper and has been published elsewhere.

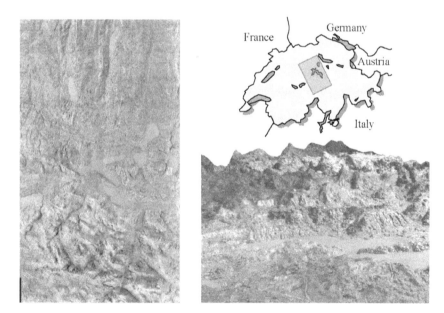

Figure 9.1   The Pfyffer relief and the related part of Switzerland

Procedures and Results

The project objectives require a high-quality 3D model of Pfyffer's relief in terms of accuracy. The overall height difference between the reconstructed model and the original may amount to a maximum of 1 mm. The procedures as well as achieved results are described in the following section.

Data acquisition The relief is situated in a cellar of the Gletschergarten Museum in Lucerne in a special temperature- and humidity-controlled room without natural light. These conditions make the image acquisition as well as control point measurement rather difficult. From a construction platform fixed at a height of 185 cm above the relief surface, 87 analogue and 50 digital 'aerial' coloured images were taken (Figures 9.2 and 9.3). In order to enable the stereoscopic processing, the

Figure 9.2   Image acquisition in progress

Camera	Analogue Rollei 6006	Digital DSC460c
Calibrated focal length	83.557 mm	28.871 mm
Number of images	87	50
Number of strips / number of images per strip	4/13 +35 additional images in mountainous areas	5/10
Image size	6 x 6 cm^2	3060 x 2036 pixel
Scale/Pixel footprint	1:23	0.6 mm

Figure 9.3   Parameters of acquired images

images have an overlap of 60% within a strip and 20% with neighbouring strips. To achieve a good illumination and to avoid the disturbing specular reflection of the shiny relief surface, spotlights in combination with dispersion umbrellas were used.

Before image acquisition, 40 circular targets of 3 mm diameter were temporarily pasted onto the relief surface. The three-dimensional positions of these 'control points' in a local coordinate system were determined using theodolite measurements with an accuracy of 0.1 mm. The purpose of control points is to establish a metric reference frame for the acquired images and the photographed object itself.

Photogrammetric processing
For more information, see Niederoest, 2002.[1]

- Photo-triangulation in a manual mode. Each block of images was triangulated in order to determine the exterior orientation of the images in a unique local object coordinate system.
- Generation of a Digital Surface Model (DSM). The comparison of a manually measured reference DSM and an automatically derived model has shown that the automatic procedures do not work properly in this case. In particular, the matcher has problems with distinct height differences in the model. As this is not acceptable as regards the project requirements, we resorted to manual DSM measurements, which gave us about 300,000 points in total. The grid calculation with an interpolation software system resulted in a regular raster of 1 cm grid width.
- Orthoimage generation, texture mapping and visualization. The original scanned images (1,270 dpi) were automatically transformed into so-called orthoimages using principles of digital image processing. For the derivation of 3D visualization products the orthoimages were texture-mapped onto the model surface (as shown in Figure 9.4).

The complete digital data set of Pfyffer's relief was archived at the Kul-

Figure 9.4   The 3D texture-mapped model of Pfyffer's relief

turgüterschutz of Lucerne for the documentation of cultural heritage. If the relief or parts of it are damaged the precise digital data can be used for physical reconstruction of the original.

Tower of Bayon, Cambodia

On the vast plain north of Tonle Sap, the Great Lake in Cambodia, is situated one of the greatest archaeological and architectural sites of the world – the Angkor complex. Angkor, the ancient capital of the Khmer Empire, dominated the region between 900 and 1500 AD, reaching its zenith in the 12th century. The whole complex spreads over an area of more than 400 km^2 and consists of many temples and other buildings. It ranks among the most spectacular sites currently included in the UNESCO World Heritage List.

Within the ancient city of Angkor Thom one can find the famous Bayon Temple, built by Jayavarman VII in the 12th century. A special feature of Bayon are its 54 towers with four large faces on each, pointing in all four geographical directions (Figure 9.5).

In this paper we present the 3D reconstruction of one of the very complex towers of Bayon. The goal of our project was to test the photogrammetric procedures for the photo-realistic 3D modelling and visualization of complex objects based on tourist-type small-format photographs.

Procedures and Results

Data acquisition   For the reconstruction of one of the Buddhist towers of Bayon, 13 small-format images covering the whole horizon were acquired with a Minolta Dynax 500si camera (see Figures 9.6 and 9.7). No theodolite measurement of control points was performed. For the determination of the object scale and the definition of

Figure 9.5   Aerial image of Bayon

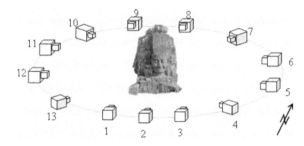

Figure 9.6   Arrangement of images for the 3D reconstruction of the Bayon Tower

Figure 9.7   One of 13 small-format images of the tower

the direction of the vertical, a scale bar was situated close to the southern tower side. Since a 360° view coverage was necessary and the light conditions were fairly extreme, the production of good, evenly illuminated pictures was practically impossible without artificial lighting. As this was not available at the site the images suffer from strong variability between the illuminated and shadow areas. Also, the dark and light parts vary from image to image, depending on the time of the day the images were taken. In order to achieve a photo-realistic 3D model, this problem had to be carefully handled during the photogrammetric processing.

Photogrammetric processing
For more details, see Gruen et al, 2001.[2]

● Photo-triangulation. After scanning of the images the photo-triangulation is set up as a semi-automated procedure. It is based on manual tie point selection and least squares geometrically constrained multi-image matching. For the absolute orientation of the whole block three control points defining the local coordinate system were used (two of them selected as marks on the vertical scale bar). In the self-calibrating bundle adjustment the interior orientation and the systematic errors of the non-metric camera used were modelled.

- Surface reconstruction, editing and triangulation. Our surface reconstruction approach works in fully automated mode applying multi-photo geometrically constrained image matching, resulting in fairly reliable and precise point cloud. Although we used the automatic blunder and occlusion detection, there were some blunders left. These were removed using a surface data editing procedure based on the iterative local surface fitting. For the conversion of the point cloud to a triangular surface mesh the Delaunay triangulation was applied.
- View-dependent texture mapping and visualization. We developed a new automated procedure of view-dependent texture mapping enabling generation of detailed photo-realistic 3D models. Based on the selection of optimal image patches for each triangle of the 3D model, it solves two essential problems of texture mapping for close-range applications: lack of image information for sloped object parts and the problem of varying radiometry of the acquired images. The results of the texture-mapped 3D model are shown in Figure 9.8.

Conclusions

We have shown how manual and automated image-based 3D object reconstruction can contribute to the inventory of cultural heritage – for high-precision applications (Pfyffer's relief) as well as for projects focusing on visualization, with lower requirements on geometric accuracy of the results but with high-level geometric complexity of the object (Tower of Bayon).

Notes

1   Niederoest, J. (2002) 'Landscape as a historical object: 3D-reconstruction and evaluation of a relief model from the 18th century', *International Archives of Photogrammetry, Remote Sensing and Spatial Information Sciences*, vol. XXXIV, part 5/W3.

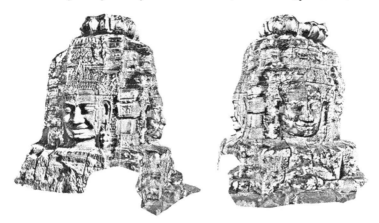

Figure 9.8   Reconstructed 3D model of the Bayon Tower (southern and eastern view)

2   Gruen, A., Zhang, L. and Visnovcova, J. (2001) 'Automatic reconstruction and visualization of a complex Buddha tower of Bayon, Angkor, Cambodia', *Proceedings of the 5th Conference on Optical 3-D Measurement Techniques*, pp. 166–78.

Chapter 10

A Virtual Open Air Museum in Three Dimensions in Latvia

Edvins Snore

Abstract

The VIRMUS (Virtual Museum) trial used 3DML (Three-Dimensional Mark-up Language) to develop virtual representation of parts of the Latvian Ethnographic Open Air Museum. The project also provides Internet users with means (3DML blocks, textures, etc.) to create their own 3D environments. The trial is a collaborative work of two partners: RIDemo, multimedia authoring company (coordinator) and the Latvian Ethnographic Open Air Museum (member).

The project commenced in August 2001 and continued for 12 months. VIRMUS involves three major phases: data gathering; data processing and interface development; and evaluation and dissemination of the results. The data gathering phase is successfully completed and the second phase, data processing, is under way at the time of writing. The initial data processing activities revealed a need to create original 3DML blocks instead of converting VRML (Virtual Reality Mark-up Language) models, as initially planned. This led the project team to the optimistic conclusion that quite sophisticated 3D environments can be generated just by writing 3DML code, which emulates HTML syntax. Therefore 3D environments can be created, for example, by museum webmasters having no knowledge of complex 3D programming.

Background

The Latvian Ethnographic Open Air Museum is one of the oldest and largest of its kind in Europe. It is a symbol of Latvian identity. During the Russian occupation (1945–1991) and Russification it was a tiny island of freedom for many Latvians who came here to speak their language, sing their songs and celebrate their 'illegal' national festivals.

Now Latvia is a free country again, one of the priorities of the local cultural heritage community and the whole Latvian nation is the preservation of the Open Air Museum and its wooden exhibits which, unlike other museums, have to resist sun, rain, wind and, indeed, … fire.

It was 26th May 2000 when the national TV and radio reported terrible news: an accident had caused a fire in the Latvian Ethnographic Open Air Museum. It spread fast and in the space of a couple of minutes a unique architectural monument of the early 19th century – the courtyard of Kurzeme – burned to the ground.

It was a shock and sorrow both to the museum's staff and to every Latvian. Soon afterwards a nationwide fund-raising campaign was initiated to rebuild the Kurzeme courtyard. People – rich and poor – contributed their money and now the Kurzeme courtyard is in place again.

If we say after 11th September 2001 that the world is not the same, then after 26th May 2000 the Latvian Open Air Museum will never be the same. The old priorities and policies were reviewed. The idea of VIRMUS was born.

VIRMUS: Introduction

Wooden architecture is like a telephone box. Today it is there, visible on our way to work, but tomorrow, in the mobile era, we will not see it any more. Although the causes are different the tendency remains the same – both are temporal phenomena that will eventually disappear. The average age of a wooden house is 200–300 years. The 850-year-old Borgund Stave Church (Norway) is the exception proving the rule.

Therefore it is highly important to preserve and document wooden architecture while it is still there. (Figure 10.1 shows an example of such a building.) Given the peculiarity of the subject, the documentation should be carried out not just in two but in three dimensions. This process is already being carried out all around the world. So, 3D documentation in itself is nothing new. There have been, however, difficulties with presenting this information to the general public.

The current practice of 3D web pages of virtual (architectural) museums focuses on complex VRML applications that have proved to be too complicated and 'space-greedy' for the average speed Internet connection. Efforts to make the 3D environment more Internet-user-friendly were made during several digital modelling projects of architectural objects. VISIRE (IST-1999-10756) aimed at creating a system which would provide the means of creating photo-realistic 3D

Figure 10.1   Typical wooden building in the Latvian Ethnographic Open Air Museum – in reality

reconstruction of a real environment from the information of the scenario contained in video image sequences. The project, 'Architectural Visualization of the Edinburgh Old Town' (ESPRIT, 24404), used HPCN to generate animated sequences of buildings. Still the computer model used made the result too 'heavy' to view it over the Internet. VISIRE envisages providing an interaction (reconstruction tool) for the web users. However, only 3D designers and multimedia professionals were considered to be targeted users.

Thorough efforts to reduce the 3D object downloadable space were made during 'The Tombs on the Appian Way' project sponsored by the Italian Government. Texture and polygon reduction techniques were used to compress VRML models. It was concluded that future work should be concentrated on making 3D architectural items easily visualized by an on-line low-power PC.

3DML: Bringing 3D Closer to People

The main idea of the VIRMUS project is to narrow the gap between the Internet user and the on-line virtual museum displaying 3D cultural heritage content. VIRMUS aims to introduce a novel approach to 3D web page development for open air museums and other institutions displaying architectural objects. The objective of VIRMUS is therefore to provide a way for ordinary museum webmasters and Internet users with limited or no knowledge of VRML or other available 3D generating tools to create interactive virtual environments in three dimensions.

VIRMUS uses 3DML technology as the main tool for implementation of the trial. 3DML is a new web publishing format that empowers users to create visually compelling rich media web pages (called 'spots'). It was selected because it uses a basic building block metaphor that enables users to create rich media environments by arranging ready-made 3D media objects and adding graphics, sounds and hyperlinks, so there is no programming or 3D modelling required.

3DML is commercially available and it emulates HTML syntax. Therefore, first-time users can create 3D pages alongside their HTML pages using the same authoring techniques, images and sounds they already know and understand. 3DML spots can be hyperlinked and include standard web graphics, animations, lighting effects, stereo-spatial audio and streaming media. 3DML is Direct3D compatible and runs on PCs with Windows 95/98/NT4.0.

Progress of VIRMUS

The project started in August 2001. The project activities are likely to take place for 12 months. The work was divided into three phases:

1. data gathering
2. data processing and interface development
3. evaluation and dissemination of the results.

At the moment (March 2002) the first phase of data gathering is already completed.

The majority of the required data was acquired during the on-site phase in the museum. Pencil sketches were made of the entire exterior. They were copied and number-coded to serve as a reference and checklist. Measurements were made via blueprints and official sources.

Digital cameras were used to capture textures of walls, roofs and other architectural elements of the buildings. Virtual panorama recordings of all the courtyards of the museum were carried out. Also ethnographic objects were photographed in order to integrate them in two-dimensional information blocks that will be embedded in 3DML interface.

The second phase of data processing and interface development is under way at the time of writing.

The gathered raw data is processed using Photoshop and CorelDRAW software for image editing and texture creating. Initially we used 3D Studio Max software to create three-dimensional objects in accordance with the data gathered on-site. We generated VRML files and later attempted to convert them into 3DML files. Although there is freeware available for this purpose, we came to the conclusion that VRML conversion did not provide the expected results. The 3DML blocks generated from VRML files were not entirely compatible with the whole 3DML spot. They also behaved strangely during user navigation through a 3DML spot, which was enhanced with blocks generated by the conversion software. These blocks used to 'vanish' when the user came 'virtually' close to them.

Therefore the 3D designers of RIDemo responsible for creation of 3DML environment proposed creating 3D objects by manipulating 3DML code of the 3DML pages. Initially this approach was not chosen for fear that 3DML as a tool for creating 3D objects might be too robust, not allowing creation of sophisticated architectural elements. In a way this was true. 3D Studio Max generated VRML objects which were far more sophisticated and detailed than those generated by 3DML. Nevertheless, display of detailed objects required substantial downloading time. To avoid this problem details were simplified during VRML–3DML conversion. So simplification happened anyway.

Another challenge of creating 3D objects in 3DML was the lack of sophisticated 3DML authoring software. Spotnik, which was available on-line, allowed manipulation of predefined blocks, but not creation of customized (in terms of shape, not textures) blocks.

Experiments with manipulating 3DML code were undertaken by RIDemo programmers with knowledge of HTML programming but no knowledge of 3D. Due to the fact that 3DML emulates HTML syntax, the operational environment was somewhat familiar. The first experiments showed that basic 3D shapes (triangles, spheres, cubes) are quite easy to create and to cover with customized textures. More work was required to create complicated objects like straw roofs and wooden gates. But it was still possible. Figure 10.2 shows work in progress.

When our experiments proved to be successful we decided to carry out the whole project – creating five courtyards of the Latvian Ethnographic Open Air Museum – only by writing 3DML code, instead of modelling VRML objects and converting them into 3DML.

Simultaneously with data gathering and interface development phases, the

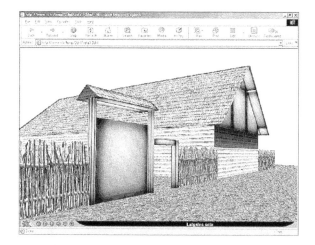

**Figure 10.2   Fragment of Latgales courtyard generated by 3DML. Textures
are not yet applied**

VIRMUS project team has started dissemination activities, providing information
about the project to the local professional community and national media.

Conclusions

The main conclusion of VIRMUS is that a virtual open air museum in three
dimensions is possible. It is possible not only for a secluded community of
professionals but for the general public. You do not need to have a super-ultra-DSL
Internet connection to be able to see and browse through a 3D environment.

Another major conclusion is that a 3D open air museum can be created by an
ordinary webmaster. No knowledge of 3D programming is required, only skills of
HTML. This was vividly demonstrated by the project activities.

Finally, it should be mentioned that VIRMUS was the first IST trial being carried
out only by Latvian members. Given the fact that Latvia was still on its way to full
EU membership, we are both proud and highly motivated to have carried out a
successful take-up action, the results of which could later be used by other European
open air museums.

Note

http://www.virmus.com/3dml_museum.htm provides a comprehensive description and
presentation of the entire results of the project, including considerable historical information
with video and audio as well as 3D representation. However, the paper was kept mainly as
originally presented in order to provide an 'in-process' project description. [Eds]

Chapter 11

The Virtual Dead Sea Scrolls and the Electronic Art Garden

Susan Hazan

Abstract

The Israel Museum, Jerusalem, perhaps best known for the famous Dead Sea Scrolls, includes permanent collections ranging from prehistoric archaeology through to contemporary art. It is the leading cultural institution in Israel and is one of the largest encyclopaedic museums in the world, annually presenting a full roster of temporary exhibitions, publications and educational activities. Enhancing the complex of galleries and material collections are the information kiosks in the galleries and computerized study rooms. Innovative, on-line electronic projects add a further dimension to the museum experience, providing the contextual information that complements and enhances the gallery experience. This paper will focus on two projects, The Virtual Dead Sea Scrolls, and the Electronic Art Garden.

Introduction

The Israel Museum in Jerusalem, perhaps best known for the famous Dead Sea Scrolls, includes permanent collections ranging from prehistoric archaeology through to contemporary art. It is the leading cultural institution in Israel, and is one of the largest encyclopaedic museums in the world, annually presenting a full roster of temporary exhibitions, publications and educational activities. The three curatorial wings of the main museum, Archaeology, Judaica and Jewish Ethnography and Fine Art extend over 22 departments, with extensive holdings of the archaeology of the Holy Land, and fine art holdings from Old Masters in European Art, through international contemporary art. In addition to the art collections, visitors throng to the Shrine of the Book to see the internationally renowned Dead Sea Scrolls, the five-acre Sculpture Garden designed by the Japanese-American sculptor Isamu Noguchi and to the archaeology collections that reflect Israel's position as a bridge between the great civilizations of Egypt and Mesopotamia.

An art or archaeological museum does not prioritize technological innovation, which in some way may even be seen as an antithesis to the museum mandate, yet it has always been clear to our institution that there is much to gain from embracing new technologies to fulfil our institutional goals. Whether we are collating digital objects in the database, electronic galleries in the study rooms, or entire virtual exhibitions on the website, we question how these kinds of augmented realities impact the museum experience. In addition to the curatorial work that goes on in the galleries that is concerned with the material collections, the information kiosks in the galleries and computerized study rooms and the innovative on-line projects all add a further dimension to the museum experience, and provide the contextual information that complements and enhances the gallery experience.

Beyond the Museum Walls

In 1991 the New Media Unit began to focus on electronic projects, identifying, visualizing and implementing new media applications appropriate for the museum environment, launching the first comprehensive website in 1995. The website published both in Hebrew and in English has since undergone three new re-designs with a fourth almost completed at the time of writing.[1]

In 2001, the Israel Museum presented several notable exhibitions and each exhibition was promoted through a specially designed web presentation. In December 2001, *Dreaming with Open Eyes* opened a comprehensive exhibition of the Vera, Silvia and Arturo Schwarz Collection of Dada and Surrealist Art, which included over 300 works by leading artists including Duchamp, Man Ray, Ernst, Breton and Goya.[2] *Written in the Stars: Art and Symbolism of the Zodiac* opened in March 2001,[3] illustrating the origins of the zodiac and its place in Western culture through ancient mosaics, illuminated manuscripts, ceremonial objects and the fine arts.

China, One Hundred Years of Treasures was perhaps one of the more spectacular of the museum's exhibitions presented in 2001,[4] and the first exhibition of masterpieces from the People's Republic of China held in Israel. It afforded a view of rare and priceless works of art spanning over 5,000 years up to the eighteenth century, tracing China's crowning achievements in bronze, jade, ceramics, porcelain and gold and silver. The website exhibition offered an opportunity to learn about the collection before the visit, while at the same time providing further information to read more about the collections in much the same way as a catalogue of the collection, but available to everyone 24 hours a day, seven days a week. For the countless others who were unable to come to the museum themselves, the web visit may be the only way of experiencing, in some way, this extraordinary collection of treasures from China.

It's About Time, a year-long exhibition for the whole family on the theme of time celebrated the third millennium, and afforded a special challenge for the museum, to engage with an abstract concept that touches every part of our lives yet, for most of us, remains vague and mysterious. 'What will happen in a thousand years?' we asked one of the young visitors. 'Well, I'm sure I'll have a husband and children by then,' one nine-year-old girl answered us.[5] In addition to the art installations, interactive displays and thematic presentation of the objects from the archaeology and ethnographic department in the 800 square metre gallery, the exhibition was presented on the website as a *Quick Time* walkthrough of the Youth Wing galleries,[6] as shown in Figure 11.1. The comprehensive walkthrough acted as a trace of the exhibition, providing a spatial representation of the moment in time before *It's About Time* was replaced by the next thematic exhibition in the same galleries.

Figure 11.1   Screenshot from the Quick Time *It's About Time* Youth Wing exhibition

The Youth Wing's annual exhibition that followed in 2002 was *Hands*, a thematic exhibition that described how beliefs, customs, images and thoughts are described through gesture where it is the hand that touches, feels, sees and communicates, mediating between us and our world.

While these different kinds of web experiences all serve to interpret and disseminate the museum message beyond the museum walls, this paper will focus on two new projects, the Virtual Dead Sea Scrolls and the Electronic Art Garden.

The Virtual Dead Sea Scrolls

The Dead Sea Scrolls, in the Shrine of the Book (Figure 11.2), perhaps the most celebrated of the Israel Museum's collections provide a compelling cultural message that for our web-designers pushes the parameters of 'old' new technologies. The Scrolls, and the other remarkable archaeological collections presented in the exhibition, *A Day in Qumran*, not only illustrated a unique archaeological discovery, but also represent the religious and cultural message of

Figure 11.2   The Shrine of the Book, Israel Museum

the Qumran community of the Second Temple and the biblical and apocryphal texts written on the 2,000-year-old parchments. The cultural legacy of these rare documents not only opens up new vistas on ancient Judaism and throws light on the background and origin of first-century Christianity, but also provides a contemporary vehicle for interfaith study and dialogue.

Educational activities at the Shrine of the Book include both traditional and contemporary pedagogic methodologies that illustrate the manuscripts and their aesthetic presence. In order to explore new avenues to disseminate the cultural and spiritual messages, the Israel Museum, in partnership with the Politecnico di Milano, is researching an imaginative digital platform to reach out to local and international visitors across the World Wide Web.[8] While still in an early stage of development, the on-line virtual reality environment will present a shared 3D space for visitors to visit the Shrine of the Book (as depicted in Figure 11.3) and the exhibits while interacting with each other in groups under the direction of a trained museum guide.

WebTalk II evolved out of an earlier project, *Leonardo*, which had been developed in JavaTalk. The SEE project (Shrine, Educational Experience) was developed as a Client and Server, and provided navigation in 3D VRML environment for the eight remote participants and a guide to meet together. In the virtual Shrine of the Book, the guide invites visitors to follow him to Qumran in an on-line adventure. This innovative net space invites participants to search for hidden objects, and to take part in team-quest in 'real time', and to solve challenges set and directed by the on-line guide. Walking in the shoes of an avatar, and using more than one set of eyes, visitors may walk or fly around the museum with a friend, or in a group, to discover the archaeological evidence of a community that once lived in Qumran. This will provide a compelling experience for the visitors to interrogate the manuscripts and artefacts, to take part in a real-time discussion on the Dead Sea Scrolls and their contemporary relevance, and to share their experiences with other remote students around the world.

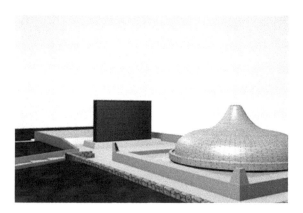

Figure 11.3   The virtual Shrine of the Book

The Electronic Art Garden

The Electronic Art Garden is a 3D, photo-realistic walkthrough of the (real) Art Garden in the Israel Museum campus, designed by the Japanese-American sculptor Isamu Noguchi. The Art Garden extends over five acres and is characterized by terraces built from agricultural heaps of boulders that recall the natural terraces, and the archaeological structures which may be found in the landscapes of the Judean Hills. The surface of the Garden is covered with a layer of small stones that recall Zen gardens in Japanese monasteries. The Electronic Garden incorporates an innovative application, designed by Innovu, a Tel Aviv-based company founded in 1999, using a combination of high-quality photography based in real and synthetic imagery supporting 56k dial-ups to broadband. Visitors may select either an intuitive walkthough of the garden or a guided tour zooming in to the sculptures to view them in more detail.

The museum continues to embrace new technological innovations, not in order to show-case emerging technology, but as a means to present the galleries and the collections in engaging and meaningful ways for our visitors. Whether visitors come into the museum campus to experience the collections in the gallery or in the art garden, or discover the collections when visiting the museum over the web, it is our hope that through these kinds of electronic architecture, and digital applications the New Media Unit provides experiences that enhance and augment the material collections and extend the museum experience beyond the museum walls.

Figure 11.4   Screenshots of the Electronic Art Garden

Notes

1. Israel Museum website at <http://www.imj.org.il/>
2. *Dreaming with Open Eyes* at <http://2002.imj.org.il/dada/>
3. *Written in the Stars* at <http://2002.imj.org.il/zodiac/>
4. *China, One Hundred Years of Treasures* at <http://2002.imj.org.il/china/>
5. Michal Broshie Ben-Levi, quoted in 'Who is Older, Daddy or Grandpa?', *The Israel Museum Journal*, Vol. XVIII, 2000, The Israel Museum, Jerusalem.
6. Quick Time walkthrough of the Youth Wing galleries at <http://2002.imj.org.il/qtime/>
7. *Hands* Exhibition at the Ruth Youth Wing at <http://2002.imj.org.il/hands/>
8. From the First Millennium to the Third, the Content is the Message! at <http://www.ichim01.polimi.it/index_e.htm>

Chapter 12

The Production of Conservation Facsimiles: The Tomb of Seti I

Adam Lowe

Abstract

Cultural tourism is a rapidly expanding market. Inevitably this has placed immense pressure on a number of cultural heritage sites around the world, with a large number now permanently closed to the public, or with access restricted to a small number of researchers. The production of high-fidelity facsimiles is seen as a means of relieving pressure on such sites. In this paper I discuss the initial development work relating to the production of conservation facsimiles for a project to create an exact copy of the Tomb of Seti I in Egypt. Previous state-of-the-art facsimiles are reviewed and related to the preliminary work in the tomb of Seti I, Valley of the Kings, Luxor.

The Development of Cultural Tourism

Cultural heritage sites are now the focal points for the rapidly growing number of cultural tourists but this comes at a cost and the cost is the preservation and well-being of the sites themselves. In Egypt these issues are particularly pressing; the tombs of the Pharaohs served a specific religious function and were never intended to receive visitors of any kind. The climate in Egypt, hundreds of years of neglect, and more recently the work of the Supreme Council of Antiquities are the main reasons these tombs still exist. Since the first rush of tourists in the early nineteenth century the tombs have suffered layer upon layer of damage.

Damage has arisen from many sources: during excavation; from the often plundering colonial approach of the British, French, Italians, Germans and Americans; repeated squeezing (casting) of the wall surfaces; failed conservation attempts; humidity from thousands of visitors; natural movement of the rock; flash floods due to inadequate drainage; over zealous researchers; greedy antiquities dealers; ignorance and, in some cases, straightforward malice.

A proposed solution, that balances the needs of conservation with cultural tourism, is to produce high-fidelity museum-quality facsimiles of tombs that are either closed to the public or inaccessible. It is important that these facsimiles, and the data gathered in their production, are of the highest standards and can be of use for both the study, monitoring and conservation of the sites. The work carried out in the Tomb of Seti I is a model for how this approach can work and be funded.

In this paper I will discuss the novel techniques used to produce a high-fidelity facsimile from an area of the Hall of Beauties and a section of Room K in the tomb of Seti I. In section 2 I will discuss examples representing state of the art in 2D and 3D facsimiles. Section 3 discusses the aims of the project and relates the Seti I facsimile to previously built facsimiles. The 3D scanning and colour capture techniques used to measure the walls of the tomb are discussed in Section 4. Issues related to the routing of the scan data and final production and printing of the facsimile are covered in Section 5. Section 6 provides an update on the current state of the project and future stages of the project are discussed.

Construction of Facsimiles in Two and Three Dimensions

The common perception is that facsimiles are either the domain of the Las Vegas-style showman, the forger, the unscrupulous dealer or the second-rate museum. Alternatively it is often thought that they lack the 'aura' of the original and are missing the complexity that years of history have bestowed upon the object, information that can be deciphered by the discerning specialist.

The use of modern digital techniques for recording and production poses several questions. Is it possible to make a facsimile that is indistinguishable from the original under museum viewing conditions? If it is possible, is it desirable to do so and would the data, in its various forms, have implications for academic research, monitoring and conservation? Additionally, would such a facsimile have implications for the conservation of heritage sites that are at risk and could tourists be attracted to visit them? Alternatively can the presence of the tourist, often a negative factor in preservation, become a pro-active force in the preservation of world heritage?

The answer to all these questions is 'yes', and is demonstrated by the recent success of both the Altamira and Tuthmosis III facsimiles. The museum at Altamira has proved to be a major success, attracting large numbers of visitors who are prepared to queue to visit the facsimile. The public response to the museum indicates that the vast majority of visitors believe that the experience significantly enhanced their understanding and appreciation of both the cave and the importance of its preservation. The success of the Altamira museum proves that people can be encouraged to appreciate the facsimile as a wonder in its own right, a positive use of new technologies that reveals the layers of complexity that become apparent under close scrutiny. Similarly the Tuthmosis III facsimile forms a central part of the exhibition *The Quest for Immortality* that opened at the National Gallery of Art, Washington and is currently touring the United States.

Review of Current Facsimiles

The use of facsimiles to represent tombs and caves is not an entirely new phenomenon. Ironically the tomb of Seti I was the subject of one of the first facsimiles to be shown in the UK. A facsimile of parts of the tomb was made by Belzoni and opened in 1823 at the Egyptian Halls in Piccadilly, opposite the Royal Academy. The squeezes, or casts, made in the tomb by Belzoni and others in order to produce this facsimile are the cause of much of the damage now visible in the tomb. The Egyptian Halls were one of the main tourist attractions in London at the time and fuelled the public interest in Egyptian culture.

In more recent years several important caves showing examples of early Palaeolithic art have been created as facsimiles. In 1983 Lascaux 11 was opened to the public. In this facsimile of the main area of the cave photogrammetric techniques were used to record an accurate rendition of the volume and surface. Using the survey information a replica was created in cement by hand and painted with natural dyes resembling those believed to have been used in the decoration of the original cave.

In 1998 Tragacanto, working in conjunction with Manuel Franquelo (one of Spain's leading realist painters and a director of Factum), were commissioned to build a three-dimensional facsimile of the painted cave at Altamira. The facsimile was to be built on a scale of 1:1 in the same materials as the original. The painted interior was measured using photogrammetric techniques to a spatial resolution of 4 mm, with unpainted areas being measured at a resolution of 40 cm. In some areas where higher detail was required, a 3D laser scanning system was used to measure to a spatial resolution of 0.9 mm. An extensive photographic survey was also conducted.

The 3D data was used as input to a CNC controlled router which cut blocks, representing the cave walls, in polystyrene. Textured beeswax sheets were then applied to provide an accurate micro-texture across the block. The beeswax-coated blocks were then cast in silicon and piece moulds were made. Pulverized limestone, taken from a site near the original cave, was mixed with resin and applied to the silicon moulds. The resulting cast was then reinforced with fibreglass. Fixings were embedded into the fibreglass reinforcement so that the finished facsimile was easy to install into a steel frame at the museum in Altamira. An ochre pigment was then applied across the casts; after preparation the surface was similar to the original in both colour and other physical properties. During the first stage of the painting, large-format photographs of the paintings were projected onto the sections of cave and accurately positioned. Using the photograph as a guide they were then drawn onto the surface of the composite before being painted, reworked, distressed and matched to the original. The entire surface was finally varnished to mimic the water that now covers the Altamira cave walls. The Altamira facsimile differs from the Lascaux facsimile in that equal attention is paid to the surface of the rock, its composition, texture and cracks, as it is to the paintings.

In June 2002 Factum Arte completed a 1:1 scale facsimile of the tomb of Tuthmosis III (Luxor, Egypt). The facsimile, commissioned by the Danish company United Exhibits Group, forms the central piece of the exhibition *The Quest for Immortality* at the National Gallery of Art in Washington. Extensive photographic data was gathered inside the tomb, the images were processed, enlarging them by 2,000 %, and the colours were retouched to match the feeling of the tomb. The data was then printed onto gesso panels using a specially adapted flatbed pigment printer. The final dimensions of the facsimile were 18 x 9 x 3.2 metres, with two free-standing square columns measuring 1.2 metres on each side. After printing the panels were hand-finished, significantly adding to the resolution and feel of the facsimile with particular attention being paid to the damage and aging that give the walls their character.

Figure 12.1   A photograph from inside the Tuthmosis III facsimile in Washington

All of the facsimiles described above have been received with great acclaim and are popular tourist attractions. However the facsimiles cannot be described as being of conservation quality as the data gathered during their production is not of sufficient resolution to facilitate accurate study or monitoring of the surface. In each of these cases the reality of the facsimile is dependent on subjective decisions that increase the apparent resolution of the facsimile. Factum Arte's approach in the recording of the Tomb of Seti I is to increase the accuracy of the data and the objectivity of the recording methods while eliminating, as far as possible, any subjective interventions.

The Seti I Project

The Seti I Project was initiated by Michael Mallinson, an English architect working on conservation projects in Egypt with some initial funding from Dr Ahmed Baghat, an influential Egyptian philanthropist. Originally a site was proposed in an old quarry near Giza within easy reach of the Great Pyramids and the New Museum of Egyptian Antiquities.

The original aim was to create a museum housing five tombs that have been closed to the public for several years. Each exhibit was to be a full-size three-dimensional physical copy replicating, in the most minute detail, every aspect of the original. A uniform attention would be paid to all elements of the reconstruction. It is the complex relationship that exists between all the elements that results in a convincing recreation. The key areas of concern are: the texture of the surface, the accuracy of the painting, the way the paint sits on the surface, its colour, the cracks and damage, the evidence of repair, scratches, graffiti and incised lines. Working to spatial resolutions of 0.1 mm, and depth resolutions of 0.02 mm, every subtle change of surface and texture will be recorded.

Other conditions like scale, smell, light levels, light sources, temperature and humidity are also important, presenting possibilities that will enhance the experience of visiting the site. The importance of the facsimile as a means of conserving the site without diminishing the impact of the experience is an important aspect of the work.

As the project developed it became clear that both the Supreme Council of Antiquities and The Friends of the Royal Tombs of Egypt, a Swiss Foundation run by Eric Hornung and Theodor Abt, favoured the location of the facsimiles in Luxor. The current position of the project is that the trial section of the tomb of Seti I has been totally successful, a site has been identified near the Valley of the Kings and political and financial discussions are ongoing. Rather than re-creating five tombs the aim will now be to start with the Tomb of Seti I and then to plan a self financed project to build replicas of the most endangered tombs.

The tomb of Seti I is the largest and most lavishly decorated of all the tombs in the Valley of the Kings. However, in the late 1980s it was closed to the public because of structural problems. It has not reopened. The creation of a 1:1 conservation facsimile of the Tomb of Seti I will make it accessible once more. The scale and ambition of this project is unprecedented. It brings together Egyptologists, conservators, scientists, technology providers, artists and the museum world. The Seti facsimile has made vast leaps in terms of accuracy and resolution; the 3D data acquisition and routing processes are some 400 times higher, and the images are printed at 1440 dpi rather than being painted by hand.

In phase 1 of the project Factum Arte was commissioned to carry out background research into the best practical methods of recording and constructing a facsimile of the tomb of Seti I at a resolution at least 100 times higher than the Altamira facsimile. These included the design and build of equipment where required, procurement and modification of existing equipment, 3D scanning and colour acquisition in Egypt and the production of the first 16m² of finished facsimile.

In phase 2 Factum will purchase or manufacture all equipment required for the scanning of the complete tomb of Seti I, train an Egyptian work force in all aspects of facsimile production, set up workshops in Cairo and Luxor and oversee the construction of the full facsimile.

Digitally Acquiring the Tomb in 3D and Colour

The project brief called for the tomb to be measured to a spatial resolution of 0.1 mm or better. An initial market survey revealed that there were a multitude of 3D scanning systems commercially available, employing a variety of different optical techniques. Several systems were investigated for suitability encompassing laser scanners, laser radars, 3D interferometry and white-light-area-based systems.

After a series of tests and benchmarks it was decided that no commercially available system fully met the project requirements. However a short-range laser scanner, REVERSA manufactured by 3D Scanners, could be adapted.

To adapt REVERSA for scanning in the tomb a specially designed movement system was required; we call the combination of this movement system and the REVERSA sensor a SETI scanner. This scanner has a high-resolution REVERSA (25H) scanning head mounted onto a CNC controlled XYZ movement system. It is capable of a spatial resolution of 0.08 mm. Normally systems of this type have the sensor facing directly down or perpendicular to what might be termed the Z-axis. In this system the Z-axis is thought of as being perpendicular to the wall that is being scanned. To achieve this, some modifications had to be made to 3D Scanners' software, hardware and calibration routines. Figures 12.2 and 12.3 demonstrate the scanning system operating in the tomb.

Figure 12.2   The SETI scanner in operation

Figure 12.3   A close-up of the REVERSA laser triangulation sensor scanning a portion of the tomb wall

The system was designed to gather a regularly positioned, or organized, point cloud arranged in a 0.1 mm grid. It was important that the grid was organized as this eliminated the need for extensive post-processing that was found with other technologies. The elimination of post-processing was made possible by the use of the Delcam software that directly routed from points. Given that the tomb of Seti I has about 2,000 m² of wall surface, and the scanner can record about 1.5 m² per day, the elimination of extensive post-processing literally saved years of man-hours from the project. The scanning is done in 52 cm² tiles with a 1cm overlap between each tile. Figures 12.4(a) and 12.4(b) show scan data from two 52 cm² tiles. Figures 12.5(a) and 12.5(b) show corresponding images with the height of the data points represented in colour to show depth from a nominal zero. These images show that while the reliefs are often only a matter of a few millimetres high, the 3D shape of the walls can vary anywhere from between 20 and 40 mm across a tile area.

Figure 12.4(a) in particular shows the need for high resolution when scanning, as the apparent noise on the scan data is actually the texture of the surface. The majority of the surfaces in the tomb have such texture, either from damage, flaked paint or from brush marks. This can be seen more clearly in Figure 12.6 where the data surrounding the snake in Figure 12.4(a) has been highlighted.

About 80% of the tomb wall area can be scanned using the SETI scanner. The areas causing difficulties are the corners, alcoves, areas with more than 10 cm of relief, the benches and door pillars. These areas will be scanned with the 3D Scanners' ModelMaker X system, a portable laser scanner with six degrees of freedom. Data from the ceilings and areas without relief carving will be made using a combination of photogrammetric survey and photographic techniques, a similar approach to that used in the facsimile of the Tomb of Tuthmosis III. Methods of

Figure 12.4(a)   Rendered scan data depicting a general scene, and 12.4(b) Scan data depicting Anubis

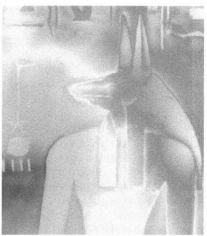

**Figure 12.5(a)   Colour map of Figure 12.4(a), and 12.5(b) Colour map of
Figure 12.4(b); colours represent depth from a nominal zero**

**Figure 12.6   Close-up of Figure 12.4(b) showing the fine detail that has been
recorded**

gathering the 3D data for the ceilings are still under consideration and will depend on the final budget for the facsimile.

When scanning of the tomb is complete the point cloud will consist of over 200,000,000,000 individual points. Each square metre of the tomb will be represented by 100,000,000 points of information. To put this into context the highest resolution that was achieved in some areas of Altamira was 1,000,000 points per m^2 though the majority of the painted area was measured to only 62,000 points per m^2. In the Seti scan each 52 cm^2 tile, when stored in ASCII format, will require

700 megabytes of memory or 1 CD-ROM for storage. The complete tomb will require 8,000 CD-ROM to store the ASCII data.

Colour recording was achieved using a Minolta colorimeter and a colour matching system designed by Manuel Franquelo. The Minolta data was subsequently discarded as being too inaccurate to be meaningful. Further colour matches were mixed by hand and compared directly to the colour on the wall. Within each area of colour there is a wide variety of hue and tone. Study areas included the nature and appearance of the gesso and paint layers, various types of damage on the walls, mattness and gloss of the surface, the character of the paint, surface qualities of the paint, the colour and variations within each colour.

Producing the Facsimile

Each panel in the facsimile is produced using an innovative blend of artistic techniques, craftsmanship and high technology. The overall production process can be broken down into twelve steps as discussed below.

1. Panels are routed in Cibafoam from 3D point data to produce positives, Figure 12.7(a).
2. Silicon moulds are cast from routed panels to produce negatives, Figure 12.7(b).
3. Gesso panels are cast from silicon moulds, Figure 12.7(c).
4. Gesso panels are trimmed and fitted by hand, Figure 12.7(d).
5. Registration marks are added to gesso panel and photographed.
6. Colour data is aligned to physical tiles in Photoshop.
7. Colour correction of photographs.
8. Gesso panels are digitally printed at 600 dpi, Figure 12.7(e) and 12.7(f).
9. Printed panels are trimmed, assembled and filled, Figure 12.7(g).

Figure 12.7(a)   A routed Cibafoam panel   **Figure 12.7(b)   A silicon mould taken from a routed panel**

Figure 12.7(c) A gesso panel cast from a silicon mould

Figure 12.7(d) Four gesso panels being trimmed and fitted

Figure 12.7(e) Printing a gesso panel using an adapted Mammoth printer

Figure 12.7(f) An individual printed panel

10. Retouching is administered to remove visible joints.
11. Final hand finishing is applied to add surface complexity.
12. The facsimile is assembled.

As can be imagined from the above description a great deal of care has to be taken at each stage of the process. However the first stage in the process, routing, is a particularly important stage since it provides the base for all production. Routing was performed by Delcam using proprietary ARTCAM software. The Delcam software directly loads the points from the scanner and calculates the tool path. As discussed, it is advantageous to cut directly from the points as the data is not

Figure 12.7(g)   A group of four panels that have been partly printed

optimized or compromised in any way. Each 52 cm^2 tile is cut into fine grain Cibafoam composite board, a lightweight material that can hold fine detail. The tile is first roughed out to a resolution of 1 cm and then a final cut is made with a 0.1 mm cutting head with a step-over of 0.03 mm. At this resolution the router was capable of cutting 0.3 m per minute, with each tile taking 81 hours to cut. Working at this resolution every aspect of the surface is visible, from tiny paintbrush marks to the coarse granules in the black, green and blue pigments. The final production process will employ 20 specially modified routers capable of cutting each panel in approximately 25 hours: even cutting at this speed with this number of routers the whole cutting process will take at least 106 weeks to complete.

An equally important stage in the process is the printing. A Mammoth flatbed printer with 1,440 dpi Epson piezo pigment heads is being used for the printing of the test panels. The Mammoth printer has been stripped down and reassembled with a linear cog to move the bed of the printer and ensure regular printing lengths. Most flatbed printers print to high degrees of accuracy on the width but over a distance of 3 metres the length can vary by up to 3 cm. The production of a cog-and-rack system to drive the bed results in precision on the length as well. If the cog is not exactly the right diameter, banding appears on the printed surface. The modified Mammoth printer can now achieve accuracy in length and high-quality print resolution.

Project Update and Future Work

Phase 1 of the project culminated in a unique conference that brought a large number of the Egyptian Supreme Council of Antiquities and the worldwide Egyptology community together in London on 17th July 2002. At the conference the initial test panels were displayed and the consequences for cultural tourism and conservation discussed. The project has now entered its next phase. Having learned from our experiences in the first stage new machinery and processes are currently being specified and constructed. This work is ongoing and constantly being improved. The use of conservation-quality facsimiles in the preservation of cultural heritage is gaining acceptance and continues to be popular with the public. However the practicalities of realizing a project of this scale are slow and complex requiring the right mix of political, institutional and financial support. Everything is now in place for the task of recording the whole tomb to start. All that is now required is for the final permissions and approvals to be granted.

Acknowledgements

All work was carried out with the permission and support of The Supreme Council of Antiquities with copyright of all material gathered residing with the Supreme Council.

Reference

http://museodealtamira.mcu.es/ingles/indexprova2.html

PART 4
DIGITAL ARCHIVING

Chapter 13

Digital Image Picture Archives: Theory and Practice in Switzerland

Rudolf Gschwind, Lukas Rosenthaler, Roger Schnider,
Franziska Frey and Jeanette Frey

Abstract

The theory and practice of picture digitization is reviewed in the light of some examples from Swiss museums. Two topics receive detailed consideration: the longevity of digital information and the necessary pre-conditions for good-quality work on large image collections.

Introduction

Photographs are found in practically all museums and archives, generally in large numbers. They are cultural heritage, an artistic medium, historical documents and a visual documentation medium of the 20th century. One of the main problems is the gradual degradation caused by the relatively limited stability of the photographic materials. In the case of black and white photographs problems arise of de-silvering, yellowing, acidity and broken glass negatives. In general, after 70 years damage is practically always present. For colour photographs the deterioration process is even more rapid, with colour fading causing visible changes after 30 years. A further problem is the number of photographs. Photography is a 'mass medium', which means that picture archives can be very large and picture collections of more than 100,000 pictures are not infrequent.

For these reasons, digital image archives are an attractive solution to the above problems for museums and archives, since a number of advantages can be obtained simultaneously:

- looking after the original
    - o optimal storage conditions for the photographic originals (preventative preservation)
    - o preventing damage due to excessive usage
    - o copying of the digital data without quality loss
- access improvement
    - o picture research, keywords, database
    - o production of copies, loans

- additional usages
  - o networking, data exchange
  - o research, reconstruction
  - o marketing (both digital and conventional media)
  - o WWW, virtual museums.

Illegibility of Digital Images after 10 Years

Every reader has certainly already had the experience when inserting a floppy into a disk drive that nothing more appears on the screen than:

The diskette is not readable – should be formatted

Thus one learns the hard way that digital data cameras have short lifetimes and that digital information – to exaggerate somewhat – behaves in a binary manner: either it is 100% present or completely absent. With the rapid advances in digital photography one should seriously ask the question as to whether digital images will not be lost in a few years?

Note that the original text of this chapter was printed on paper with an expected lifetime of approximately 100 years. Then consider the expected longevity of various other media, as suggested in Figure 13.1.

Medium	Expected longevity in years (dependent on the storage conditions)
CD	5–100
Newspaper	10–20
VHS tape	10–30
DAT	10–30
Magnetic tape	10–30
Microfilm	10–500
Kodachrome	100
Acid-free paper	100–500
Egyptian stone table	2,220 +

Figure 13.1   Longevity of storage of various data media compared

The 'degradation curve' of digital data is very different from the degradation of analogue data (such as photographs). Analogue data shows a continuous fall in quality, which can be slowed down but not stopped by optimal storage conditions. Digitally stored information is either readable (and thus available without loss of quality) or the information is not readable and thus 'completely degraded'. A gradual loss of quality by digitally stored information is impossible. The causes of degradation/loss may be as follows:

1. The data medium is defective due to natural ageing
2. The data medium is defective due to wear and tear
3. The corresponding data reader (hardware) no longer exists
4. Defective service.

In order to present the highest possible lifetime for digitally stored information:

1. all parts must be within the minimum/maximum possible lifetimes
2. the weakest link of the archival chain must be known.

The extremely short lifetimes in the information technology industry, due to the short product cycles of both hardware and software, are currently certainly the biggest problem facing the archivist. Today people expect a product cycle of one to two years from computers and data storage! Storage capacities are continually increasing and computers keep becoming faster, but this leads to problems regarding the compatibility of the storage media when a new type of successor appears on the market:

● one generation before: it can be written on and read with the current equipment
● two generations before: in general it can only be read
● three generations back: in general, incompatible – the data medium cannot even be read.

If one compares these times with the estimates of the data medium lifetimes (Figure 13.1), a system lifetime is today calculable at five to seven years. The stored data becomes unreadable, not because the medium is short-lived but because system changes are so fast. It is only because of digital storage that we will know in 250 years what the year 2000 looked like.

In order to guarantee the long-term availability of digital data regarding digital information, it is interesting to make a comparison with written information. If we look at history then we see that a large part of our cultural heritage and our knowledge of it has been and will be handed down in written form. This knowledge has survived for hundreds of years:

● It has been produced in symbolically coded form (text, letters).
● Books and texts have been regularly copied and written out, thus making them independent of the medium. The quality of the medium is of secondary importance so long as the 'code' can still be decoded.
● The information was spread widely. Above all, after the invention of printing by Guttenberg, mass distribution of information occurred.
● Writing contains considerable redundancy, so that even with degradation of the text medium it is always still readable.

For pictures, especially, the digitization of documents and image materials of all kinds has the same importance as writing and the art of the book for language. For the first time it is possible to code originals of this type, for example, pictures in symbolic form (as a number 'bundle') and to transport and replicate this immaterial code.

The digital revolution can be regarded as a true revolution, since it makes time and place in a certain sense meaningless and eliminates the concept of 'Unikats'. Writing corresponds to symbolic coding whereas mass processing, possibly thanks to data processing, is analogous to the importance of the art of book printing for language. The properties of every digital code and thus all digital multimedia data are therefore as follows:

- Digital code is in principle independent from the medium on which it is recorded. The medium may be changed at will, even if (for example) a digital code in chiselled stone is relatively inconvenient.
- Digitized information can be replicated without data loss, in other words, it can be copied. This leads to the conclusion that the term 'Unikats' for digital data becomes senseless. A further important consequence is that a theoretically unlimited lifetime for digital information results from its loss-free copying property.
- Redundancy is important since it provides greater security in the case of damage to the medium, but for this it requires more 'storage room'. Our Latin script has relatively high redundancy (circa 64 characters = 6 bit), compared, for example, with the Chinese script (circa 20,000 characters). Digital information can become particularly redundant through appropriate procedures (using error correction code or ECC) and thus protected against 'missing bits'.

Rules for the Longevity of Digital Information

The key rules are as follows:

- The medium used must demonstrate a lifetime of over 10 years. Today this can be provided by practically all media.
- The medium should possess a system lifetime which is as high as possible. This condition is met by those media showing the maximum possible dissemination and use; in practice these are as follows: CD-R, DVD, floppy disk and magnetic tape of the following types: DLT, DAT and Exabyte.
- The medium must be usable with all hardware platforms and readable regardless of the operating system.
- The medium should be as tolerant as possible regarding changes in reading equipment; that is, it should be readable not only on the equipment on which it was written. Systems which put high requirements on mechanical precision are in this regard particularly sensitive. Magnetic tape, for example, uses a helical scan (rotating magnetic heads with sideways recording).
- The media and formats should have the highest possible redundancy. Today's storage systems all apply error corrections: sometimes (for magnetic tapes) the possibility exists to determine the number of corrected reading and writing errors. As regards data formats, compressed formats should be avoided since the following is valid: 'Compression = Elimination of Redundancy'.
- User errors are a major source of data loss. In this category belong errors such

as unintentional deletion, no control of the entered data or wrong handling of the data medium (for example with CD-R: fingerprints, dust and sticky marks).

• Right from the beginning a strategy should be foreseen for the periodic control of the data storage and for data migration to new data storage.

Considerations in the Digitization of Large Image Collections

Definition of Quality

The quality necessary in digitization of analogue data is a many-faceted problem. It is dependent on the nature of the initial analogue data's condition and the requirements for reproduction correctness.

For text data it can, in some cases, be important that the text is readable as a facsimile copy, but in others that it is only the content which is of interest. In the latter case Optical Character Recognition (OCR) may be used, in order to transform the text into searchable form. The quality of image data is in comparison more difficult to determine. It may for example be important to be able to find again the smallest details of the original in the digital image, or that the digital image should be optimized for either screen display or printing. The digital image will require different qualities depending upon the objectives.

The basic decision must be taken as to whether the digitization should be carried out in-house or should be contracted to an external organization. In either case a specialist knowledge in the archive itself is necessary in order that the correct decision is taken and to be able to recruit the right people or correctly evaluate the suppliers.

Requirements for the Production of Good Quality

There are various requirements which must be fulfilled in order to produce digital images of good quality; two of the most important points are the design of the work environment and the selection and training of staff.

Design of the work environment Since the end of 1999 there exists an ISO Standard for the form of the work environment (ISO 3664, Viewing Conditions for Graphic Technology and Photography). The most important points may be summarized as follows:

• The 'white' of the screen should be D65, i.e. corresponding to daylight.
• The room lighting should amount to approximately 32 lux, at a colour temperature of up to 6,500k.
• The immediate environment of the screen should be kept neutral (grey or black).
• The screen should be placed so that no reflections appear on the screen. In particular it is important to pay attention so that peoples' clothes in front of the screen do not cause reflections. Ideally, all the walls, floor and furniture in sight of the person sitting in front of the screen should be grey.

Staff selection and training   An important point in discussing quality is the selection of suitable people. For this it is naturally important which parts of the work are performed in-house and which parts of the work are carried out by an external supplier. Experience from other projects has shown that it is often assumed that the same person may be employed for all the work tasks that occur. The areas of digitization, cataloguing and long-term maintenance each require special knowledge which it is rare to find together in one person. Above all therefore it is necessary to bring together a suitable team of people.

It has been shown that for the scanning of documents and pictures it is best to recruit people who have been visually trained. It is also necessary to ensure that the staff are trained in dealing with awkward documents of all kinds (for example, glass plates). Since most damage to objects occurs through improper handling, it is very important to set down guidelines in this area and also to check that they are closely followed.

For cataloguing, staff are required who have specialist knowledge regarding the content of the documents being digitized; for example, historians, sociologists, etc.

The long-term maintenance of the digital data, as well as the building up of the computer system infrastructure, requires staff with sound information technology knowledge. It is also important to understand that in this area, different tasks such as database design and programming or specific Internet problems on networks often cannot be handled by the same person.

Special problems of image data   In contrast with text documents for which, due to the need for readability, clear scanning quality minimum requirements can be established, the situation for images is much more difficult since no such 'lowest common denominator' appears (such as, for example, the smallest letter in a text document). Therefore the scanning parameters for each class of images are changed and again optimized. Picture variability is very high (for example, image sharpness, image type, contrast range, etc).

In the production and evaluation of digital image data there are four important parameters which must be taken into consideration: tone reproduction, colour reproduction, digital reproduction and 'noise'.

Quality control and inclusion in the workflow   Quality control is an internal component of every project. Here we shall briefly describe which points can be controlled. It is, however, dependent on the project as to which points should be considered and which points should be attributed more weight. The staff must understand, accept and regularly execute the quality checks.

In the control of digital facsimiles (direct scan at the highest resolution) it must be very clear that the user receives the raw data only in exceptional cases. The digital image, with which the end-user works, is in most cases prepared to be optimal either for the screen or printing (but not both simultaneously).

In addition to the above mentioned parameters (tone, colour and detailed reproduction such as 'noise') quality control includes the following points: edge correctness, dust and dirt, and completeness, that is, the image is not trimmed).

Quality control must be carried out at different places in the workflow. In this there are various areas to be paid attention to, as indicated above:

- Firstly, one must check whether or not the digital data has been produced in accordance with the instructions.
- A particular issue for attention is the correct naming of the files. Errors in this area often require substantially a high level of effort to correct, since often it is necessary to search through a large number of images in order to find the 'missing ones', that is, those with incorrect names.
- A further point is the cleanliness of the scanner (for example, dust specks on the glass screen). Old materials in particular often leave marks on the scanner which appear in the images of subsequent pictures and this causes time-consuming retouching work.

Digitization of Stocks of Pictures in Swiss Museums and Archives

A considerable number of museums and archives undertook digitization projects for their picture archives in cooperation with the University of Basle. The scope of these projects ranged from pilot studies to the systematic digitization of the entire stock, the corresponding pictures covering the entire photographic spectrum. Figure 13.2 provides just some examples.

Institution	Picture Stock
Swiss Landesmuseum, Zurich	Ektachrome 4" × 5", albums, black and white originals
The National Archives, Berne	Glass negatives 13 × 18 cm to 18 × 24 cm
The Land Library, Berne	Medium formats and 135 mm colour slides
Museum of Communications, Berne	Colour microfilm (CMM) (A6, 35 mm, non-perforated)
Swiss Archive for Monument Conservation, Berne	Glass negatives 10 × 15 cm to 24 × 30 cm, aerial photographs
Open Air Museum, Ballenberg	Small picture slides and negatives (collection objects)
Canton and University Library, Fribourg	Black and white enlargements, postcards, albums
Art Museum, Berne	Ektachrome 4" × 5" and 8" × 10"
DRS Radio, Berne	Black and white enlargements, albums

Figure 13.2   Variations in picture stocks under digitization or completed

The Swiss Archive for Monument Conservation, EAD

The approach for the digitization of the EAD collection, as also representative for the other collections, is now described in more detail.

Restoration documentation has been kept in the Swiss Archive for Monument Conservation for over 110 years since the beginning of the national government's support for monument conservation work. The holdings – extended by donations and purchases – consist of over 1.8 million photographs and negatives (including about 70,000 glass negatives) as well as plans and reports on the history of the architecture, monument conservation and of urban and landscape protection. With its numerous private collections of important Swiss photographers, the EAD has developed from being just a documentation centre for monument conservation to a real 'Swiss Picture Archive'. The EAD is open to the public. In 1998, the project InfEAD was launched for the recording, digitization and dissemination of the collections of the EAD. In the course of 1999, prototypes were developed for recording and presentation on the Internet.

The major part of the collection of digitized pictures consists of glass negatives in 13 cm x 18 cm format for the period 1890 to 1950. Our experiences in their digitization led to the following conclusions:

- Glass negatives make special demands regarding digitization. A Scanmate F8 Plus scanner was installed for the digitization. Glass negatives cannot be placed on glass: the two layers 'stick', quickly scratch and in the worst case there is glass breakage. A special non-glass frame was therefore constructed in which the glass negatives were laid. Following digitization the glass negatives are packed in acid-free cartons for conservation reasons, not in the original greaseproof packets.
- The glass negatives were scanned at the highest quality level (digital master) which corresponds to the photographic resolution. An analysis showed that the emulsions used at that time appear to have a low-resolution level and high granularity, compared with modern photographic materials. Cameras and lenses of those times also showed lower performance data. A resolution of 1,200 dpi was sufficient for the digitization and in most cases the emulsion granularity was clearly visible.
- The negatives – and the historical glass negatives above all – show extreme variability regarding lighting and contrast. All kinds of over- and under-lighting occur as well as a contrast range of 1:4 (extremely weak) up to 1:10,000 (extremely rich contrast). It was observed that the light parts of the picture (which are often important) in the positive are dark in the negative. This makes a very high demand on the scanner regarding the photometric resolution, (> or = 14 bit) since only thus is it possible to have an accurate resolution of the dark parts on the negative. In order not to lose this information, the 'original'/'raw' digitized files are stored as 16 bit Tiff files.
- The 'raw' digital files (about 100 MB per glass negative) were stored on magnetic tapes (DLT). For security back-up reasons two or three copies were produced and stored in different locations. Annual control readings of the tapes are planned, with migration to a new data carrier (or medium) anticipated in five to seven years.

- Since the 'original'/'raw' digital data can hardly be processed, the digital 'negatives' were transferred into positives and adapted in contrast for optimal appearance on the screen. Simultaneously the image sizes were enlarged (for example, to sides of 2,000 pixels) and stored in JPEG format on CD-R. The entire process was implemented in batch form on cost grounds, since manual processing of these high data volumes is still very time-consuming even with powerful computers. Digitization, batch processing and storage was carried out each time for reason of efficiency on particular computer systems (digitization on Mac or PC, batch processing and storage on Unix machines). General experience shows that the post-processing takes much more time than the digitization itself, which points to the importance of an optimal work flow.
- The separation of the functions of archiving and usage is also important for digital images. For archiving one needs full resolution (digital facsimile), an uncompressed image format (Tiff) and a non-manipulated image (original 'raw' scanned data). For usage of the pictures on screen one requires suitable resolution for both the application and the computer, and data and image formats optimally adapted for the particular application with the image being 'corrected' (for example, automatic colour and contrast correction).

It is noteworthy that in the digitization of large volumes the same problems always appear:

- Errors in the file names, due either to data entry problems or because the cataloguing has not been performed in a 'computer correct' form, thus leading to inconsistencies.
- Check, check, check … Continuous quality control is vital. There is nothing more irritating than when it is necessary to yet again unpack, for example, 500 glass plates and compare each with the digital image file until the mistake is found.
- Mixtures of very different picture materials and formats which inevitably lead to errors.
- The materials are not 'scanner-friendly'; for example, albums and general formats greater than A3. For these there arises a source of danger of damaging the original through faulty handling.
- Insufficient computer and storage capability. As a guideline it is sensible to have available a storage capacity of at least two weeks' production.

The dangers of errors may be minimized if care is taken by using the above procedures.

Conclusion

The spread of digital imaging of photographs appears sure to continue even though increasing proportions of new images are digital. Therefore, it is important to follow good practice in digitization and in this paper we have tried to show our views based on a variety of practical experiences in a cross-section of leading Swiss institutions at the turn of the millennium.

Reference

Further information may be found at http://www.abmt.unibas.ch/downloads/wien_
2003_a_digi.pdf.

Chapter 14

Museum and Archive Software for the BMW Corporate Archives

Wolfgang Mueller

Abstract

This paper describes the application of a content management system (CMS) for the historical archives of a leading automotive manufacturer, BMW. It describes the entire project process from the initial client requirements definition to implementation. It is noteworthy that the archive content types include audio and film, as well as 200,000 images and other company archive materials such as promotional brochures and instructional documents. Provision is also made for the library containing technical periodicals, video cassettes and CD-ROMs as well as books. Provision is made for public as well as internal access with extension planned for an eShop facility.

Introduction

Firstly a quotation from the 'Memorandum of Understanding', signed both by the International Council of Museums (ICOM) and also by CMB. This points to museums' responsibility to:

> obtain the widest possible access to the resources of museums and galleries through multimedia communication systems – all schools, universities, research institutions and public libraries should have privileged access to public collections over electronic networks.[1]

Now another quotation:

> It is proposed to call a meeting of the curators of a few provincial museums to discuss the possibility of obtaining – a compendious index of the contents of all provincial museums and collections …
>
> H.M. Platneur, 1888[2]

This idea (over a hundred years old) to create both internal and external links for collections is now more realistic than ever before, thanks to the possibilities of modern information and communications technology (ICT).

Project Participants – A Partnership

In 1996 the 'Tradition Section' of the Munich-based BMW AG decided to undertake a restructuring of its historical archives. The Tradition Section is part of the PR Department and consists of the BMW Museum, the Historical Parts Service and the Picture and Media Archive as well as other departments.

CMB has been engaged since 1993 in the production of content management systems (CMS) for galleries, collections, museums and archives. Its gallery software 'Portfolio Manager', the 'CMB Storager' and CMB's flagship product 'ArteFact' are well known in the German-speaking museum world. The CMB software house, with three companies in Austria, England and Germany, is strongly focused on the museum field; for example, the Museum Computer Network (MCN), MDA (formerly the Museum Documentation Association), ICOM, and the Consortium for Interchange of Museum Information (CIMI).

The Starting Point

The case study presented, that of the implementation of CMB software, is well suited as a 'showcase' since as well as being successful it is also comprehensive, as shown by comparison with our other projects. Whereas in most CMB projects a number of clear main points emerge as priorities, in this case almost every individual aspect had to be addressed:

- Quantity:
  o a specific amount of data to be archived in a specified time-period
  o a large volume of data to be managed electronically, thus leading to the hardware requirements.
- Functionality/quality:
  o image database (with e-commerce functionality)
  o inclusion of the entire archive holdings
  o inclusion of the entire library database
  o seamless connection of an Internet enquiry with e-commerce functionality
  o stock control, inventory taking (physical administration of the objects and archive materials)
  o exhibition organization and loans (to and from)
  o restoration management, condition descriptions.

Project Objective[3]

The BMW Historical Archive should become a Service Centre for historical documents and information. Moreover, the supply will be extended in the future from product-related documents to historical company documents and a library. The marketing of the Historical Archives will increasingly be carried out using 'new media'. Users will be able to research the archive materials with the new system and also to partly order online. A preliminary themed selection will initially be provided on-screen, with the help of digitised image information and images will be able to be printed out for lay-out purposes. Furthermore, detailed information will be transferable on-line to the customer or alternatively 'printed-on-demand' directly to a high-quality printer. A significant reduction in staff costs will thus be achievable. In the future it is planned to develop more extensive user services.

Specific objectives were then as follows:

- Conservation of the materials. The original items held in the archive system must be stored professionally. For the daily operational work a manual archive will be created.
- The content of the archive will be provided on the network.
- Reduction in the time required for research. This requires both a systematic archive structure and a detailed registration of the archive materials.
- Provision of an overview of entire archived materials even when they are physically stored in decentralized archives. It must be possible to find all the historically relevant materials with an archive system.
- To provide a higher transparency of the materials requested. The provision of statistical information on the desired materials can be determined and made available in a user-oriented manner.
- To develop an archive policy, which specifies what archive materials should be held and how the company-wide supply is to be effected. An archive structure in the form of a Guideline is to be developed, which should be acted upon by all the future decentralized locations worldwide.

Project Steps

The BMW staff responsible for the project invited six leading content management system (CMS) suppliers to demonstrate their software and an initial solution to the internally produced requirements specification. A weighted points-scoring scheme was used to provide a comparative evaluation from which CMB was selected.

The first step was the cooperative refinement of the requirements specification produced by BMW. All key staff were interviewed at their workplaces and CMB experience drawn upon to add to the requirements specification. In general, customers are not 'at the state of the art of CMS technology' and it only became clear to both partners what should be the way ahead after a joint survey of, on the one hand, the project requirements and, on the other, the possibilities which a particular software offers.[4] The original 20-page BMW requirements specification grew into a project planning document with over 60 sides.

The installation of ArteFact was carried out in 14 partly decentralized (Munich, Steyr) workplaces in the BMW Archive. Then followed data transfer from third party systems (a FAUST database, several Microsoft Access databases as well as data from an ORACLE database). Operational work began after a one-week training programme. In parallel with the tailoring of the ArteFact system, work was carried out at BMW on a hierarchical thesaurus and process definition for the Archive.

During the initial data entry and the work with the ArteFact system, Phase 2 of the project was started: connection of the database to the Internet. In April 2000 the Internet access system went on-line.

The Archive

Taking into account the original Eisenach factory, BMW's historical development covers a time-frame of some 100 years. The task of the Historical Archive is the comprehensive collection, access provision and scientific interpretation of all those documents which are important in the company's history. They include, for example, approximately 200,000 pictorial images, 4,000 promotional brochures and 2,000 instruction documents. Production data permit research on nearly all cars produced since 1923 from the delivery books. The Library consists of over 2,000 volumes and considerable numbers of technical periodicals. In addition there are numerous video cassettes and CD-ROMs. The Archive also includes a collection of nearly all the products ever produced by BMW. The data assets grow continually through manual data inputs and very large quantities of pictures. The pictures were digitized externally at about 40 megabytes per image, read into the database using the automatic image import routines of ArteFact and linked with other data (such as object data).

The BMW Archive uses in fact almost all of the different data types which an ArteFact database offers. In the main it thus handles about every type of data that is found in most museums and archives.

- *Object data*   In this data type all of the products produced by BMW are placed, divided into different collection areas and provided with detailed descriptions.
- *Persons*   Data about people who at some point had a connection with the firm or who had an influence on the firm are recorded in detail.
- *Archive materials*   Here all the written documents regarding the firm's history or products are stored, for example, thousands of catalogues and brochures, work instruction documents, spare part lists, price lists, accessories lists, press packs, workshop handbooks, and about fifty successive delivery books.
- *Audio-visual materials*   ArteFact evidently has to manage the broad collection of sound recordings and film material. So the BMW Archive has available numerous video and sound documents, which later on will need to be transferred in digital form into the archives.
- *Library*   The Archive's own book collection (about 2,000) and about fifty periodical series are managed in the Library module.
- *Historical events*   Historical events which are important for the company (such as general historical events or anniversaries, etc.) are recorded with detailed information.
- *Papers and documents*   A comparatively large number of historic papers and documents form a major part of the area of the company's history.
- *Files*   ArteFact also facilitates the inclusion of electronic computer files in the Archive. Thus Excel and Word files or PDF documents are conserved in the databanks.

- *Pictures* An important component of the Archive data bank consists of pictures (some 75,000 prints as well as about 25,000 colour slides among others) which were digitized, annotated and registered in an optimal tailored workflow for input into the Image Data Library.

Requirements for the Successful Implementation of an Electronic Archive System

As a building block for the successful conversion of the whole archive to an electronic system, process definition was regarded by the BMW management as a necessary basic requirement.[5] (The complexity of the task can be assessed by looking at Figure 14.1.) Only through an investigation into new procedures in the Archive could an awareness of the internal administrative requirements be obtained. In turn these were put into the workflow for the collection management system. Process-oriented core tasks as classic archival functions were defined as follows: securing the sources (collection, documentation input), evaluation, recording and archiving, conserving the stocks as well as the preparation of all the relevant materials. Research and establishment of archives and information for internal company and external enquiries are also valid as tasks for the historical customer services.

The Strengths of the ArteFact CMS as the Main Pillar of the Project

Fast implementation was an important requirement in the BMW project described above. ArteFact is a software package, which only needs parameter setting, not programming, in order to adapt it to the needs of the client and so the installation could be implemented a short time after the order was placed.

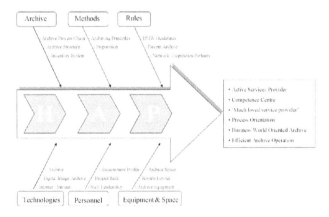

Figure 14.1   Historical Archive Process (HAP) definition

The data processing needs in a content management system are almost always underestimated. There is a widespread opinion that thorough detailed documentation plays a central role in the work whereas tools to raise the efficiency are in general neglected. A CMS presents, so to say, the core of a collection. This institutes a core which efficiently manages the data, in order to subsequently extend, edit, publish and integrate in many different administrative tasks.

A CMS requires considerable investment. Calculations show that, for example, the J.P. Getty Museum had to invest 17.5 man-years to deal with 100,000 object data records.[6] This order of magnitude indicates the importance of holding the data in a suitable way in order to serve as a basis for meeting the many requirements.

More important than directly fulfilling concrete data description or data maintenance standards (which anyway in the museum world at best can be described as 'quasi-standards') is to provide a flexible system for the data description which supports any desired standard and an open system for data maintenance with, also, an easy-to-produce interface with the external world.

Figure 14.2 shows a detailed view of the object data type (R 32) with corresponding text, list and date fields, related to other connected data records which may be seen to the right in the middle of the panel. (Here we can see the R 32's relations to other motorcycle products, people and events.) The inventory number (at the top) and title remain always on view while, in the form, the detail, continuation, administration and user-definable classes of fields can be changed. Notable is the fact that ArteFact is available in several languages. This screenshot shows software and data in English, whereas BMW's main language is German, of course.

A content management system not only has to satisfy efficiency aims but also should maximize the value of the included data. Information value may be defined by its quality and availability. For the former the key issues are the documentation content and error-free data input. The accessibility of the information depends upon the search and display possibilities. For this the accessibility of the data is increased

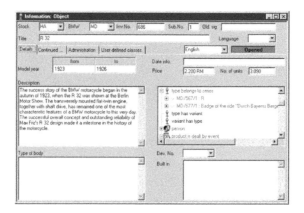

Figure 14.2   Detailed view of the object data type (R 32) with corresponding text

in ArteFact in so far as one may create information from them (that is, transfer them into a structure) which is understandable by both people and computers. It is also possible with ArteFact to provide the information again in a structure through an intelligent connection mechanism. A knowledge base is formed through the linkage of data records following desired relationships, chosen by the user. Only through these steps to creatively maximize the capital investment in the data entered is it achievable.

OPAC (Online Public Access Catalogue) Connection – The Gateway to the External World

The OPAC software WebMill, as an add-on to ArteFact, enables data to be published over Internet browsers by utilization of many search possibilities. This OPAC data bank enquiry is used by both BMW staff on an intranet and by different user groups on the Internet. The information architecture (see Figure 14.3) is designed for this, so that any data source can be connected, its data prepared and made available online over Internet browsers.

WebMill applies solely the ArteFact database as the information source (except for user verification of employees as internal users, which is the Internet LDAP). The preparation of the data is such that Internet access is made on a data warehouse and not on the operational CMS database. The data warehouse is being generated on a regular basis by WebMill's distribution manager. This is done for security and performance reasons. Data is put into a standard form and relevant results are provided such as, for example:

- the generation of pre-view screens
- the selection of data for which publication is permitted
- information on which prices for information are payable by which user groups.

In order for BMW to achieve the not inconsiderable goal of efficiency

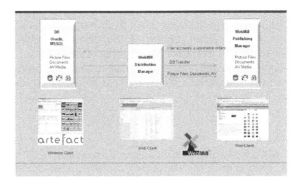

Figure 14.3   System architecture scheme: CMS with WebMill OPAC

optimization, various content is available over the Internet. This concerns above all enquiries regarding picture materials from agencies as well as from journalists or private individuals who are interested in BMW's history. For this purpose e.pic can be extended with the e-commerce module e.max (Latin: keen on buying). e.max consists of a session-independent shopping basket and also offers, 'at the other end', orders and administrative enquiries to be processed, up to the inclusion of electronic payment options and order processing.

The collection management system ArteFact can thus also be simply used as such. In the general content management field, functionalities arise that a CMS need not address as primary issues; for example, data multilinguality or the possibility of differing presentation forms for certain content. However the integration of these functionalities into ArteFact provides additional advantages for the collection management system itself. The data is located in a central pool. Using an additional authorization level one can determine which data may appear on the Internet. Through the high-volume data processing interface provided by ArteFact, all the data relevant for publication can be efficiently altered. The image database integrated within ArteFact supports from the beginning the automatic generation of various image qualities, from the low-quality one suitable for Internet use to the necessary high-quality one in the CMS, with embedded watermarking as an option.

The operation of a maintenance-free, always up-to-date Internet database is thus achieved by an ingenious system architecture and an optimal symbiosis between the ArteFact application and the WebMill Internet publishing tool.

The shopping basket functionality integrated in the Internet application permits the person seeking information to order electronically certain data, at first limited to pictures. These images will be marked as being orderable in the ArteFact database and various alternatives offered (such as a small image, slide, CD-ROM, etc.). ArteFact includes a fully featured DRM (digital rights management) module to cater for the right usage of pictures as well as to calculate pricing. The detail level achievable is shown in Figure 14.4: with a single click all the search types, the list of search results (in colour) or data related with the retrieved data record can all be obtained.

Thus the way ahead is set in the on-line collection, for the marketing of a picture archive and for an automatically generated and integrated museum e-shop.

In the collection management system, ArteFact has the possibility of providing data in different languages and qualities (such as different educational levels). The Internet application accesses again precisely to the data cross-section that the user wishes to have presented (for example, data records in English).

The overall application thus represents successful application of content management systems in 'industrial cultural heritage' to industrial service standards.

Notes

1   Memorandum of Understanding of the European Commission, April 1996.
2   Platneur, H.M., cited in Stiff, M. 'Developing digital museum collections', in *Digital Resources for Humanities' (DHR), Proceedings of the DHR Conference*, Oxford, 1997.
3   Objectives statement in the original text of the first Requirements Specification of the BMW Archives.

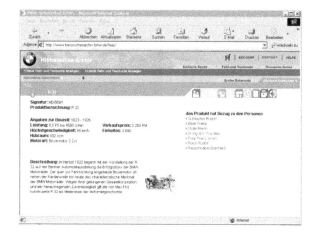

Figure 14.4   Detailed view of the data record of R 32 in an Internet research usage

4   See Waetzold, S. 'Museum documentation and data processing. On the Report of the Museum Documentation Working Group' in *MuseumsKunde*, no. 40, 1971, p. 1211f.

5   Raiger, J. (Manager of the BMW Archive): *Process definition 'HAP'*.

6   Noel, A. (1996) 'Reflecting the years of actual automated data at the J. Paul Getty Museum' in *Museum Computer Network (MCN) Spectra*, vol. 23, no. 4, S. 28f.

Chapter 15

The ICCD Catalogue's General Information System: A Tool for Knowledge, Preservation and Valorization of National Cultural Heritage

Maria Luisa Polichetti

Abstract

The ICCD (Instituto Centrale Per Il Catalogo e La Documentazione) is one of the world's largest cultural heritage documentation centres with over five million catalogued items. The paper describes how an integrated modularized system has been developed, benefiting not only from internal systems work but also from taking advantage of broader Italian national, European and international projects.

The project for the creation of the Catalogue's General Information System (Sistema Informativo Generale del Catalogo – SIGEC) is based on a concept that has been consolidated through time by the Central Institute for Catalogue and Documentation, which views the world of heritage as a 'system'. The wealth of Italian heritage is spread throughout a territory characterized by goods of incalculable cultural significance, in association with those preserved in museums, making systematization a necessary condition in order to guarantee an organic knowledge of heritage.

SIGEC is developing an integrated system that jointly manages functions and processes carried out at the different levels of the Italian Ministry for Cultural Resources and Activities' operational structure in charge of cataloguing. The system integrates both the tools and products already released by the ICCD, and an impressive amount of data that has so far been loaded into the system, such as the 1,000,000 catalogue cards that have been dealt with by the ICCD during the current year and another 834,000 that are going through the process. The expected increase is 4,100,000 catalogue cards, which have already been computerized and that are ready to be integrated into the system in a short while.

The architecture of the Catalogue's informative system is modular and divided into four subsystems: *alphanumeric*, *multimedia*, *cartographic* and *user*. The first three subsystems manage the data's entire production cycle (textual, multimedia, cartographic). The last, the user subsystem, does not operate on the data, but processes it on the basis of diversified handling requirements, and allows access to it. The methodology employed allows both the commencement of the cataloguing process, from any one of the remaining three subsystems, and the integration of all the available data on a given resource into a single context.

The *alphanumeric* subsystem, which deals with the textual data related to a given resource, also contains the module for management of national cataloguing standards issued by the ICCD (GENORMA). The module helps the automatic update and alignment of the data entry, control and management tools belonging to databases. In addition, the Alphanumeric subsystem enables the integration of data related to different standards and to different versions of a specific standard into a single environment.

The *multimedia* subsystem manages a broad genre of documental attachments (pictures, audio files, video files, CAD drawings) and allows query through related images, by means of integration with the other subsystems. This function is useful, for example, when procedures to send cultural resources abroad are carried out, and also in optimizing visual research on stolen or recovered cultural resources.

The *cartographic* subsystem enables the association of different types of geographical information with various resources in relation to their characteristics. The location of every single resource can be expressed through coordinates or, in an indirect manner, through alphanumeric data: for this reason 'geo-vocabularies' that take advantage of geographical data processed by other institutions, such as ISTAT, have been created. The subsystem also enables the performance of cartographic research and the implementation of spatial analysis of a geographical territory, by relating the resource to every available type of cartography.

The *user* subsystem makes the ICCD's data accessible through technologically advanced query and utility modes, organized on the basis of predetermined processing that optimizes functions of navigation and, consequently, the process duration. The subsystem also informs and directs the user within the General Catalogue's system, where the system is understood as being that of the databanks distributed throughout the national territory, inclusive of information on data stored in systems that are external to the Ministry, following the signature of specific institutional agreements. Special requirements pertaining to data security issues, related both to intellectual property rights and to the legal status of the resources catalogued, are also considered in this context. Specific channels of access have been taken into account for this reason, based upon the type of users that have been determined: general users will be given access only to minimal information, while more specific information will be given to registered users and, finally, complete access will be reserved exclusively to the Administration.

The implementation of a multimedia environment for cataloguing cultural resources in the national territory, capable of integrating inspections based on the ICCD referral standards, is among the main benefits of possessing a computerized modular integrated tool.

Thus, the evolution of cataloguing activity, along with the constant guarantee of quality, begins to take shape, by offering simplified cognitive processes to the world of cataloguing, through the introduction of incremental elements of knowledge:

- The objective of the *identification module* is primarily to provide the identification of a cultural resource in an unambiguous way within the system. It is composed of a set of minimal descriptive elements (brief description and portrayal of the toponym, in other words, the place name) and it is the initial moment in the cognitive process of a cultural resource. All the information components are linked to this first cognitive item: the information module (described below), the catalogue card, the multimedia documentation, the relationship to other cultural resources and the relationship to other documental components. Such information components may be progressively increased by including data on the state of preservation of a resource and, in general, of anything considered to be useful in enriching the cognitive outline of the cultural resource itself.
- The *information module* is composed of the first nucleus of validated data relevant to the resource. It permits a first rapid survey of data, through the use of terminological controls, and it ensures the unequivocal identification of the resource. Its essential objective is an immediate visibility of the resources throughout networks.
- The *catalogue card*, at its different levels of analysis, is the most extensive moment of cataloguing and, through the process of data alignment and final validation, it corresponds to the final moment of the process of knowledge, thereafter launching the data towards complete and integrated use by different types of user.

The system is able to share the information resources with external bodies through pre-arranged definition of data and metadata transfer protocols. Cooperation is carried out at a dual level: a methodological-institutional level, in which the characteristics of the reciprocal exchange and the aspects related to the quality and the availability of the catalogue data are defined by the means of conventions, and a technological level where the most appropriate modalities in the creation of a shared environment are enabled and updated from time to time.

Thus, much useful experience has been derived from the methodologies proposed by the European Commission's Aquarelle project, in which the ICCD was involved, and also from those of the Ministry for Cultural Resources and Activities' Information Network project, which is the latter's tangible realization at the national level. This exercise involved not only the Institute itself, which promoted it, but also other institutions exemplifying the different realities that operate in the sphere of cataloguing (Superintendencies, local bodies, Italian Episcopal Conference, etc.), who have been given due attention within the Information System.

The SIGEC system has been developed in a strong relationship with two European projects: TRADEX and CHANCE. It is the technological scaffold of the CHANCE[1] project (Cultural Heritage Access through Networked serviCes for Edutainment market), that aims at validating a European-wide service for on-line access to the cultural data repository and intends to offer a uniform content base to multimedia applications and special tools to be used primarily in the educational, edutainment and tourist market segments. The SIGEC will benefit also from the results of the TRADEX project,[2] that focuses on the on-line multimedia object transfer, considering available copyright marking technologies for solving the illegal copying and proof of ownership problems in the context of multimedia objects.

Notes

1   CHANCE is a TEN-Telecom project (no. C26785) where five of the most active EC countries in the cultural domain (Italy, France, Germany, Greece and Spain) are involved. In each country there is at least one partner in charge of content provision and one technology supplier. The CHANCE Consortium is composed of the following organizations: Engineering Ingegneria Informatica (Italy); Istituto Centrale per il Catalogo e la Documentazione (Italy); Scuola Normale Superiore di Pisa (CRIBECU) (Italy); Producteurs (France); Netimage (France); Fundació Catalana per a la Recerca (Spain); Direcció General de Patrimoni Cultural (Cultural Heritage in Catalunya) (Spain); Eutelis Consult (Germany); Staatliche Museen zu Berlin (Germany); Museum of Cycladic Art (Greece); ATKOSoft S.A. (Greece); METAWARE (Italy); Consorzio Pisa Ricerche Centro Meta (Italy). The website http://www.project-chance.net provides information on its activities.
2   TRADEX is an IST trial action project (no. 1999-21031). The TRADEX consortium is composed of the following organizations: Multimedia and Telematic Research Centre (META) – Consorzio Pisa Ricerche (Italy); Engineering Ingegneria Informatica (Italy); Netimage (Normes Et Technologies pour l'Image) (France); ICCD (Instituto Centrale per il Catalogo e la Documentazione) (Italy); Dipartimento di Elettronica e Telecomunicazioni, Università di Firenze (Italy); CENTRICA s.r.l. (Italy); and Digital Archive Japan Alliance (DAJA) (Japan). http://www.tradex-ist.com.

PART 5
DESIGN, RETRIEVAL AND PROTECTION

Chapter 16

The Cleveland Special Exhibitions Tool – An Elegant Solution to a Common Requirement

Ben Rubinstein and Holly Witchey

Abstract

The Cleveland Museum of Art (CMA) pursues an ambitious programme of special exhibitions. The need to produce sophisticated web features for blockbusters precluded properly supporting lower-profile exhibitions. The museum commissioned Cognitive Applications to create a master design that could be reused for exhibition web features. A content editing and management tool supports this process. The tool's potential quickly became apparent. It proved possible to use the first prototypes to develop and publish content-rich special exhibition websites in record time. A more sophisticated version of the tool proved so successful that it was quickly put into use for many other elements of the website. It was then put into constant application for prototyping as well as for creating final versions of many features within the site. This paper describes the process by which the tool was conceived and analyses the factors that have led to its success.

Introduction

The Museum has an ambitious exhibition schedule (12 major exhibitions a year) as well as a stimulating programming and events schedule (events include lectures, tours, children and adult classes, family programmes, community arts festivals and events, symposia, film series, two major performing arts series, a new music series, chamber music, and classical music and organ concerts).

In the fall of 2000 the New Media Department was formed as a division of the Information Technology Department. This two-person department is responsible for the development, care and maintenance of the museum's website (www.clevelandart.org) as well as for the development of interactive displays relating to special exhibitions and the permanent collection. This paper is about a special exhibitions editing tool that was commissioned and developed in the first quarter of 2001.

Fall 2000

In the fall of 2000 the New Media Department of the Cleveland Museum of Art was at a crossroads. Like many such departments, with co-workers clamouring for features on the website we were so swamped with the immediate work that we had little opportunity to consider where we were going.

We had a 5,000 page website in serious need of a makeover. It had grown organically over a period of about three years and was the loving work of two staff members who managed to fit it into their schedules despite the demands of their regular full-time jobs. The site was clearly a labour of love but, due to restrictions imposed under previous administrations, had few images and little to give a web visitor a sense of the depth and breadth of images, information, resources and programming that the Cleveland Museum of Art had to offer. The redesign of the website was clearly the most important of our tasks.

Added to this was the continuous pressure to provide a CMA web presence to market our major exhibitions. The museum experimented with contracting out special exhibition features to independent developers. Although these features were often lovely, the percentage of dollars and time spent developing them meant that there was little or no time, money or energy devoted to the many smaller but important scholarly exhibitions hosted by the museum.

The presence of a new director at the helm of the institution, Katharine Lee Reid, brought a renewed commitment to all exhibitions large and small – though her arrival at the museum mid-calendar year meant that budgets for 2000 were already in place. Complementing her vision was the strong belief among the members of the inter-divisional web team that no curator should give several years of his or her life to researching a subject and then be allotted a single paragraph and a single image on a website under a banner entitled 'Also Showing' .

Business people know that there are three basic variables in any project – time, people, money. We were not going to be getting more money, we were not going to be getting more people, and – exhibitions are scheduled – so we could not count on more time. We needed a solution – how to keep our internal commitment without going crazy.

First we went looking for that magic software package which would make all our dreams come true. There were any number of software solutions on the market – two we particularly looked at were Dreamweaver and Net Objects Fusion. The problem with commercial solutions is they required a time commitment to a learning curve that the department simply did not have at that moment.

The Cleveland Museum of Art needed a software solution that put the majority of the organizing of content into the hands of the content generators (or at least someone who had a great familiarity with the content). The content generators were spending way too much time outlining for developers, technologists and programmers how they thought information ought to be organized. Later in the process when content generators would determine a better way of presenting information (as frequently happens the closer an exhibition is to opening and a larger number of staff members have grown familiar with the material), reorganization would cost the museum in terms of both time and financial resources. We needed a software solution which would allow us to spend more time creating content and less time negotiating details.

We needed a software solution which would allow us to accommodate a large number of internal clients. These internal clients – the group of people involved in the creation and use of special exhibition websites, including curators, educators, exhibition coordinators, registrars, event programmers and development officers – have a clearly defined set of reproducible needs. Each exhibition is different, and each may have a new challenge, but the bulk of the job is very simply *routine*. The theory therefore was that we needed a software solution that would allow us to reduce the amount of time spent on routine (boring) tasks and give us more time to spend on the creative (fun) part of all our jobs.

Another requirement was that we needed a software solution that was easy to learn and easy to use. We needed a software solution that could accommodate the inclusion of a variety of different media – audio, video, images – with ease. The goal was a software solution that would provide maximum flexibility for the New Media Department to create special exhibition features quickly and effectively.

The Request for Information and the Response

In January 2001 the department crafted an RFI (Request for Information) about bids for the redesign of the website. Into this RFI we included a separate component describing the tool we felt we needed:

> To work with CMA to create a scalable exhibition tool into which the CMA can load content, according to our needs, for special exhibitions and permanent collection features. In general, the museum would need to have three of these modules up on the website at any given time (current special exhibition, upcoming special exhibition, current permanent collection highlights). The module would need to accommodate text, images, audio and video according to the various needs of the exhibition.

This was accompanied by an outline of the exhibition we wanted to use as the model for building the tool. The RFI was posted to chosen vendors and, two weeks later, we had bids back on this component alone that ranged from under $50,000 to $500,000. Based on conversations with the various developers and the bids, we chose Cognitive Applications for the project.

Cognitive Applications' Response

We have been making websites and web features for museums for many years and, almost from the beginning, found that even for static sites it was almost always worth creating tools to generate pages in a consistent way – but then, we always had programmers available, with suitable tools to hand. Generally for each project we developed a custom tool, but always borrowing ideas, and often code, from the previous one. Less often we had tried to pass these tools onto the clients to help them maintain the site – but usually with insufficient budget to make them really usable by people with different skills.

So when we received this brief from the CMA, it chimed well with many of the things we had been thinking about for some time, and we were excited to have the opportunity of working out some of these ideas.

Initially, we took the brief for the first special exhibition site, and developed a design which catered for all the requirements of that brief, with an eye to how the design would be generalized to apply for future exhibitions. For this we used a simple tool (in fact adapted from the tool we had used for a previous web feature we had created for the CMA) and extended it to create the first site.

In the process of this we went beyond the standard use of templates for pages, with different templates for different sections, to the concept of components; elements of a page which repeated either on the page or across many pages; and which could have their own micro-templates.

We then turned round almost immediately to working on the second exhibition feature for CMA, which proved the strength of the design, and helped indicate some of the ways the tool needed to be generalized.

With these two web features published, we took a deep breath, stepped back a bit from the tool we had built ... and threw it away. As we had worked through the first two features, we had inevitably modified our first ideas and, with the constraints of a deadline, had needed to bend the tool to fit. We were now able to recast our concepts, take a clearer view of what concepts could be merged, which were really trying to yoke together two different things and should be split, which were relatively unhelpful frills and should be dropped – and which were really key.

We then started from scratch creating a new tool, which cleanly represented the new system. This has been refined and extended since then, over the course of some twenty or so projects at the CMA, and half a dozen completely different websites constructed by Cognitive Applications for other clients – but the basic architecture has held up.

How the Tool Works

Some of the terminology needs to be clarified. We use *pages* to refer to what you would expect: an HTML web page. Such a page is made up of *elements*, according to the content and design. Some elements are *components*: they are nuggets of unique content. Other elements represent no special content: for example, a graphic button to go 'home'. Looked at as an HTML page, this distinction makes no difference; it is all text, images and layout code, regardless of whether it is a running feature of the navigation or design, or some content unique to this page. But it is important to us, because a primary goal is to separate the content and content editing from the design and HTML coding.

We wanted to support richer designs than can be accommodated with a simple template (which frequently has some navigation and identity elements across the top, bottom and left hand side, leaving the rest of the page for the editable content, which is often then limited to very basic styling). In pursuit of this, we allow components to be created out of several atoms of content (so a component need not be a single paragraph of text, but might for example be the combination of an image, a caption for the image, and an associated paragraph of text); we allow components to be grouped together into agglomerations, ultimately into pages; and we support 'micro-templates' assigned to each component.

The design for the Cleveland Exhibition features and the tool developed in parallel: we developed the design so that templates could be applied to individual components, and implemented the tool so that components could be linked into pages.

Some examples should make this clearer. Figures 16.1 and 16.2 show two pages from this first exhibition feature. In Figure 16.1, the area in the top left which gives navigation 'up' in the feature is an element repeated across all pages. The title and introductory paragraph is considered to be one component; the style of this is common across many pages. The illustration on the left, with the title, image caption

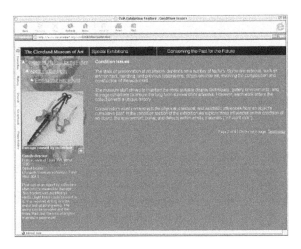

Figure 16.1   A page from CMA's first exhibition feature
(http://www.clevelandart.org/ConsExhib/html/condit.html)

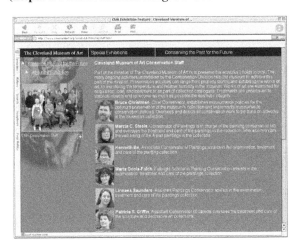

Figure 16.2   Next page in the CMA feature
(http://www.clevelandart.org/ConsExhib/html/A2staff.html)

and text, as well as the '+' control which displays a larger version of the image, is a single component – again, the style of this is common to many pages.

The page in Figure 16.2 has most of the features of the previous page. In addition, there is a component for each staff member, consisting of a photo, title and description; these components repeat down the page.

A third example page in Figure 16.3 illustrates some more variations. Again, there is the 'up' navigation element in the top left of the page, a title and some body text on the right, an illustration in the left margin. Here the illustration does not have an image caption, but is otherwise the same. The remaining elements on the page are actually not components of this page; they are components of the pages that are children of this page. The hierarchy here is:

About the Exhibition

    Making a Case for Preservation
    Finding your way around
    Cleveland Museum of Art Conservation Staff
    Learn More About Conservation
    Guest Lectures

One of the principles of this system is that the authors editing the content of a web feature should not have to enter redundant information. For example, the title of a page should only be set once, although it may need to appear many times: in the title of the window for that page, in the page itself, and also as shown here in an 'index' listing on the page's parent, or for example in a 'bread-crumb' trail or other navigation element (here, in the top left and bottom right of the pages). This is to save the author effort and to reduce errors. When it is decided to change 'Making a Case for Conservation' to 'Making a Case for Preservation', we should not rely on

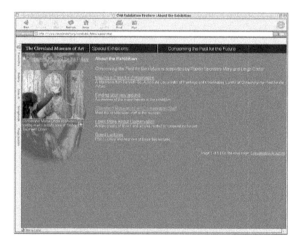

**Figure 16.3   Another sample page from the same feature
(http://www.clevelandart.org/ConsExhib/html/About.html)**

the user remembering to change it in all these places. So we wanted to provide a way to support the common requirement of displaying an index to sub-pages, and felt that this should not involve editing information about those pages except directly in relation to them. So in this case, even the 'subtitles' shown here belong to the individual pages – but they only appear on this parent page.

Now that you have seen some of the pages, let us show you the tool that generates them. The most interesting view is the component editor. A user operating at the content level need never see any HTML: instead they edit content in the component editor, and for each component, select a template. This is the component for the page about the CMA Conservation Department Staff (Figure 16.4). This component is using a template 'StdPage' (which in fact is shared with every other page in this feature, except for the front page). That template includes the standard furniture of every page, including the 'up' navigation tree in the top left corner; it places the title and body text defined by this component; then places any child components, which can be tagged to different areas of the page, and each of which can use its own template; and finally places child components (which themselves represent pages) into an index, and adds the 'next' navigation link at the bottom right of the page. This single template can represent the rich variety of pages in this web feature because of the way that it can dynamically address related components, and because the related components can each specify their own templates for their own portion of the page.

Looking again at the component editor, we can see some of the child components of the page. Both these components are 'illustrations', which means that they have four elements: an image filename, an alt tag, a caption and body text. They use two different templates, as shown in Figures 16.5(a) and 16.5(b): one is the standard for an image with a caption, and possibly a body underneath, and a control to view a larger version; the other does not use the caption at all, and places the body text on the right of the image. The other difference is in the 'role'; the group picture of the

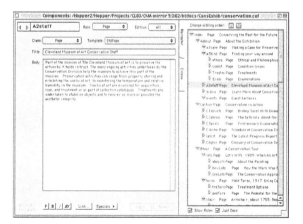

Figure 16.4   Component editor editing the 'A2staff' page, with navigator showing hierarchy

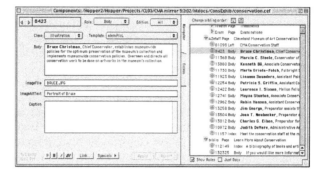

Figure 16.5(a)   Component editor editing the 'Bruce Christman' component

Figure 16.5(b)   Component editor editing the staff group picture component

staff is tagged with the role 'left'; the standard page template drops the first 'left' component it finds into the left margin, under the 'up' navigation tree. The component describing Bruce Christman, and the similar components describing the other members of staff, is tagged with the role 'body', which ensures that the standard page template places these components in the main area of the page.

This is a brief glimpse of the content editing side. As well as the component editor, in which the content unique to each page is edited, there are a set of properties associated with each 'publication' (for example, a special exhibition feature) which can be used by the templates on every page: these properties are used to give each special exhibition feature a different tone; for example, by setting such things as the background and font colours and background image for the pages. Not shown are the template, role and class editors, which supply the other half of how the tool works. In the case of the CMA exhibition features, these are rarely modified, except when a new special item is needed, although the template for the front page of each feature is sometimes edited directly.

Process

The internal process used by the CMA to develop a special exhibition website is fairly standard. First, an outline is based on previous exhibitions, advance press release material and advance in-depth articles – which precede the exhibition by at least a month – from the museum's member magazine. Using this information, a prototype site is built to show to the curator and other colleagues as appropriate. During these discussions other features are identified and included to enhance an exhibition web feature (highlights tours, video clips, flash trailers, in-depth features, expanded information and content) and the prototype site is re-generated to include placeholders for these features.

Images, text and other assets are then gathered by appropriate staff members and inserted into the tool. When the site is complete it is posted internally for review. At the same time hard copies of the site are distributed to the curator, the chief curator, the exhibitions office, the education office and the external affairs office for final review. When everyone has signed off, the exhibition is posted to the Web. This usually happens on the day the exhibition opens to the public or, with large special exhibitions, on the day of the press preview. The process is, in general, remarkably painless.

Features of this Tool

The tool does two useful things:

1. It separates content (text) from design and code (HTML) – so content creators can concentrate on content, not worry about code or macro-level design.
2. It economically supports templates to handle cases where many pages or parts of pages are represented in a consistent way.

There are therefore two ways in which it can be valuable:

1. When a website has a strong design in which elements of mark-up are repeated across many pages and/or parts of pages. In this instance the value is even greater if the design is not closed, as changes to the design can be applied economically across the site.
2. When the content of the site must be edited (or even created) by users who are not comfortable with HTML coding, or who are not authorized to create or implement the site design.

The tool has several valuable aspects:

- The ability to re-use structure from successful previous features. Obviously this is key to the original requirement for a tool to edit special exhibition features, but it has also led to the success in other parts of the CMA website.
- Template authors can add support for arbitrary kinds of media (QuickTime, Flash, etc.) with no load on content creators.

- It allows template authors to implement relatively sophisticated navigation within the sub-site, with little effort (especially from the content creators) and without incurring overhead when changes are made. The CMA exhibition features show this with the bread-crumb trail in the top left corner of each page giving navigation back up the tree, the annotated index for pages lower down the tree, and the numbered and labelled link to the next page at each level. All of these items are automatically generated correctly without requiring any maintenance as pages are added, deleted, or the structure is rearranged.
- If a design change is made, the entire sub-site can be regenerated in seconds.
- Boring production tasks are taken care of, such as checking image sizes, generating derived pages (for example, 'larger view' image pop-ups), auto-generated indexes and navigation.
- The tool ensures consistent application of the site design and (provided the templates are correct!) the tool can be relied upon to generate clean HTML code, in the hands of non-specialist content editors.
- Components can be used in multiple contexts, so that there is less content to check and fewer typos to fix.
- Templates can be used in multiple contexts, so that the maximum value is achieved from careful coding.
- The tool supports variant editions: for example the original *Conservation* exhibition feature appeared on a kiosk in the exhibition as well as on the Web. The kiosk edition is almost identical, but misses out a top navigation bar relating it to the main site, and there are a few pages which are unique to each edition. The two editions are maintained in a single file, so when a change is made to a common page, both editions can instantly be regenerated – each will have the appropriate navigation, indexes and so on.

Why this Tool has been Successful

One of the key success factors must be its simplicity and the tight focus of its ambitions. This does not set out to be a large-scale content management system. Nor is it a layout tool, or a graphic HTML editor. These are all useful features, and there are systems which address them, but they are accordingly more complex and, in our experience, less capable within this tight arena. It is aimed squarely at the context in which a small team is working on a relatively small site or sub-site, and probably with the profile of an intensive development phase leading to publication, and then only intermittent and occasional updating.

It is a single-user application; and there is no attempt to address ownership or history at the component level. The entire definition of a 'publication' (a small site or a feature sub-site) is stored in a single file containing the text content, component class definitions, templates and so on (images and other media assets are stored separately). It runs on a single desktop computer, does not require network access while a publication is being edited (for example a user can take it on a laptop to work directly with a curator), and the file defining the publication can be e-mailed from one person to another – for example from the author working on content to a specialist who can tweak the HTML code. (The editor runs on both Windows and

Macintosh, and the publication files can be moved back and forth between the two without issues.)

The tool has a low learning curve, at least for content editing. It is also easy to deploy, because it generates absolutely standard static HTML pages, with no server dependency.

Return On Investment (ROI)

Businesses look for ROI – return on investment. Given what we had been spending on special exhibition features contracted out to web developers, it took less than 12 weeks after delivery for the tool to be completely amortized. To date, we have built more than 20 special exhibition features and, in addition, we have used it to create many other portions of the web for departments which would otherwise still be in the queue waiting for development funds to be made available.

We continue to develop the tool, adding features and streamlining it to make it easier to use. This tool has changed the way we work and think about web development. Most importantly the tool has given us the time and the freedom to concentrate more on content and less on construction.

Reference

The results of the work represented in this paper may be seen at www.clevelandart.org. Readers can make their own judgements [Eds].

Chapter 17

Prometheus: The Distributed Digital Image Archive for Research and Education

Sigrid Ruby and Ute Verstegen

Teaching and learning in the academic disciplines of art history and classical archaeology traditionally rely on the image as the main medium of discourse. In these branches there is hardly any lecture or course session held without darkening the room for a slide show. However, the procedure of slide shows means expenditure of time. It is expensive and limited, because hardly anybody owns about 100,000 slides.

Out of this uncomfortable and old-fashioned academic tradition Prometheus was born. It is a cooperative university project launched on 1st April 2001 and financed until March 2004 by the German Federal Ministry of Education and Research. The partners were the University of Cologne, the Humboldt University of Berlin, the Justus-Liebig-University of Giessen and the University of Applied Sciences of Anhalt at Dessau/Koethen. Each of them contributed their specific professional skills in the fields of art history and classical archaeology, information technology, media didactics and design. Prometheus has set out to develop an Internet-based knowledge platform that brings together a whole range of distributed digital image archives. Moreover, it provides a variety of didactic units to support academic teaching and learning.

Prometheus is considered to be one answer to the challenging developments in information technology. It seeks to offer an easy-to-use learning environment for academic education that effectively uses the genuine properties of the Internet. Prometheus may smooth part of the way in the ongoing discussion of media change, its circumstances and effects, and it might open perspectives for the future. In contrast to the traditional way of studying which is restricted within subject-specific borders, Prometheus tries to break these limits by integrating neighbouring disciplines. By doing this we hope that not only the media competence at universities will increase but also that scientific research for classical archaeology, art history etc will attain new fertile impulses.

The aim of Prometheus is to connect various heterogeneous and distributed digital image archives via the Internet. In contrast to some earlier impractical attempts, Prometheus does not try to impose a particular database upon all museums and institutes. The only precondition is that all databases define three basic elements (the work's title, the image itself and information on the copyright). XML is used as the only web-based standard that does not depend on any further specification. Even a standard such as Dublin Core cannot be presupposed for all databases. Instead, the central information broker holds profiles of the individual databases. These profiles specify how the consultation of each single database has to be formulated and how the answer has to be processed in order to guarantee smooth adjustment.

In accordance to the different databases each archive has its own specific focus and the individual objects administered range from archaeological monuments to today's computer art. These databases are:

- The 'Digitale Archiv' at the University of Applied Sciences of Anhalt in Dessau/Koethen,
- 'IMAGO' and 'Virtuelle Kunst' at the Art History Department in Berlin,
- 'EikOnline' at the Department of Classical Archaeology in Gießen,
- the 'Digitale Diathek' and the 'Interactive city plan of Rome – Piranesi' at the Art History department in Gießen,
- and 'DaDa – The Associated Image Archive' in Cologne.

In addition to these databases two important German image archives, 'Foto Marburg' for art history (www.fotomarburg.de) and the 'Scientific Archive for Antique Sculpture' (www.arachne.uni-koeln.de) in Cologne must be mentioned. Both have been associated partners of Prometheus since the very beginning; we cooperate with Foto Marburg and have already integrated Arachne. Today (January 2005) 22 databases can be consulted via Prometheus.

The plan was to make available about 185,000 images by the end of 2004. This goal has been achieved.

But how does Prometheus work? Prometheus follows the concept of Internet based Metamachines and, thus, gives access to the various databases. Via a single web interface each associated partner can use the system.

Prometheus differentiates between two functional fields: retrieval (search and find) and presentation. The simplest and best known version of retrieval is the textual inquiry with the results displayed in a list. In addition to textual lists Prometheus tries to break new ground by the usage of the Internet's media-specific qualities. It is planned to integrate a so-called image-in-an-image inquiry. The company Cobion in Kassel has developed an image indication program, which helps companies in their search for logos and the Federal Office of Criminal Investigation to find people. We are in permanent contact with the Technical University Clausthal and the ETH Zurich who both do research in this field as well. Art history and classical archaeology would profit enormously by this type of visual identification. The inconvenient, laborious and time-consuming consultation of catalogues and specialized encyclopaedias might become superfluous. For the system it would be no problem to find f.ex. all the drawings or plaster copies of the 'Apollo Belvedere' without having to depend on metadata and their possible sources of error.

The Internet not only offers new possibilities in the area of visual retrieval but also as regards different types of results display. Designers and computer scientists at the University of Applied Sciences of Anhalt have cooperatively developed the so-called TimeLine – a highly efficient retrieval tool, which visualizes the results not as a list but graphically in a point set distribution on a 'timeline'. The works of an artist are arranged on a chronological timeline and can be picked out and enlarged with a single mouse click.

In addition to image retrieval, Prometheus offers the possibility of compiling a digital image presentation which can be projected on the wall as part of a lecture or other kinds of presentation. After the login the user has the possibility to choose all, one particular, or a group of databases from those which are integrated in Prometheus; he or she may f.ex. choose 'only classical archaeology' or 'only museums'. The chosen images can be collected and arranged in a folder. From this folder the presentation can be prepared – as with slides in a slide box. Some time-consuming work can also be done off-line, because being connected with the system is not necessary for sorting. However, the Prometheus plan is not simply to transfer each traditional work step on a one-to-one basis into the digital world. An individual presentation with a single image or with various images side by side as well as the attachment of text and audio is possible. Each user can decide which form of presentation he or she prefers. Both the classical 'double projection' as well as the extended possibilities of the digital world are available.

Prometheus generates single HTML-pages from the assortment. These HTML pages can be saved on-line on the server or locally on the hard disk. They can be represented independently from the distributed digital image archive by any browser. Thus, the visual apparatus that accompanies seminars and lectures can be prepared with moderate technical effort. Any user is able to prepare his/her lecture or presentation from wherever he or she likes to and present it via beamer subsequently. This allows a highly flexible mode of teaching and learning.

In 2003 the first version of Prometheus was set up so that our associated partners were also able to test it. This first beta-version contained the textual research and list display as well as the possibility of first putting an unsorted choice in a folder and then ordering these images for a presentation. Since summer 2003 we have incorporated the TimeLine and – as a didactic module – an interactive unit for describing the wall paintings in the Romanesque basilica of Altenstadt as well as a learning platform called ILIAS.

Prometheus not only provides a distributed digital image archive but also tries to stimulate self-instruction by the introduction of subject-specific teaching and learning units. One problem is the fact that there exist no standard textbooks for art history or classical archaeology. Against that backdrop, Prometheus offers two types of teaching and learning units: Some deal with particular subjects, while others offer tools. With these tools the teacher can provide his students with exercises and information via the Internet.

We have already started with the development of learning units concerning the description of architecture and the training of expert terminology. Preparatory units that deal with the methods of Art Historicy and Classical Archaeology respectively as well as with different artistic genres shall follow.

One aim of Prometheus is to cooperate with associated partners from different institutions – universities, museums, image archives etc. Within this process of cooperation the independence and genuine character of individual databases and institutions are to be preserved. In addition to the founding partners, several associated partners such as the Scientific Archive for Antique Sculpture in Cologne, the Diocesan Museum Regensburg and the University Library of Cologne have already joined us. They are building up their own digital image archives parallel or in cooperation with us. Many other potential partners have indicated considerable interest and are ready for cooperation. In addition to universities, there are also image- and video archives, museums, organizations for the conservation of historical monuments, libraries and scientific institutes (such as the Bibliotheca Hertziana and the German Archaeological Institute) which are interested to cooperate. It is especially important that the participating institutions are willing to make their images available for education. One of Prometheus's further endeavours is to support and promote a variety of professional qualifying academic programmes that deal with digitalization and database administration.

After the successful integration of many additional associated partners in the course of 2003 the system was evaluated, the educational units were improved, and the final version was produced.

When the project started in April 2001 only a handful of German university teachers had actually integrated digital images in their art history or archaeology courses respectively. The opportunity to participate in a virtual teaching-and-learning-programme did not exist. In order to firmly establish digital presentation as well as the potential of e-learning in academic teaching, Prometheus has been working on differentiated concepts of implementation and sustainability right from the start.

At present Prometheus is pursuing two strategies to guarantee long-term impact and benefit: on the one hand we use our remaining resources to further integrate existing image archives and to introduce even more prospective users to Prometheus, thus broadening the community of interests involved. The considerable number of cooperative agreements with image-holding institutions (museums, archives, libraries, research institutions, media centres etc) as well as user institutions (universities, schools) that are already completed or right now in the process of being prepared speaks for itself.

On the other hand we have already been developing structures destined to carry and to support Prometheus in the future. On the 24th March 2003, the association ('Verein') 'Prometheus – the distributed digital image archive for research and education e.V.' was founded to guarantee the long-term existence and further development of the project. The early founding of the association presents the possibility to enter negotiations with potential licence takers and to sign contracts independently. A smooth passage from project status to independent association and an uninterrupted work-flow will thus be ensured. A new head office takes care of the server management, coordinative issues and the integration of databases. Furthermore, the association creates structures that allow for changes in personnel without serious consequences for the work of Prometheus.

A secure legal situation is crucial for the existence and further development of Prometheus. As regards potential restrictions for the free use of digital images in academic research and education, the recent amendment of the copyright law according to EU-guideline 2001/29/EG pertaining to the harmonization of certain aspects of the copyright and related safety rights in the information technology society ('Informationsgesellschaft') was of particular importance. By means of opinion statements and signature collections Prometheus pleaded for a modern academic teaching in the disciplines of art history and classical archaeology. This activism found broad public support. On the 11th April 2003, the German Federal Parliament voted in favour of the respective amendment to the copyright law and thus also agreed to § 52a, the paragraph most dear to the interests of academic science, research and teaching. On the 11th July 2003, the German Federal Council agreed to the copyright law's modernization as well.

Reference

www.prometheus-bildarchiv.de

Chapter 18

HITITE: IST-2000-28484
The Heritage Illustrated Thesaurus:
An On-line Resource for Monument
Identification

Phil Carlisle

Abstract

HITITE, the Heritage Illustrated Thesaurus project, concerned the development of an on-line thesaurus of monument terms illustrated with images from the National Monuments Record's (NMR) archive, the public archive of English Heritage. Uniquely, the thesaurus included three-dimensional models, and a novel image-based search facility.

It was anticipated that the thesaurus would serve the needs not only of heritage professionals wishing to search for specific terms and view images associated with them, but also encourage access by a much broader range of users; for example, people who are unfamiliar with thesauri or heritage terms, but who could, through the use of HITITE, increase their understanding of the historic environment in which they live.

The NMR Thesaurus of Monument Types contains c.6300 terms, and HITITE provided a variety of mechanisms for users to access the data:

- *Key word search. Using Boolean terms users could query the thesaurus by typing in known terms. As well as enabling a search on the terms themselves, the images contained within the thesaurus were referenced with comprehensive meta-data. This metadata related not only to widely-accepted heritage terms, but also to descriptive terms such as shape, size etc.*
- *Expert system. The thesaurus provided a facility whereby users could search for terms by answering a series of simple, high-level questions, each illustrated with generic photographs or diagrams. Each question helped the user to rapidly filter out inappropriate terms (and associated images), and ultimately provided a refined list that related closely to the user's query.*
- *VR search. The project explored the possibility of providing three-dimensional VR worlds in which users could explore, intuitively, different monument types and their associated terminology.*

The HITITE project was a joint project between English Heritage and Adlib Information Systems Ltd. It received funding from the European Commission's Information Society Technologies (IST) Fifth framework programme, and development took place between October 2001 and September 2002.

Introduction

The HITITE project was initiated to develop an image-based thesaurus for the built heritage. Historically, thesauri have tended to be the preserve of specialists working within a given field and, as such, the terminology contained within them can often bewilder the interested lay person. This is particularly true of thesauri relating to the built and buried environment where one person's tumulus is another person's barrow.

The Thesaurus of Monument Types which is currently available to the heritage community in the England, and used in the national databases held by the National Monuments Record Centre, attempts to classify the structural remains of archaeological cultures as well as the more commonplace structures of the everyday built environment. It contains over 6,300 terms relating to archaeological and architectural sites and monuments, many of which would be unfamiliar to the lay person.

Initially, using a subset of the terms contained within the Thesaurus of Monument Types, the HITITE project built an interface which allows the user to interrogate a database of images indexed with terms from the thesaurus without the need to understand the terminology. This was achieved by allowing the user to search for images of monuments or buildings by answering simple questions and then providing them with the appropriate term relating to the resulting images.

Finding Information

The Internet is a powerful information resource and an excellent medium for knowledge sharing. However as more and more information is published on the Internet, it is becoming increasingly difficult for a user to access relevant information on a chosen subject. The ability to search the Internet is reliant upon the user being able to ask the right questions.

Keyword Searching

There are a variety of search engines available on the Internet but by far the most common are those where a user enters a keyword or phrase to search on. These rely upon the automated indexing of websites using keywords contained within the documents or URLs.

Although the results of such a search will always include some relevant sites, the user may have to scroll through many irrelevant results to get to the information they require or refine the query further by including/excluding more keywords. This is particularly problematic where homographs occur in the search language or a word has been adopted as a trade name or brand (Figure 18.1).

Intuitive Searching

A recent attempt to solve the problem of erroneous results has been the development of intuitive search engines, for example www.ask.co.uk. These interpret the

Figure 18.1   A simple search on 'pillbox' retrieves sites relating to pillbox hats, fortifications and hand painted containers for pills

keyword(s) and return results asking the user to refine the query by selecting the category, which matches the original query most closely. In this type of search the results, though fewer in number, should include more relevant sites. However, more often than not the question the user has asked will have been rephrased by the search engine and the sites, which the new query would retrieve, may no longer be relevant.

Subject Gateways

One solution to the problem of retrieving erroneous or irrelevant websites is to use a subject-specific gateway or portal. Querying on such a resource ensures that any sites retrieved will at least be relevant to the subject area. One example of this kind of portal is the Archaeology Data Service (http://ads.ahds.ac.uk/) which provides archaeological information from a variety of sources across the UK.

However the main drawback of these portals is that they are reliant upon the information provided to them and as a result the quality and depth of the information contained within the sites and databases that they use as source materials can vary. Likewise such portals can be limited in scope.

Informing the User

All the methods described above rely, to some degree or other, on the user having some knowledge of the subject area. This is particularly true when the subject area has its own specialized terminology.

So how does a user know what keyword to use when searching for information on the humps and bumps which scatter the landscape of southern England, when they do not know that, what they are actually interested in, are barrows?

The Solution

The HITITE project is one attempt to allow the non-specialist user access to information about the built and buried heritage of England without him/her having to know or understand the terminology used to record it. To achieve this, the project initially built a demonstrator which stores images relating to 500 terms used to record monument types in the National Monuments Record Centre database. These images were then indexed with metadata relating to their shape, size, function, age and building materials.

By asking the user to answer questions relating to these criteria it is possible for him/her to retrieve images which resemble the monument they are interested in. (Figures 18.2 and 18.3).

These images are linked to the terminology used to record such monuments which in turn allows the user to retrieve text-based information from any source by simply using the terminology provided.

As well as enabling the user to retrieve information through the use of images the project also provides access through two other user interfaces:

• The first interface, aimed at the professional user, will allow quick text based searches for those already familiar with the terminology. This will allow direct access to the images without having to answer questions relating to the metadata.
• The second interface allows the user to browse the thesaurus hierarchy and view images.

A third interface, aimed at the casual user, was originally proposed as part of the project. It was envisaged that this interface would take the form of a series of VR landscapes each of which relates to one of the classes used in the Thesaurus of

Figure 18.2   Questions linked to metadata associated with the definitive images

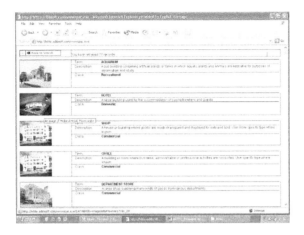

Figure 18.3   A sample of the results retrieved using the criteria: Modern, concrete

Monument Types. For example, the user would be able to 'fly' over a virtual religious, ritual and funerary landscape populated with a church, graveyard, barrow, henge etc. By hovering over the 3D image, users would be able to get further information about the monument type as well as see images associated with it. Although it was not possible to develop the VR interface within the given timeframe of the original project it is hoped that this will be developed at some point in the not too distant future.

Lessons Learned

The project initially involved images associated with only 500 of the most commonly used terms from the Thesaurus of Monument Types. This sample proved that the concept could work in practice but highlighted the need for more focused metadata.

The most problematic area of the project was the indexing policy. As time was of the essence, it was necessary to use images which had already been digitized and were currently available rather than selecting the most appropriate images and indexing those. Many of the images therefore included more than one monument type and as such it was often difficult for the indexer to decide which was the most appropriate metadata to attach to the image. For example an image of a Georgian Terrace might also include a 1930's Telephone Kiosk. Should both periods be indexed or just Georgian? Should Cast Iron be included as a material?

The concept of *size* was particularly difficult to assign to images. User testing undertaken by children in the 5–10 age range highlighted this with many children choosing to call a 2 storey house "Very Large". This was overcome to a certain extent by including comparative illustrations which included people drawn to scale. Similar issues arose with the concepts of *original use* and *period* – the what and the when – and again the inclusion of illustrated examples helped.

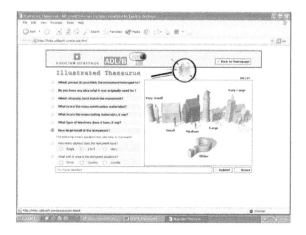

**Figure 18.4   Comparative illustrations aid the user in determining which
term to choose**

Conclusions

The concept, from which the HITITE project stems, of answering questions to
identify a given thing is not new, one need only look at botanical field guides and
taxonomies. However, we believe, this is the first time such an approach has been
used for the identification of monument types.

A programme of system testing and the availability of web-based access to the
prototype have provided a great deal of positive feedback and widespread approval
for such a search mechanism, indicating that further development of the interface
would prove to be a worthwhile endeavour.

The experimental nature of the project facilitated the exploration of concepts,
practices and methodologies, such as the various possible approaches to indexing,
which would be employed in the development of such a search facility. As important
as proving the workability of certain concepts was the elimination of others as
approaches to future development.

Since the development of the prototype HITITE interface, English Heritage have
been investigating the possibilities of using illustrated thesauri not only as tools for
indexing and information retrieval but also as encyclopaedic resources in their own
right.

The new corporate knowledge organization system planned for 2005–2006 will
allow the development of more complex thesauri and will address the issues
which have arisen from the HITITE project. It is hoped that a successor to HITITE
will be developed focusing on the use of illustrated thesauri as an educational
resource.

References

The NMR Thesauri are available on-line: http://www.english-heritage.org.uk/thesaurus/thes_splash.htm

The HITITE website is available at: http://hitite.adlibsoft.com

Chapter 19

An Approach to Adding Value while Recording Historic Gardens and Landscapes (Valhalla)

John Counsell

Abstract

This paper considers the Hortonet and Valhalla projects, designed to link European historic gardens on the Web. The team at FBE/UWE, Bristol, investigated uses of spatial information systems to store, manage and visualize records of historic sites, enabling interactive off-site access to interpretative information and real-time video.

Introduction

This paper is based upon the work of a team in the Faculty of the Built Environment at the University of the West of England (FBE/UWE) in developing 3D computer models and related databases over a period of years. The recent Hortonet and Valhalla projects are described. It argues that spatial digital information forms a new medium best deployed in new forms and not simply in replicating previous approaches to recording heritage sites. It is suggested that in many cases records are neither integrated nor adequate, nor are the necessary resources for such recording easily justified. It is necessary to identify sufficient immediate and longer-term uses to provide a justification. Among these is the provision of a factual basis for interpretation to persuade the public of the value of conservation.

Major new roles include the remote capture of information, and interactive off-site access to interpretative information. Existing records are mostly inadequate for such use since they are often accrued in an ad hoc manner, and are incomplete without external contextual reference to the physical heritage site to complete understanding. In this sense they are 'uncoordinated' and tend to lack stand-alone off-site coherence. By contrast explicit classification and codification of similar digital data is necessary for stand-alone remote access. This coherent integration of simplified records of a real place creates a model – however abstract.

Such use necessarily starts with acquisition of an archive of data but ought to proceed to being able to answer locational questions such as 'where' and 'when' and ultimately to the support of strategic analysis and 'what-if' speculation. This process from archive to analysis is at the heart of the development and maturation of geographic information systems (GIS). It is argued that data has to be recorded appropriately to support these longer-term applications. While buildings are relatively slow to change and decay, so past records and now computer-modelled analogues stay valid in the long term, yet their contexts, settings, gardens and grounds are open to rapid change, and often not adequately recorded. The capture and display of fleeting diurnal and seasonal change is a particular challenge. Effective recording of potentially rapid change is highly resource-intensive, justifying exploration of automated data capture, usually satellite imaging at the macro, and remote controlled video at the micro levels. Yet automated capture creates additional problems for record management, storage and retrieval in which few heritage organizations have achieved maturity. Experts often cannot obtain the precise interpretation from a photo that they can make on-site, so melding interpretative information with rapidly changing imagery is also discussed in this paper.

Recording and Interpretation

Recording and interpretation are held to be integral parts of the process of achieving sustainable conservation by determining significance (and establishing environmental capital). So creating a record of the built cultural heritage is part of that process of establishing its significance. It is held here that these principles apply equally to the gardens and landscapes that both form the context and setting for historic buildings and are often fragile and at-risk works of art in their own right. The maintenance and development of an accurate record underpins the effective management, care and protection of the built cultural heritage, from defect analysis to visitor management. Within these processes computer modelling (including GIS) may add value and consistency through its capacity for support of multiple relevant uses (models) based upon appropriate selections from the same set of data. This data may either have been accrued or have been recorded in a single exercise.

The first objective of a survey should be to record what is necessary in order to understand and illustrate the history of a building, its plan, structure, development, use and decoration. The ICOMOS guidance also says that

> The record of a building should be seen as cumulative with each stage adding both to the comprehensiveness of the record and the comprehension of the building that the record makes possible.[1]

The team at FBE/UWE have argued previously that heritage site records are a mixture of description and interpretation and that recording is not a 'one-off' event but a continuous process that is a prerequisite of many conservation management activities.

> Decisions on how and what to record will involve varying measures of subjective judgement of the relative values embodied in, or represented by, the heritage site. However it is also clear that the process used to communicate or disseminate the analytical record may in itself influence the interpretation of the site and therefore the understanding of its significance.[2]

The task of computer modelling, in the sense of creation of an analogue of a real site or building, may also assist by revealing flaws in or the incompleteness of records, and thereby challenge habitual working practices and procedures.[3]

It is considered possible to make some generalized observations that apply to a range of sites. Access is often limited to the visible and safely reached. Record techniques that rely solely on such access at one point in time tend to be incomplete without other forms of data. (Recording is desirably a continuous process.) Remote imagery together with photographs and earlier 'historic' records are likely to form part of, and require accurate location and integration into, the overall record. Consequently different types of data will require to be amalgamated in the sense of integrated multimedia to provide a coherent record.[4] Recording digital data without its accurate spatial location is perceived as likely to offer no more than short-term benefits. It is still easier to encapsulate 'virtually-real' images with audio and associated information off-site than to deploy 'augmented reality' on-site to locate the physical on-site object on which a visitor has focused and deliver a visual superimposition or audio commentary alone. Visual augmented reality still has major problems of registration of the superimposed image on the real. Given the technology, however, it is argued here that the spatial referencing and metadata issues are the same and that it takes longer to acquire and structure sufficient data than for advances in computing and visualization technology to be realized.

Interpretation and Accessible Analogues

Interpretation is also clearly an essential key element in enhancing public understanding, appreciation and engagement in determining the values represented by the built cultural heritage; that is, to help to educate visitors 'not so much about their history, but in how to explore, interpret and respect' heritage sites.[5] Binks et al. state that for non-specialist visitors to museums and galleries, the aim is to give them an overall picture, to explain what is happening, what is being revealed, and what its significance is. For repeat visitors it is necessary to also explain what has changed since the last visit. They add that the interpretation will need to be presented at a variety of depths. They suggest that themes and stories presented in a logical sequence relating to route from the human angle, which are participatory, which explain the detective story, effectively provide living history for the visitor.[6]

Other research has also shown that animated and interactive exhibits are more valuable than static presentations.

> Above-expected interest was shown in the dynamic, animated, or changing presentations represented by movies, changing lighting, and audio sequences ... all the sequences with less-than-expected interest involved flatwork, suggesting a greater preference for three-dimensional presentations.[7]

Sharpe uses this research to argue that an interpretative audience prefers those interpretative media that are most closely associated with entertainment, and that the dichotomy of education and entertainment parallels that of inertness and animation. He also records that participation increases retention and that multimedia is necessary to cater for a variety of levels of information. Reading, while looking at objects, has been found to discourage visitors, who prefer an audio commentary.[8]

Off-site interpretation is not suggested as an alternative to first-hand experience, but may be the only substitute. While first-hand experience of parts of heritage sites is possible for many visitors there are additional problems of access for the disabled and the elderly. Howell argued that if we considered people in our profile who have perceptual problems then an analogue within the CAD system can be used, with careful consideration, to present that part of the building which cannot otherwise be perceived.

> I have to say that a description of a cathedral by, say, Willis or le Duc is often a brilliant analogue. It is almost inevitable that words will have to accompany the visualisations and auralisations ... the words ... could be transcribed into signing alongside a picture or subtitles provided for the deaf or hard of hearing.[9]

> Off-site interpretation may or may not succeed in arousing in its audience a wish to conserve an area but it will almost certainly arouse a desire to go and see it.[10]

These arguments were posed before the impact of the Web and new media offered the potential for worldwide remote interactive access to virtually real environments.

Hortonet – Network of Historic Gardens

FBE/UWE recently worked on a multimedia pilot study funded by Trans-European Telecommunications Networks to create a network of linked historic gardens and landscape parks (project ref. Ten 45612 FS). One prime goal of this project was to enhance public understanding by enabling the visual display on the Web of comparative design influences and planting across Europe, for both primary and secondary interpretation. As Thompson put it,

> The best basis for understanding a ruin is therefore a wide knowledge of structures of the same period, whether ruined or not, since the mind is consciously or unconsciously making comparisons, and the larger the stock upon which it is possible to draw, the more reliable the result is likely to be.[11]

Landscape design influences in particular have often been pan-European or global, so it was argued that understanding for most was hampered by the constraints of opportunity and distance, which the Web might serve to overcome. The popularity of gardening books and of garden visits demonstrated the market.

This process assisted in identifying useful GIS-based techniques for recording and retaining original digital imagery with associated metadata. Most of the data with which to create a credible sense of presence were digital video, digital panoramic images and high-resolution digital photographs, together with associated botanic and historic information. It proved possible to capture sufficient photographic imagery to create a credible sense of presence for a site with two staff in one day. (The same staff can process and edit the material within a week.)

However the critical conclusion was that the ongoing data management of a website of the predicted eventual size and complexity would be challenging, since a major goal was to acquire a continuing record set of images for each stage of growth in each season, each year.

Thompson went on to say 'study of the relationship between written sources and visible remains is like the reciprocating action of a piston'.[12] For similar reasons of understanding it was considered necessary to relate images of the planting in the gardens to other more abstract information on history, soil type or species. Yet manually associated hyperlinked explanatory information proved too resource-intensive to apply, let alone maintain. One approach explored was to create polygonal overlay hotspots to associate relevant information with each image. This was possible but, given the scale of the project and the number of images in video and other forms involved, the association of data with overlaid polygonal boundaries proved impractical. It was intended to keep adding increasingly higher-resolution imagery over time to the site, which would entail regular re-association and resizing of the hotspot polygons. Conflicting overlaps were found between the boundaries of information that are required to be coded onto an image in HTML. While HTML still does not support overlaps (multiple levels of detail) for hotspots, this was found to be effectively supported in VRML.

Accurate identification by experts of botanical information from photographic images alone also proved impractical. It proved necessary to map botanical and historical information on-site as a separate expert process, prior to the definition of the hotspot associations. This made clear that images without associated explanatory information would be of little use in interpretative use by the public. For these reasons a GIS spatial database approach was subsequently tested to determine its suitability for recording, explaining and retrieving heterogeneous information in conjunction with images, including video.[13] The team at FBE/UWE used proprietary software (Pavan[14]), written within the commercially available Mapinfo GIS environment, to enter spatial data about buildings, sites and landscape into the GIS and (as one output use) Pavan to generate 3D interactive VRML models. These models can be imported to proprietary software such as 3D Studio Max for photo-realistic display, but are held in an open standard, capable of multimedia deployment on the World Wide Web.

Valhalla

This project is a continuation of the previous work at UWE in linked VRML and spatial databases, applied to visitor information and heritage site management. It ran from October 2001 to November 2002, funded by the European Commission Information Society Technologies programme (IST-2000-28541). It was a partnership between UWE, the Gardeners Exchange Trust (who have promoted physical exchanges between historic gardens staff over the last few years), and the gardens of Hatfield House in the UK, and the Chateau de Villandry in France. The goal was to promote comparative study and discussion between staff at each site (a virtual Gardeners Exchange), and put real-time interpretative samples on the Web, with hotspot information generated in matching VRML viewpoints from a 3D spatial information system. This involves a form of remote data capture, followed by spatial referencing and retrieval of digital images with other associated descriptive information. The project team therefore installed prominently placed remotely controlled video cameras overlooking the gardens. Staff could control the cameras during interactive on-line discussion to illustrate or seek information, or the cameras might follow scripted routines to capture matching images for later time-lapsed sequences showing diurnal and seasonal change. It extended the previous work in two directions: that of real-time remotely controlled acquisition of digital imagery, and that of the relationship of heterogeneous information to the images to explain and interpret them based on VRML, the whole managed by GIS.

There were six major elements to the project: recording and updating information about the gardens; video cameras with a controllable real-time overview of the gardens; 3D models of the gardens that link through to a database and serve to interpret the video images; a website for 'virtual' visits and to discover more information about the gardens; higher-quality video highlights than can be viewed on the Web recorded on DVD; and staff enabled to share experience on-line (virtually).

Recording Locational Information about the Gardens

Recording information on the gardens took more time than planned due to the lack of usable surveys or planting plans. No suitable plans of Hatfield House Gardens existed. The French cartographic maps of Villandry are not detailed enough to show planting areas in the gardens, nor are the Ordnance Survey 1:1,250 scale maps of Hatfield. Aerial photographs were purchased but proved insufficiently detailed at a resolution of 50 cms to transcribe (12.5 cms resolution is only just becoming commercially available and does not cover the Hatfield area yet). Geometrical measured surveys were completed of the selected area of each garden in the field of view of the cameras, and a 1992 3D survey of Villandry was purchased from a local geometrician. For both gardens the logged data then had to be translated into the Mapinfo GIS. Steps, walls, copings and other distinctive architectural features, and the edges of changes in hard and soft landscape surface materials, such as grass, paving, flower borders and paths were separately identified in the GIS.

Recording Planting and Accessibility Information

The purpose was to 'map' information about plants, trees and hard landscape features within the field of view of each camera, into the GIS, from which the VRML 3D web-based models are generated, to enable comparative identification of the elements visible in the video. (Common plant names in French and English are linked by the Latin index as a key to assist identification despite the different languages involved.) Plant location and accessibility information for the gardens was not readily available and proved more difficult to acquire than anticipated. Compaq IPAQs were acquired for the task of hand-held data logging at each site, with ESRI Arcpad GIS software (on investigation found more usable than the comparable Mapinfo pocket PC product). These had both wireless networking connection and docking station transfer of data to and from the server. The Arcpad software was loaded with spatial mapping of both gardens and with templates developed for logging the location, characteristics and spread at different seasons of each distinctive plant feature. GIS standards for exchange are robust enough for it to be simple to exchange mapping and data between Arcpad on the IPAQ (or Desktop) and Mapinfo at UWE.

It proved difficult to identify people local to the gardens with both the necessary specialist expertise and also the confidence to use computers for entering the data. It therefore became necessary to provide assistance in entering the data to computers, and to print paper plans and forms on which information is recorded. The information then had to be transcribed to computer. Staff at FBE/UWE thus spent more time than planned in recording plant labels at Hatfield, linking the data to the mapped survey information in Mapinfo and searching for detailed information about the plants at both Hatfield and Villandry in garden and botanic books and on the Web.

Video Cameras with a Controllable Real-Time Overview

Gardens were chosen that are designed to be seen from the windows of the houses, so that a camera mounted on the house as a vantage point would give a similar view. Both a fixed and a motorized camera were installed because there was no suitable position from which the whole of the selected area at either garden could be viewed by a single camera. Initially it was intended to install as the motorized camera a conventional pan-and-tilt motorized camera mounting with a Sony FCBIX47 Camera (460 TV lines) with auto focus and 18 x optical zoom, in a heated weatherproof housing, but on investigation and testing it became apparent that the conventional motorized mountings used in the security industry are only suitable for a limited range of pre-set views or for direct control by keypad and joystick by an on-site operator and do not enable the precise telemetry required for remote control over the Web. It was found that the Dome Camera (Dennard 2050) (Figure 19.1) was capable of precise telemetry, but required programs to be written to remotely control the camera. Unfortunately the Dome Camera is also more prone to reflection, glare and raindrop distortion.

A C program was written and tested by Oggle Ltd, from whom the cameras and Web upload utilities have been leased, to control the Dome Cameras. Shell scripts were developed by FBE/UWE to enable the cameras to be remotely controlled by clicking on a map or panoramic image on a web page, with a slider to control zoom. These worked effectively as shown in Figure 19.2.

'Models' of the Gardens that Link through to a Database

The Parallelgraphics Software Development Kit was bought in order to customize and simplify the Cortona VRML browser to display modelling in conjunction with video clips. The browser was customized to export the current VRML field of view and

Figure 19.1 The Dome Camera in a window at Villandry

Figure 19.2   Web-based camera control with live video

directional vector data to provide control data for the search routines (and requests for camera targets) and to enable comparative display within the browser, between the current visible video image and a matching view of the VRML. A 'calendar' program was written by UWE to control the cameras based on the data in the Mapinfo GIS, and simultaneously archive the video clips tagged with data on viewpoint and zoom. The program calculated and exported field of view and directional vector data from the GIS, (based on optimal viewing times and locations for features within the spatial database), to prepare scripted directional information to control the path and field of view of the video camera. The same program responded to date–time triggers tagged onto plants and objects in the GIS to operate the Mpeg2 capture card (to avoid over-filling the local server hard drive) and write the results (tagged with viewpoint data) to DVD for transfer back to UWE. This program recorded vector and field of view metadata with each image file to enable video sequences to be selectively archived with associated VRML seasonal modelling.

A search program used the metadata or a view match in the VRML model to invoke an archived video clip. This helped to address the issue of data management of potentially very large quantities of images: partially by planned 'scripting' to capture in a selective manner; but also by use of the GIS to assist in the content description, management, archival storage and retrieval by place, time and objects within the field of view. The data on the plants and planting enabled a sequence of seasonal composite three-dimensional digital models with hyperlinked plant and feature identification information to be generated (for example, as shown in Figure 19.3). Data on 'mature' plant sizes was entered into the GIS based on research in books and on the Web, and compared to the actual sizes recorded at survey. A further routine was tested to generate the current size on a monthly basis from this data.

A Website for 'Virtual' Visits and Discovering More Information

The video cameras were linked to a specialist compression card (from a French company Com1) incorporated in a Linux web server on each site, which served the images in 640 by 480 resolution motion JPEG format on the Web, and archived the

Figure 19.3   3D VRML model with plant data in frame

video in clips, set at five-minute intervals throughout the day. (The archived clips were transferred nightly to a server at UWE, Bristol, to avoid limiting bandwidth during the day. A scriptable secure FTP program (CuteFTP Pro) was used to automate the transfer. A British Telecom always-on ADSL service with five fixed IP addresses and an upload speed of 256 kb/s was connected to the servers at Hatfield House, and the servers were also linked to the Local Area Network at Hatfield House, enabling access to the servers and the cameras from any PC on the network. No ADSL was available at Villandry so the minimum suitable France Telecom product was ISDN, a 128 kb/s upload facility with 3 fixed IP addresses and always on, at a cost four times that of the superior ADSL provision at Hatfield House. The remote location of servers and cameras in the unused wing of the Chateau also required the installation of a wireless Ethernet bridge to connect the servers (and cameras) to the Local Area Network in the separate administration building approximately 100 metres away, and thence to the ISDN router.

The web-based interpretative real-time samples and archived or time-lapsed sequences linked to matching 3D model views were intended to enable the comparative study of similar information within both gardens from a web browser, so broadening public access to this part of European cultural heritage. A website was created in February 2002 – http://environment.uwe.ac.uk/valhalla – for public information about the project on a server at UWE, with threaded discussion forum, and links to the video footage and the VRML modelling added as they became available. This was designed to:

● enable users at the Visitor Centre or on the web on request to view information identifying the plant, landscape, or architectural feature visible in the live or archived video feed

- provide comparative information about both sites on the Web;
- enable staff and visitors at one site to see what is currently happening in real time at another European site and to search for and view similar landscape features or plants.

Video clips, taken while walking through the gardens, supplemented and enhanced the aerial real-time views, and these (with historic images) were incorporated at both sites. Active server page scripts, and cookies generating questionnaires to frequent users, audited visitor use of the website at the garden or on the Web.

Expertise from professional gardeners for display on the World Wide Web was added through:

- recording specific video interviews with gardeners at both sites
- timetabling staff use of the video conferencing and recording the process on video
- adding 'Frequently Asked Questions' to the website
- higher quality video highlights on DVD.

Higher-Quality Video Highlights on DVD

The cameras generated higher-quality video than can be seen currently on the Web. The additional occasional upload of high-quality Mpeg2 (approximately 45 m/bytes for 1 minute) is possible but cannot be relied on. Transferring the archive of web video clips per night is approximately 500–600 m/bytes per day for the two cameras on each site, which would take about 5.25 hours at 256 kb/s upload (the ADSL at Hatfield), and twice as long for the 128 kb/s upload (ISDN at Villandry). It proved necessary therefore to write scripts to record the Mpeg2 in real time on site, archive it onto rewritable DVDs on site and then send the DVDs by post to UWE for editing and archive. The calendar program also handled this. Therefore a second server (running Windows 2000) was installed at both Hatfield and Villandry and linked to a splitter in the feed from the cameras. This server incorporated a specialist Amber Video card which encodes analogue video in real time into Mpeg2 format, and a Pioneer DVD recorder. Windows 2000 terminal services were used to remotely control the server, the Mpeg2 card, the DVD recorder and the hard disk space from UWE, Bristol. This process was found to work effectively.

Staff to Share Experience On-Line (virtually)

Phillips USB Video cameras and software (Net-Meeting and Yahoo) were tested and installed, to enable staff to videoconference between the two gardens to exchange knowledge and skill, while reviewing real-time video imagery of selected aspects of the gardens. It took longer than anticipated to reach the point where staff could deploy the remotely controlled camera during discussion, due to the difficulties in achieving web-based camera control discussed above. However it was satisfactorily tested between the head gardener at Hatfield and the owner of Villandry.

Conclusion

This paper describes an investigation into the marriage of long-term data with what might be called more ephemeral imaging data, using a common key of spatial and temporal location, and served by a spatial information system or GIS, to create a meaningful whole. The physical and historical complexity of heritage sites is held to be better recorded in 3D than 2D to ensure commonality of understanding between all those involved in its care and with the wider public who fund it. A common approach to spatial and temporal referencing across a range of sites will enable comparative search and simultaneous display to envision the broad range of examples that Thompson described as so important to enable reliable understanding of what is seen on site. This broad understanding can only be obtained asynchronously by first-hand experience at present.

VRML has been found to be a useful de facto standard for defining and interacting with such models on the Web. VRML models based on spatial databases have the potential to become actively served with appropriate associated detail and data on demand. VRML is a useful de facto standard both for defining and interacting with such models, and for enabling the process of selection and presentation of appropriate information with images to the viewer.

A common underlying coordinating geometric structure or primary model to which all objects relate is likely to emanate from the lowest level of detail at which such spatial data can be captured without extensive reinterpretation. Much more locational and time data requires to be captured and entered into a database with visual images and information than is currently the norm, in order to enable a common relationship.

A spatial database can be used to serve appropriate information with images or video clips on demand. There appears little difference between the data management and retrieval issues that apply to web-based multimedia interpretations of historic environments and those that are particular to large-area 3D computer models. In both cases more effective use can be made of video or high-resolution images in many instances where resources are currently put into 3D modelling alone. Yet there remains a question of when it is appropriate to model instead of or in addition to experiencing first-hand.

The Grand Canyon is cited in support of the argument that some sites need no interpretation, although this is not held to preclude the need for informed professional understanding.[15] The Grand Canyon might be brought to a remote off-site audience using video and audio alone. However, many other sites are enhanced by interpretation and for these, remote access or (in the future) augmentation of the reality on-site will require on-tap synchronized abstract information in addition to that directed at the senses. It takes a long time to commission and procure useful records. To meet these future developments it is desirable to record locational and temporal metadata with such records now. The Valhalla project suggests that this can be done, and that the process can be made resource effective, by enabling public access to the information gathered in interactive and interesting ways.

Notes

1   ICOMOS (1990) *Guide To Recording Historic Buildings*, Butterworth, London.
2   Worthing, D. and Counsell, J. (1999) 'Issues arising from computer-based recording of heritage sites', *Structural Survey Journal*, vol. 17, no. 4, pp. 200–10. ISSN 0263-080X.
3   Washburne, R.P. and Wagner, J.A. (1972) 'Evaluating visitor response to exhibit content', *Curator*, vol. XV, no. 3 pp. 248–54.
4   Binks, G., Dyke, J. and Dagnall, P. (1988) *Visitors Welcome, A Manual on the Presentation and Interpretation of Archaeological Excavations*, HMSO.
5   Virtual Heritage web site at http://www.virtualheritage.net
6   Binks et al. (1988) as above.
7   Washburne et al. (1972) as above.
8   Sharpe, G.W. (ed.) (1976) *Interpreting the Environment*, J Wiley and Sons Inc.
9   Howell, P. (1995) 'Perception, disability and the conservation element', *Journal of Architectural Conservation*, no. 2, July, pp. 63–77.
10 www.pavan.co.uk
11 Thompson, M.W. (1981) *Ruins, Their Preservation and Display*, British Museum Press.
12 Thompson, M.W. (1981) as above.
13 Counsell, J. (2000) 'Recording and retrieving spatial information with video and images', in E. Banissi, M. Banatyne, C. Chen, F. Khosrowshahi, M. Sarfraz and A. Ursyn (eds), *IEEE Information Visualisation IV 2000*, IEEE, July 2000, pp. 589–96. ISSN 1093-9547.
14 www.pavan.co.uk
15 www.pavan.co.uk

Chapter 20

Copyright Protection and Exploitation of Digital Cultural Heritage

Dimitrios K. Tsolis, George K. Tsolis, Emmanouil
G. Karatzas, Dimitrios A. Koutsomitropoulos and
Theodore S. Papatheodorou

Abstract

The main issue addressed in this paper is the design and implementation of a framework for the copyright protection and exploitation of digital cultural heritage. The framework consists of an Advanced Digital Image Repository, which offers specialized services and a dedicated user interface for the protection and management of the intellectual property rights of digitized material. Another main research area of this contribution is the implementation of a web-based library, supported by advanced technologies, for the proper presentation of digital cultural content. The work described in this contribution has been carried out as part of the Praxitelis Project.

Introduction

The evolution of technology is challenging the status quo of intellectual property (IP) protection and management in many ways. In recent years we have seen the exploration of many technical mechanisms intended to protect IP in digital form, along with attempts to develop commercial products and services based on those mechanisms.[1] These mechanisms include interchangeable metadata (data describing data) to characterize the digital object and its IP rights (IPR); unique global identifiers (a permanent identifier given to a digital object-file) for the digital objects; watermarking techniques to mark, detect and prove the existence of the copyright of a digital image, audio or video; and encrypted and secure data transfer through networks. The primary target of the current phase of the project is the implementation of an Advanced Digital Image Repository which, except for the above capabilities (metadata, unique identifiers and watermarking), provides specialized services and user interfaces for efficient and resourceful retrieval, including search by image content. In addition, this phase equally focuses on the creation of a web-based library, structured upon the Digital Image Repository, for the proper presentation of digitized material of the Hellenic Cultural Heritage.

Advanced Digital Image Repository

The design and implementation of the Advanced Digital Image Repository for this information system is a very important task. A repository fully capable of serving as a platform to this system should incorporate the following basic characteristics:

● Scalability – that is, the capability of gradually improving its performance in accordance with the platform and the number of computing resources used. The information system is a distributed one. Independent repositories already exist throughout Greece and are installed in the Ephorates and other authoritative agencies of the Hellenic Ministry of Culture (HMC). The integration of these independent installations requires a scalable and modular repository.
● Internet orientation, providing secure and easy access to data and metadata via the Internet and corporate intranets. The Hellenic Ministry of Culture already has a corporate intranet (designed and implemented by the High Performance Information Systems Laboratory) and, as a result, the integration of the digital repository to this already existing infrastructure is considered necessary.
● Support for applications and interfaces for data and metadata manipulation. These applications do not only include the built-in mechanisms of the database management system, but also user interfaces developed and customized in a way that meets the needs and requirements of this project.

The Advanced Digital Image Repository is implemented using the IBM DB2 Universal Database (Version 7.1, Fix Pack 3) with the AIV (Audio, Image and Video) and XML Extenders.

Metadata – Digital Images and IPR Management

The need to adopt international standards is essential, especially for applications aiming at cultural content exchange and on-line transactions. Following these guidelines results in an open information system ready to be integrated into an expanding global, multilanguage and multinational network in which the digital objects and the metadata coupled with them are uniquely identifiable and interchangeable.

The DIG 35 Specification 'Metadata for Digital Images', Version 1.1[2] has a very important role in the selection of fields and tables, as far as the metadata for the digital images are concerned. This metadata standard is already being widely used from simple end-user devices to worldwide networks. The database structure has a special focus on metadata for intellectual property rights management. Consequently, the definition of sets of metadata, which are tightly coupled with the high-quality digital surrogates of objects of the Hellenic cultural heritage, was a significant research area for this project. In particular, these sets are divided into five major sectors: the technical metadata, the image creation metadata, the history metadata, the content description metadata and the IPR-related metadata.

The most important metadata set is the one related to intellectual property rights management. This metadata set includes information about names of the copyright holder, important dates, contact points, the restrictions of use and the watermark ID (identity). The watermark ID associates the digital image with a unique identifier, which is imperceptibly incorporated in the image using watermarking methods. The Digital Image Repository is implemented in accordance with the described metadata sets and will be distributed in regional Ephorates and authoritative agencies of the HMC.

Watermarking and the Image Repository

Invisible watermarks are one proposed solution for the protection of intellectual property rights and for dealing with the problem of illegal reproduction of content of multimedia objects.[3] Numerous watermarking schemes have been proposed and implemented and the performance evaluation has resulted in the selection of the best watermarking tools for this information system.[4] These tools have been obtained in SDK (Software Developers Kit – a set of programs used by a computer programmer to write application programs) format and the watermarks are being automatically embedded in the Digital Image Repository using technologies that the database management system provides. The goal is for the watermarks to be embedded in the digital images when the digital image is being stored in the central repository. This general strategic planning is focusing on the following:

● Distributed management of the watermarking process and scheduled synchronization of the regional databases.
● The watermarks should be embedded only into the high-quality digital surrogates of photographs of objects of the Hellenic Cultural Heritage.
● The watermarks should carry two ID numbers. The first number will be common to all digital images and will identify the Hellenic Ministry of Culture as the copyright holder of the digital image being processed. The second number will identify the instance of the transaction, containing the digital image and the name of the persons involved in that transaction. This number is a reference that points to specific IPR-related information in the database.
● The watermark should be robust to attacks and detectable over Internet-oriented environments. This is ensured by the exhaustive evaluation, which has been conducted.[5]

This watermarking schema is being implemented via the creation of dynamic link libraries (DLLs) that are available with the dedicated user interface.

Dedicated User Interface for the Repository

The images are managed by archaeologists using a dedicated user interface. The selected GUI (graphic user interface) development tool is Microsoft Visual Basic 6.0. Custom-developed dynamic link libraries (DLLs) are being used extensively for the interconnection of the GUI with the database system. The capabilities supplied to the end-user include operations that allow import and export of high-quality digital images as well as searching for digital images and metadata and management of image metadata. The most important features are:

- The watermarking: this is embedded transparently into the digital image. The user has the facility to initiate the detection of a watermark.
- The application under development creates XML documents containing information from the advanced digital image repository. (Extensible Markup Language or XML is a flexible way to create common information formats and share both the format and the data on the World Wide Web.) For this project the usage of XML is recommended as the standard metadata interchange format.[6] The XML documents are produced by user-defined SQL queries. The XML documents are based on an XML schema, which derives from that of the DIG35 Metadata Standard. The XML schema is modified in accordance with the needs and specifications of the Hellenic Ministry of Culture. The output files are automatically populated using XML template files. These template files transform the database schema to the XML schema. The presentation of the results is accomplished through the transformation of XML files to HTML, using Microsoft XSLT Processor. (XSL Transformation is a standard way to describe how to transform the structure of an XML document into an XML document with a different structure.)

Web-Based Image Library

The web-based image library is structured upon a digital image repository. This digital image library is not only the gateway of the information system to the world, but also provides numerous basic and advanced services. The basic features include news, information and helpful documents and on-line help that depends on the web page the user is exploring. As well as the basic features the advanced web-based digital image library implements advanced services for the user. These services include:

- Advanced methods for searching the digital content. The search methods consist of:
  - o Search for metadata and free text. The user is expected to fill in the required fields. The fields reference specific database columns and produce dynamic web pages. The user is able to search the database using relational constraints (AND, OR) and free text queries.
  - o Query by Image Content (QBIC). This advanced feature allows the user to send a query to the database in terms of colour and/or layout. The layout search provides for queries that are created by the user and represent basic shapes (circles, rectangles etc) filled with the preferred colour.
  - o Zoom-in collections are those that give the flexibility to the Internet user to zoom into certain images.
  - o Copyright notices and protection.
- A thematic-based catalogue that organizes the digital content in categories.
- Collections and selected cultural presentations. Selected digital collections are created and enriched with accompanying information.

Implementation Principles

The most advanced web technologies were exhaustively tested and evaluated. The largest part of the website interface is built on pure web technologies, avoiding impressive but high bandwidth technologies like Flash or Quick Time VR. The principles of human computer interaction and usability were taken into particular consideration.

Dynamic web pages, for the search results, are created with PHP (PHP or Hypertext Preprocessor is a script language for creating dynamic web pages). The descriptive pages of the artefacts (containing large images and detailed information) are created using Java technologies implemented as user-defined functions (UDF) in the database. Zoom-in collections are presented through Java applets.

The database repository of the digital images and their metadata is implemented using the IBM DB2 Universal Database, with the assistance of the IBM DB2 AIV (audio, video and image) Extenders. The system provides support for the streamlined implementation of the aforementioned XML schema and the advanced services for searching and retrieving digital images. QBIC searches are created by Java applets with the support of the AIV extenders.

Implementation Paradigm

The Query by Image Content search engine is an advanced feature that allows the user to explore new ways of accessing the database content. The search engine is developed through the combination of web technologies such as PHP and Java applets, embedded SQL, C++ and dynamic link libraries (DLLs are collections of small programs, any of which can be called upon when needed by a larger program that is running in the computer), all presented with simple HTML and XML forms.

For example the Query by Image Layout functions as follows. Because the web server is installed on a different platform from the database server, in order to improve performance, scalability and interoperability, a Query by Image Layout involves the following steps:

- The user draws up his query with the support of a Java applet.
- An ActiveX Control is initiated by PHP through a COM (component object model). The ActiveX Control is a component program object that can be re-used by many application programs within a computer or among computers in a network, which is a system-registered dynamic link library (DLL). The main functions of the ActiveX Control are the connection with the database, the necessary file format conversions of the temporary image (like preserving the transparency colours), the import of the image into the database and the disconnection from the database.
- An SQL statement is used for fetching a result set using success indicators and percentage of similarity, deleting the temporary fields and tuples (fixed-size collections of elements).
- PHP is used to format and present the result-set in HTML tables and to delete all the web server's temporary images.
- The QBIC Layout search is a multi-user search tool.

Indicative Scenario

The main purpose of the indicative scenario is to present an overview of the system's everyday use. It is assumed that training of the necessary personnel of the administrative agencies of the HMC is completed successfully, the system is installed in three selected organizations supervised by the HMC and that a certain time for adjustment and performance optimization has passed. In everyday use the system supports:

- the distributed insertion and management of surrogates in the selected organizations
- automated and imperceptible embedding of watermarks for the copyright protection of the digital content.
- the insertion of twenty high-quality digital images per day and per organization
- once a month and when the HMC's network is not overloaded, the transfer of these digital images safely through the network to the central database server
- automatic presentation of 'low'-quality, watermarked copies through the Praxitelis website.

The above scenario is based on the assumption that a trained user in every organization will be using the system five hours per day.

Conclusion – Future Extensions

The work reported above is in line with a proposed framework for the protection of digital image copyrights[7] and also includes innovative approaches such as content based queries. The future extension of the system should aim at the implementation of value-added services for the exploitation of the digitized material. These services could aim specifically at the financial exploitation of the content. A system for on-line sales of digital images has already been pre-designed. In addition, a B2B (business to business) system dedicated to museums and other cultural organizations is under consideration. Furthermore, electronic editions and CD-ROMs should be supported.

Notes

Praxitelis Project website: http://www.hpclab.ceid.upatras.gr/en/projects/praxitelis.html
1   ACM Publications, *Intellectual Property in the Age of Universal Access*, 1999.
2   Digital Imaging Group, *Inc: DIG35 Specification – Metadata for Digital Images*, *Version 1.0*, 30th August 2000.
3   Computer Science and Telecommunications Board, National Research Council, *The Digital Dilemma – Intellectual Property in the Information Age*, National Academy Press, 1999.
4   Petitcolas, F.A.P. and Anderson, R.J. (1999) 'Evaluation of copyright marking systems'. *Proceedings of IEEE Multimedia Systems*, vol. 1, pp. 574–9.
5   Bartolini, F., Cardelli, R., Capellini, V., De Rosa, A. and Piva, A. (2000) 'Digital

watermarking: a solution to electronic copyright management systems requirements', WWW9 Culture Track, Amsterdam 2000.

6   Tsolis, G.K., Tsolis, D.K. and Papatheodorou, T.S. (2001) 'A watermarking environment and a metadata digital image repository for the protection and management of digital images of the hellenic cultural heritage', International Conference on Image Processing 2001 (ICIP 2001), Image Processing and Cultural Heritage, Thessaloniki, Greece, October 2001.

7   Voyatzis, G. and Pitas, I. (1999) 'Protecting digital-image copyrights: a framework', *IEEE Computer Graphics and Applications*, January/February, pp. 18–24.

Chapter 21

Protection of Intellectual Property: A Must in Digital Content Exploitation

Jean Barda and Claude Rollin

Abstract

Protection of intellectual property (IP) is required for at least two main reasons: firstly it allows for the respect of the moral rights attached to the creator of an original work, and secondly it allows for tracing use and therefore gives the creator or rights-holder adequate remuneration. The paper will look at the technical state of the art in the security domain for digital content. It will highlight the technology issues, the applications and finally the typical uses of those applications. As an example, for the first time, a system called CAVEAT (Controlling the Authenticity and Versioning of Electronic documents by Accessing a Trusted third party), will be demonstrated.

Introduction

Since December 1996, when the World Intellectual Property Organisation issued its Treaty on Copyright, a number of countries have ratified the text and implemented it in their national laws. However, introduction of the Treaty in operational contracts and practice is much slower than expected. This is due to the slow migration of ideas towards 'all-digital' exploitation. For example, the fact that a digital copy is as good as an original has been quite easy to accept for traditional photographers, but the additional fact that it is impossible to distinguish a digital original from its copy has taken much longer and has created a huge fear about intellectual property.

Two ISO working groups have been working on protection of IPR (intellectual property rights): MPEG and JPEG. MPEG is concerned with motion pictures and has now produced an MPEG 21 working draft which is taking the studies on IPMP (IP management and protection) to DRM (digital rights management). JPEG has started a more technical approach with its new offshoot JPSEC (JPEG 2000 Security) (see References).

In this paper we examine the different technical and application issues that JPEG has raised in terms of security, illustrating them with typical uses in the cultural heritage domain of visual assets exploitation.

Technical Issues

The first work that JPSEC as an ad hoc working group did was to consider all different types of protection that could be applied to still pictures, in order to make certain that:

- an image delivered is exactly a copy of the original
- no unwanted copies are circulating
- non-qualified users cannot access the content
- allowance is made for DRM systems to carry on their content management tasks.

An Exact Copy of the Original

This requirement means that there is a need to be able to compare the copy to the original: this is done by registering the original document and taking a digital signature of this document as proof that it has not been altered in any way. Therefore there is also a need to identify the original document (and its different versions if any), with a unique identifier.

No Unwanted Copies Circulating

Now that original and certified copies are defined, we try to avoid having copies circulating on the Web without due authorization; therefore we need to be able to trace the documents in circulation and identify them to check for illegal use.

Only Qualified Users can Access

This restriction of access is ensured by using the techniques of access control, where a content has a profile and a user also has a profile, only those users having the right profile being able to access the content for which they are qualified.

Content Management Issues

In the context of IPR this includes all that was called ECMS (electronic copyright management systems), recently renamed DRM (digital rights management). But this also includes content management, both in-house and in the marketplace, involving a reliable way of identifying the contents and logging the uses, variants and versions of the same document, together with any amendment to the related metadata, for instance when the rights-holder changes.

As pre-requisites to these requirements the JPSEC ad hoc group has identified the following basic techniques:

- signature generation and verification
- watermark insertion and detection
- encryption and decryption (includes scrambling)
- 'medialiving' and 'demedialiving'

- key generation and management
- identification and registration.

Let us take a look at each of these techniques and see what kind of use situations they can address in IPR protection.

Signature Generation and Verification

This protection mode consists of taking a computed extract from a file and organizing the extract so that it changes whenever there is a change in the file. Even addition of a space inside a text would make a difference to the signature and be detected when the checking operation is activated. Similarly to human identification, this technique is often called fingerprinting, but there is a confusion with some applications where fingerprinting serves as an identifier for the end-user.

When verifying the authenticity of a file, only a 100% identical content would get a positive answer, thus giving the end-user the secure information that the file has not been modified. In the case of multiple versions for the same content, each version has its own signature and the verification can tell which version it is.

Typical uses Thanks to this technique, one can check whether a file has been modified or whether it is still the original version, without having to transfer the whole file with its signature. This is very useful to protect the moral right attached to the creator of a work. The signature must be kept in a safe place in order to be called back when the checking takes place: the operation is quite fast, just a few seconds even for a very large file, and the answer is OK or NOK according to the positive comparison of the real-time signature with the registered one.

An example of such an operation is given at the end of this paper with CAVEAT, the system allowing for Control of Authenticity and Versioning of an Electronic document by Accessing a Trusted third party.

Watermark Insertion and Detection

A watermark is typically an invisible mark, hidden inside the image itself, and therefore not visually detectable nor erasable, unless you have the algorithm and the secret key that has been used for hiding the information. Inserting a watermark is an operation done at the most upstream level in an application, then the file goes on its way carrying the mark for any downstream control.

There are parameters for a watermark, according to its main goal: two different types are well known, one for authenticity and/or integrity control, called a 'fragile watermark' and designed to be erased or altered if any modification occurs (same goal as the signature); the other one has a strong presence and resistance to small modifications or geometric transformations, and is called a 'robust watermark', designed to carry along with the file an identifier or a link to another source of information about the file. In addition to the strength, the secret key and the payload length are two other parameters for a watermark.

Typical uses Watermarking is used mainly to convey information that can be used as a link to a place where additional information can be securely stored and occasionally updated, under access control, by authorized individuals. The main characteristic of such a watermark is robustness to what is called attack: this could be malicious or aggressive attack designed to erase the watermark or friendly attack for non-voluntary results of content modification.

Another line of application with a fragile watermark is used to check the integrity of a file, when any modification would change the content of the payload and show the presence of the modification, without telling which type it is. However, in this domain, a digital signature is preferred to a fragile watermark.

Encryption, Decryption and Scrambling

Encryption is a generic term meaning that the content of a file has been changed following a rule making it unreadable or unusable under normal conditions. For example, scrambling the file, by operating a rotation in the bytes addresses, is an encryption, as the reconstruction of the original file can only happen if you have the 'key' that has been used when operating the encryption. Another encryption mode makes use of a reference table giving the correspondence between the codes actually sent and the codes actually meant. Note that both encryption and scrambling convey all the information to the end-user, with the risk that when the coding is cracked the content appears in 'clear'. Encryption and decryption are operations that are applied in real time to the content that has to be protected on one side and displayed on the other side.

Typical uses   One of the most frequently used encryption processes is designed for TV programmes going on air or on a satellite link, where anybody can anonymously grab the content. The same situation happens on the Internet; for example, where encrypted data is used for on-line trading, to avoid misuse of your banking information. Encryption is generally used for applications requiring access control, when information could be broadcast without being able to exclude users, but you give the decryption key only to those users with the right profile. This is why encryption is very often used in subscription-based public services.

'Medialiving' and 'Demedialiving'

This technique avoids part of the problems encountered with encryption, due to the fact that all of the information is actually on-line, even though it has been transformed. Indeed, hackers (Internet pirates) know that it may take time but they can finally end up with the encryption key, especially if they find some reference content that reads easily, allowing for guessing the way encryption has been applied. In fact, using a very large encryption key may avoid this but with medialiving there is no risk at all, because from place to place small parts of the codestream are taken off and replaced by 'lures', non-significant content which jumbles the encoded data. This is why 'medialiving' takes place inside the codestream, destroying the coherence of the content: the user is unable to reconstruct the content unless he gets the missing pieces and their address from a specified secured website.

The technique used in medialiving allows also for selective decoding of the content: for example one might be decoding a black and white version of a colour image or a low resolution of a large image, or even a low-quality area inside an image. Depending on the mode in use, the user can work out where the missing pieces have been taken off, and which of them have been returned.

Typical uses   Medialiving is a very new technique which has few references in use at the moment, but we can talk about two typical uses. The first one is when a CD-ROM or DVD is disseminated and there are missing pieces that a low bandwidth link can convey to the user after verifying payment or access clearance. The second one is when a watermark is added during the reconstruction process to identify the end-user, who is now responsible for further use of the reconstructed content. The payload for the watermark identifies the reconstructing session and the secure server only talks to identified users: there is a direct link between the session and the user and the distribution path can be controlled.

Another way of using medialiving is to force users to be on-line when they want to decode a real-time broadcast, and to send them during the broadcast (through a parallel link) the missing codes as they need them. For real-time transmission, this process is perfect, under access control, allowing for identification of the user.

Key Generation and Management

Keys are used in many protection systems as described above. A key has a length and is applied to a given algorithm. A long key (with a large number of bits) makes the protection system more secure as it takes too long to find out what the key is. However, for national security reasons, some countries have limited the length of encryption keys to avoid unwanted messages being transmitted on public dissemination support.

Key management concerns the way keys are transmitted and conveyed to the qualified end-user; for instance a secure surface mail would be used to send the code associated with a credit card, while all ATMs (automatic teller machines) are able to check whether you have the right key to get money from a given account. The general schema for key management is using two different paths for the content and for the key giving access to the content.

Typical uses   Watermarking, encryption and medialiving make intense use of keys, coupled with their own algorithms, thus allowing the same algorithms to be disclosed while giving access to content only to those having the right key. Secret keys are devoted to a single user while public keys are able to open content for multiple users. In many cases, secret keys are kept by the generator of the key and disclosed only when needed; for instance when a monitoring operation is required to read the watermark of a protected content. In such a case, only a court can ask for key disclosure, under legally safe conditions.

When subscribing to a paying service you are supposed to get a key for your payment contained in a smart card, for example. Such a process is used in most set-top devices for paying TV or for paying mobile phones. In that respect key use is close to the addition of a password to user identification, and only when the couple (that is, both identification and password) is coherent are you allowed in.

Identification and Registration

Tracing the circulation and usage of content can only be done if there is a machine-readable identification of the corresponding content. For this reason, most of the above protection systems are making use of a unique identifier for the content they protect. This unique identifier is often called a licence plate (LP), by analogy with the way cars (mobile objects circulating on a public path) are identified – spotted in real time when passing by. The problem with a unique identifier is that it must be certified by an authority, which delivers the LP and logs all reference information about the mobile, describing it and giving the name of the owner. All this information is kept for digital content in a secure place called the IPR database, which would contain the following items as a minimum:

- title
- creator's name
- creation date (in case precedence is critical)
- contact for exploitation
- copyright mandatory mention
- restrictions of use related to moral right.

Additionally, information such as price, access conditions, special descriptions and other type of metadata can be stored in the IPR database.

Typical uses   You create a digital object (such as a digital photograph) and before you show it on your website you register it with a registration authority, which sets the date of registration at default as the date of creation, and delivers a licence plate (LP). You can then use this LP to protect the object by inserting it as a watermark hidden inside the image. In any case, the LP will make it possible to link to the IPR database and therefore to be able to find out who is the owner and with whom anybody can get in touch to obtain clearance for further use of the content. Ideally, when displaying an image, the copyright mention and the licence plate should appear on the side of the image. More information can then be accessed using the LP as a link to the IPR database, all this being automatic on a single button request. Indeed a typical LP, as defined by JPEG, contains an identifier for the country where it was delivered, then a second part carries the identifier of the registration authority inside the country, then the actual registration number. Note how similar this structure is to a phone number, a number that you can call from anywhere and that always gets you to the same individual.

IPR Protection Applications

Legal Aspects of IPR Protection

When dealing with valuable content, implying IPR protection, legal aspects should be considered: building an application requires observance of the official texts of the following:

- Bern Convention on Intellectual Property
- WIPO Treaty (World Intellectual Property Organisation, www.wipo.org)
- DMCA, the Digital Millennium Copyright Act (USA)
- European Directive on Copyright
- some national texts on copyrights, often derived from the WIPO Treaty.

But quite obviously this is a matter for specialists on legal issues, and a lawyer is needed whenever a dispute may occur between a user and a provider or content owner. A number of authors' societies, such as SACD in France, have decided to step into the digital era and give their members all necessary information and provide advice on how to deal with digital content. In particular, model contracts can be obtained for digital content trading. Similarly the music business found out that illegal copies were having a significant negative impact on their turnover and they began to move forward seeking efficient protection and legal punishment for counterfeiters.

CAVEAT – An Example of an IPR Protection System

CAVEAT stands for Controlling the Authenticity and Versioning of an Electronic document by Accessing a Trusted third party. The process has a protection phase and a verification phase. When registering the content to get a unique identifier, an electronic signature of the document is taken and kept by the registration authority together with the rest of the IPR information. The content owner can then ensure that the object is an original version by linking to the registration authority (which must be a trusted third party) and uploading both the identifier and the computed signature. When both are corresponding to the registered couple, the answer is positive. This is the basic process, but additions are needed, for instance when a content owner wants to modify the content without having to register for a new identifier, because it is only a new version of the same document. In this case an additional signature is added to the IPR information and, when checking, the authority answers giving the number of the version that has been submitted, together with some information, for example the date of registration of the new version.

Access to the control is anonymous and open to all; however, access to the IPR database can be secured with the need to identify the user. This type of security is present to bring trust in digital content exchange as it is well known that digital images can be modified easily. If a watermark was present in the original file, the CAVEAT control also includes the watermark and if it has been maliciously removed the authenticity control does not give a positive answer. Moreover, when trying to register a new version of an existing document, the registrant must prove that he/she is in possession of a previous version from which the new one has been derived. This process avoids registration of a so-called new version by someone who did not have access to the previously registered versions or to the original document.

Distributing a document featuring CAVEAT protection ensures that only an original file can be delivered and that if any variant is present, it has been edited by an authorized operator and referenced as a new version, with the same identifier but a different signature.

Security Applications in the Cultural Heritage Domain

In general, protection is applied to bring trust in transactions on-line, either by providing a way to check identity and registration of the files or to check integrity or authenticity of the content. This is required when the document value is considered high enough. Besides, DRM systems can only work with secure content, because otherwise the cost for using the content could be billed to the wrong user and the credit for fees paid to the wrong owner. Identification of both content and users is therefore a critical process that systems like those described above are able to operate securely. As a reminder, the main applications are listed as follows:

- integrity check showing the completeness of a document
- authenticity compared to original or registered versions
- access control with user profile, identity and password
- IPR database access to check the registered information
- secure transmission, including error resilience
- DRM operations to automatically bill and credit actors
- physical protection with indelible watermark.

What kind of transactions are we talking about? In the cultural heritage domain, protecting IPR is absolutely mandatory for living artists who do not have resources other than reproduction rights, as it is for their rights-holders, agencies or galleries showing their works to try and sell them. But the most frequent use of images of all is on the Web when presenting, exhibiting and offering to sell copies of the most wanted images, showing them and offering a download function for a given reproduction fee (for example when an image is published in a magazine, a newspaper or a book). The law says that the copyright credit should appear, and also that the link to the IPR database should be available at all times. This will return to art creation the high status that it had when copies were made by hand and clearly identifiable. If you look at museums' bookstores and souvenir shops, all they sell is IPR-related and copies can be (and actually often are) made at lower cost, bypassing the IPR. If you consider their turnover you realize that there is substantial money involved in exploitation of documents based on cultural heritage IPR.

References

Readers should check the WIPO website (www.wipo.org) and the website below for the latest information.
General information on ISO/IEC procedures may be found in http://www.jtc1.org/directives/copyrite.htm.

PART 6
SPECIAL NEEDS

Chapter 22

On-Line Access to Cultural and Educational Resources for Disabled People: An International Challenge

Marcus Weisen

Abstract

The e-Europe Action Plan says that public sector websites must be designed to be accessible to disabled people, whereas UK statistics (2003) show that only approximately one third of websites meet basic web accessibility standards. This article shows that:

- *large numbers of disabled people face substantial access barriers to on-line culture and e-learning*
- *on-line culture that is accessible meets technical web accessibility standards and presents content in ways that are accessible – examples are presented*
- *web accessibility is compatible with attractive websites and benefits all users*
- *disabled people have a right to access websites*
- *policy, funding, strategic and capacity building initiatives are needed to achieve significant progress.*

Equal Access for Disabled Citizens: An Urgent Need

2003 was the European Year of Disabled People. Funding invested in e-learning and on-line culture is set to grow exponentially. In the UK, the Government has allocated significant public funding to projects such as Curriculum Online and Culture Online. Access to these new resources will increase dramatically over the next few years for the majority of people. E-accessibility has become a key European priority. But how accessible really are on-line cultural and educational resources for the 40 million EU citizens who are disabled?

This paper argues that:

1. Large numbers of disabled people face substantial access barriers to on-line culture and e-learning.
2. Web accessibility of on-line culture is more than a matter of meeting technical web accessibility criteria and comes fully to life only when the content has been presented in ways that are accessible to diverse groups of disabled people.
3. Disabled people have a right to access websites.

4. Initiatives at policy-making, funding and strategic levels and in the cultural and educational sectors are needed to achieve significant progress.
5. There is an urgent need to pilot best practice projects and disseminate guidelines to set trends for the future.
6. Some resources exist already: we look at links with examples of good practice.

The Council for Museums, Archives and Libraries (MLA), is a strategic UK government-funded body established in 2000. It promotes good practice and standards in museums, archives and libraries and acts as an advocate for the sectors; it also undertakes research and initiates strategic developments and acts as an adviser to government. Public access has become a high priority. In February 2002, MLA appointed a Disability Development Officer, who is one of MLA's Learning and Access Team, which has a staff of six. MLA has always demonstrated a strong commitment to promoting web accessibility standards. This paper passionately affirms the need for a socially and culturally inclusive on-line culture, and focuses on the accessibility of the content of on-line cultural and educational resources for disabled people – an issue which has hitherto received scarce attention.

Barriers to Access

This paper calls for *a person-centred definition of on-line access to cultural and educational resources for all*, in line with the UK e-government 'Quality Framework for Government Websites' guidelines. Such a definition does not yet seem to be in place; it is now proposed that the definition:

- complies with web accessibility standards
- is purpose designed for a range of target audiences
- allows for independent access and use
- communicates meanings (and thus text, digital images and interpretive commentary) in a way which is meaningful to target audiences
- engages target audiences
- provides both inclusive and specific resources.

This definition, susceptible of being fine-tuned, needs to be linked to the development of a framework for the evaluation of on-line cultural and educational resources, which would incorporate existing standards, management processes, approaches to content creation and user involvement. The recent Cultural Content Forum mapping project of the evaluation of on-line cultural resources (2002–3) is heading in this direction.

Using the above definition, it becomes clear that only a very small number of museum and heritage websites meet several or all of the above criteria in relation to disabled audiences. Where content accessibility for disabled people has been purposely built in for disabled people, the amount of collections presented in an accessible manner represents only a fraction of all resources available and seldom exceeds a dozen or two dozen objects. No portal exists as yet which would provide easy access to these scarce resources and these remain little known by users and therefore under-used. Currently, every new on-line cultural resource risks widening the exclusion zone and unwittingly contributes to installing a new form of cultural apartheid, which must be energetically dismantled; or, to put it in other words, *barrier-free resources need to built on a large scale.*

What are the barriers faced by disabled people to on-line cultural and educational resources? Currently there do not seem to be any systematic audit tools available which would bring together technical standards and the presentation and interpretation of digital collections from an audience-centred perspective. Audit tools exist for technical standards and in the UK the Disability Rights Commission has been auditing a wide range of 1,000 websites for their technical accessibility. Case studies on the technical accessibility of websites are available on the website of the Web Accessibility Initiative (see References). Compelling examples of barriers, seen from a person-centred perspective, are easy to provide:

- A blind person can surf the Web endlessly before finding an on-line museum or heritage collection with (audio/text) descriptions of digital images. To her or him, such cultural materials will remain an arid abstraction in the absence of description. If technical web accessibility standards have been ignored, the navigation of the website will be a tortuous, if not a hopeless task.
- A deaf person who does not read – and many do not – will find little joy with cultural websites. Whilst he or she will see the digital images and perhaps analyse them visually, their meaning cannot be fully decoded, because the necessary information has been denied them in sign language – which may soon become recognized as a minority language by the Council of Europe.
- A person with dyslexia will benefit from audio.
- For a person with a learning difficulty and very limited literacy, navigation is likely to present serious issues – because it fails to engage her or him with the quality of immediacy; and what's the point?: all this information in scholarly and curatorial language on the museum website is of no relevance whatsoever!
- Society, especially its disabled people and teachers, pays a high price for these barriers. Teachers in special schools and teachers working with disabled pupils and students spend vast amounts of time individually crafting educational and cultural materials again and again, which could be made available with the right expertise on the Web for many more people. Whilst the notion of cost efficiency has entered everyone's minds, it has as yet to be put into practice for the benefit of disabled people and cultural access.

Solutions

The challenge to overcome access barriers is manifold and requires interdisciplinary approaches:

- Web designers need to engage with web architectures that provide smooth access to diverse audiences of disabled people

- Content providers and writers need to learn to write for new audiences, commission freelancers and work with communities
- Managers need to build technical and content accessibility for disabled people into web design contracts, and budget for it!
- All need to develop a knowledge of their audience; community participation is a prerequisite.

In addition to addressing current technical web accessibility, on-line cultural and educational resources need to evolve ways of providing access to content:

- Descriptions of images for visually impaired people. These will allow blind people to form a mental image of an object and to make sense of interpretive commentary. They will enable all people who have limited sight to see images better. Descriptions may be embedded into inclusive presentations for all or made optional – which allows for more detailed descriptions for visually impaired people. Descriptions can be visual or technical (for example, for science and technology exhibits).
- Image magnification, heightened tone/colour contrast, detail against contrasted background and visual analysis of art works will interest all people who have some sight.
- Text and subtitles will assist people with a hearing impairment.
- Outline drawings can be downloaded and copied as raised images in schools with young visually impaired people.
- Sign language could be provided for deaf people.
- Images could be supplied as a communication support for people with learning difficulties, featuring situations, beings and objects with which they engage. The use of plain English is essential.
- Audio resources will help people with dyslexia.
- A friendly and welcoming design and style could prove beneficial for everyone, including people with mental health issues – this prospect remains little documented.

The challenge is to meet new communities, to learn from them and involve them and to translate this into accessible websites. There is much expertise among teachers, disability organizations, sub-titlers, sign language interpreters and audio describers for TV, video, film, theatre and live events (such as in Australia, Canada, Germany, Greece, Finland, Italy, France, Spain, Sweden, Japan, UK, US) etc. It is a whole new way of thinking! It is a time to lay apartheid to rest. [As an example, Germany is making significant efforts in these areas, as reflected in a special EVA 2002 Berlin workshop at which there were six papers, including one by Marcus Weisen. Ed.]

Access is a Right

> Everyone has the right freely to participate in the cultural life of the community …
> Universal Declaration of Human Rights, article 27.1

Cultural Rights and Policies

In the 1990s, a number of countries started developing policies to put in place the implementation of the cultural rights of disabled people. One example is the UK Arts Lottery, a distributor of £300,000,000 annually, which makes access for disabled people an essential criterion for cultural funding. Similar policies are needed for new national e-learning and on-line cultural resources infrastructure, content creation and funding programmes. This is a fundamental requirement, if Council of Europe Recommendation R92(6) is to be implemented: 'Government institutions, leisure and cultural organisations should develop comprehensive access policies and action programmes designed to bring significant and lasting access improvements for all disabled people'. In May 2003, the European Council of EU heads of state has for the first time passed a resolution on access for disabled people to Europe's cultural riches and infrastructure.

Disability Rights and Policies

The Treaty of the European Union commits the EU and member countries to combat disability discrimination and EU funding programmes to be eligible for disability projects. The European Disability Forum calls for an EU anti-discrimination directive, which would create a right to access to goods and services; this already exists in anti-discrimination legislation in, for example, the US, Australia, UK, Italy and Germany.

Access to Technology

The European Commission DG XIII TIDE fund (Telematics Initiative for Disabled and Elderly People) has promoted inclusive design principles for a decade. The e-Europe Action Plan, agreed by all Member States, says that *Public Sector Websites* and their content in Member States and in the European institutions *must be designed to be accessible by 2005* to ensure that citizens with disabilities can access information and take full advantage of the potential for e-government. In relation to 'designing-in' accessibility to all information society technologies, training for designers in this area is relatively new and therefore fragmented across Europe. There remains much scope for *mutual learning between centres of excellence* to build a coordinated and high quality approach. The European Minerva project, supported by the European Commission, is pursuing ways of achieving this aim.

What is an On-Line Cultural Resource?

In terms of US, Australian and UK anti-discrimination legislation they are a service, like all publicly available websites. In the UK, service providers need to make reasonable adjustments and provide 'auxiliary aids and services' under the Disability Discrimination Act (DDA) which make a service more accessible to disabled people. The government DDA Code of Practice on 'goods, services and facilities' specifically mentions websites as an example of a service. The UK e-Government 'Quality Framework for Government Websites' states that 'websites must be accessible to disabled people'. The Quality Framework strongly emphasizes usability, user-centred design and consultation and is mandatory in the UK public sector.

On-site (non-virtual) museum and heritage education programmes are currently more responsive to providing access to cultural resources for disabled people than are on-line cultural sites and e-learning resources. There are three main reasons for this discrepancy:

● Public and education services in museums and heritage sites have a longer tradition of awareness of cultural access policies and disability policies. They have experienced this development over a decade and have generated organizational and creative responses, as well as invaluable expertise.
● On-line cultural resources are a very new service, and it is probably a fair comment that they have been more ICT-driven – which brings with it a lesser focus on cultural policies and practices.
● Even where awareness of (technical) web accessibility standards is high, these have often been seen as the answer, whilst they are simply a starting point for cultural access. In addition to meeting legal obligations, it does take human, intellectual and experiential engagement with the ways in which disabled people use or are barred from using the Web.

Rapid progress can be made, if on-line cultural resources are being seen by all stakeholders as a service to which disabled people have a right and as being part of the broad family of cultural services (and can thus assimilate their traditions and experiences of cultural access policies and practices).

Then ICT can transform, like a Sleeping (but rather useless) Beauty, into actualized potential.

Strategy and Implementation for On-Line Access to Cultural and Educational Resources for Disabled People: An International Perspective

To make on-line access to cultural and educational resources a reality, a number of measures are needed. Here are some suggestions for solutions, whose combined effect should be designed to set the foundations for the significant and lasting improvements called for by Council of Europe Recommendation R92(6).

Strategies

● Build (technical) web accessibility standards into funding agreements
● Build content accessibility into funding agreements
● Make these an essential funding criterion for all strategic projects
● Research existing good practice, develop evaluation tools, develop good practice guidance
● Foster a critical mass of accessible resources; for example, promoting new innovative schemes and up-grading existing e-learning resources
● Build capacity in the areas of ICT, human interface, culture and disability

access, harness existing and yet under-used skills, develop new skills and training
● Provide easy access to accessible resources; for example, via portals to cultural websites
● Foster good and innovative practice in design, content development and consultation, possibly via award schemes
● Develop information on resource requirements; human, technical and financial and project management.

Cultural and Heritage Organizations; Software Industry

● Develop disability access policies and plans, to include websites
● Ensure that websites are designed to enable access.

Resource advocates that the issue of the accessibility of the content of on-line cultural and educational resources for disabled people be given heightened priority in England and in Europe, beyond 2003, European Year of Disabled People. We would like to hear of projects, research and policy and funding initiatives.

Resources and Links

Web accessibility standards and guidance:

● www.w3.org/WAI
● Reports on how disabled people use the Web:
www.w3.org/WAI/EO/Drafts/PWD-Use-Web/Overview.html
www.abilitynet.co.uk
http://bpm.nlb-online.org/

Access All Areas: Disability, Technology and Learning; edited by Lawrie Phipps, Allan Sutherland and Jane Searle; published by Association for Learning Technology, JISC and TechDis; July 2002. Available as PDF at www.techdis.ac.uk. See also www.alt.ac.uk and www.jisc.ac.uk

On-line access to cultural and educational resources:

● www.datyonartinstitute.org/accessart/access.cfm
● www.ukoln.ac.uk/nof/support/help/papers/writing-web
● www.mencap.org.uk/html/easytoread/easytoread/htm

Special Educational Needs and the Internet: Issues for the Inclusive Classroom; edited by Chris Abbott; published by Routledge Falmer, London/New York, 2002. See also www.routledgefalmer.com and www.culturalcontentforum.org/intro/html

A few on-line cultural resources:

- http://tours.daytonartinstitute.org/accessart/
- www.tate.org.uk/imap (BAFTA Award 2002; commended for its innovative approach to content accessibility by the Jodi Mattes Award for the most accessible museum, gallery of heritage venue website 2003)
- www.fng.fi/hugo
- www.louvre.edu
- www.24hourmuseum.org.uk/nwh/ART13481/html
- www.americanhistory.si.edu/disabilityrights/welcome/html
- www.thebritishmuseum.ca.uk/compass (National Library for Blind 'Visionary Design Award' 2002)
- www.nmm.ac.uk (Visionary Design Award 2002, Jodi Mattes Award 2003)

Examples of good practice (in all languages) are welcomed by marcus. weisen@resource.gov.uk to help widen the pool of experience in this important field.

References

RNIB and Vocaleyes (2003) *Talking Images Guide: Museums, Galleries and Heritage Venues Improving Access for Blind and Partially Sighted People* and *Talking Images Research Report*; RNIB, May 2003, £14.50 (total for both publications); www.rnib.org.uk/leisure, telephone 0044-20-7388 1266.
See also www.resource.gov.uk/action/learnacc/00access.asp#3.

Chapter 23

Web Access to Cultural Heritage for the Disabled

Jonathan P. Bowen

Abstract

Physical disabled access is something that most cultural institutions such as museums consider very seriously. Indeed, normally there are legal requirements to do so. However, on-line disabled access is still a relatively novel and developing field. Many cultural organizations have not yet considered the issues in depth and web developers are not necessarily experts either. The interface for websites is normally tested with major browsers, but not with specialist software like text-to-audio converters for the blind or against the relevant accessibility and validation standards. We consider the current state of the art in this area, especially with respect to aspects of particular importance to the access to cultural heritage.

O world invisible, we view thee,
O world intangible, we touch thee,
O world unknowable, we know thee,
Inapprehensible, we clutch thee!

Francis Thompson (1859–1907)

Introduction

A cartoon in *The New Yorker* magazine on 5th July 1993 showed a picture of a dog at a computer talking to his friend and saying:

On the Internet, nobody knows you're a dog.

Peter Steiner

A significant number of people using the Internet in general and the Web in particular have some form of disability that may affect their use of the technology. Of course the World Wide Web Consortium (W3C),[1] the main web standards body, is aware of the issues but many sectors still have little awareness of the access problems to their websites. Museums and related cultural institutions normally pride themselves on the accessibility of their physical buildings with expensive lifts, induction loops for audio access, special toilet facilities etc – see in Figure 23.1, for example, the prominent ramp for the River and Rowing Museum at Henley that is

Figure 23.1   Disabled access ramp for a museum

raised well above the ground level which is in the flood plain of the River Thames. It would not be untypical to spend around 10% or more of a building's overall cost on improved accessibility. This is both a legal requirement in many countries and also a moral duty for public-spirited institutions such as museums. What is more, perhaps around 10% of the population have some sort of physical disability that impairs their activities in some way. However, many heritage institutions have yet to make an equivalent effort for their on-line facilities, despite the fact that legislation covering this mode of access is in the offing or already exists in most developed countries.

Since many web designers come from a graphic design background, they may not be expert in non-visual forms of access. In addition, web tools do not necessarily enforce or even greatly aid improved accessibility. Indeed some are positively detrimental because their output often does not meet the basic HTML coding standards laid down by the World Wide Web Consortium (W3C). Instead they tend to aim at the latest web browsers and try to maximize the use of new features, with little concern for backward, cross-browser or cross-platform compatibility issues, let alone the problems of accessibility. To confound the issue, customers (not unreasonably) know even less about the issues than the designers. What is more, the situation is getting worse because of the increasingly diverse set of technologies available on the Web and rampant 'featurism' as commercialization increases. Of course, this is somewhat overstating the case and there are pockets of highly accessible web material from both museums and other organizations. Awareness is improving and most cultural heritage institutions are keen to improve the accessibility of their web facilities once they understand the issues and the fact that it is possible to do something about it, often at little cost if it is considered during a major website redesign.

With the increasing importance of the Web as a communication medium, cultural institutions should ensure the widest possible accessibility of their resources on-line. This does not just mean making cultural information available on-line in any form, as is thought by some less informed designers. It means thinking about the issues of different means of access (whether by blind, partially sighted, deaf, paralysed or otherwise disabled users).

As multimedia access increases and is improved through higher-speed access to the Internet and faster computers with better facilities, it is important that several modes of access are available for different users. For example, if audio is provided, a text transcript should also be available. If an image or video is presented, a text description and perhaps subtitles should accompany it.

Accessibility is a special case of usability. Computer users have understood that the 'friendliness' of computers could be much improved for decades and of course the technology has progressed remarkably, with Windows-based display, interactive keyboard, mouse access, stereo sound, etc., now being the norm.[2] Improved usability aims to make use of technology (such as the Web) more efficient, enjoyable, easier to remember etc. Improved accessibility explicitly aims at widening the number of people who can use the technology, minimizing the barriers that will always exist but that can also always be reduced. Jakob Nielsen provides an excellent website on web usability issues in general (www.useit.com), as well as writing leading books on the subject.[3] Here we concentrate on accessibility, in particular to cultural material where commercial pressures may be less and where there is a moral as well as a legal imperative to widen accessibility.

Legal Issues

It is likely that having an accessible website will become an accepted legal requirement for public institutions in most countries. As an example, the original website for the 2000 Olympics in Australia was not accessible for the disabled, especially the blind. A complaint was made in the case of Bruce Maguire, a blind person, versus the Sydney Organizing Committee for the Olympic Games (SOCOG) (www.contenu.nu/socog.html). In this case a single individual won against a large organization under the Australian Disability Discrimination Act. The case, known as 'Maguire vs. SOCOG', was the first of its kind in the area of web accessibility. The statement of Tom Worthington, one of two expert witnesses, is available on-line (www.tomw.net.au/2000/mvs.html), together with a paper.[4] The Olympic website was actually deemed unlawful and the Australian Human Rights and Equal Opportunity Commission (HREOC) (www.hreoc.gov.au) ordered that it be made accessible to the disabled in time for the Olympics. However SOCOG ignored the ruling because its partner IBM said it would be too expensive and time-consuming to update the site, and thus were subsequently fined A$20,000, around

£8,000, which is a fairly small sum for such an organization. However the effort involved in correcting the site was also in dispute. An irony is that the International Paralympic Committee, in parallel with the International Olympic Committee, even organizes games explicitly for the disabled (www.paralympic.org). On the positive side, the accessibility of the website for the 2004 Olympics games in Athens (www.athens2004.com) was much improved as a result. However a check with the Bobby accessibility checker (see below) revealed three 'Priority 1' (top priority) errors with missing alternative text for three images in the main homepage, a very basic accessibility mistake that was easy to correct.

In the United Kingdom, the Disability Discrimination Act (DDA) of 1995 (www.hmso.gov.uk/acts/acts1995/1995050.htm) applies to many bodies including museums and other cultural institutions. The UK government's disability website gives a useful and more friendly introduction to the Act (www.disability.gov.uk/dda). This phased legislation came fully into force in October 2004. Essentially, disabled access to services should be provided by institutions where possible. Part III of the Act (covering 'Goods, facilities and services' amongst other aspects) makes it illegal for a service provider to treat those that are disabled in a less favoured manner because of their disability. 'Information services' are explicitly covered under section 19(3) of the Act. Services should be adjusted by reasonable means to ensure that they are not impossible or unduly difficult to access, as covered by section 21(1) on the duty of providers:

> **2.1** - (1) Where a provider of services has a practice, policy or procedure which makes it impossible or unreasonably difficult for disabled persons to make use of a service which he provides, or is prepared to provide, to other members of the public, it is his duty to take such steps as it is reasonable, in all the circumstances of the case, for him to have to take in order to change that practice, policy or procedure so that it no longer has that effect.

An associated Code of Practice[5] is also available from the Disability Rights Commission (DRC) (www.drc.gov.uk). This is a more approachable document than the Act itself and may be a better place to start for a non-lawyer needing some general guidance on the legal aspects of service provision.

More recent legislation explicitly covers web services under the Special Education Needs and Disability Act 2001 (SENDA), available from HMSO on-line (www.hmso.gov.uk/acts/acts2001/20010010.htm). The new rights came into force on 1st September 2002, with some exceptions, including the provision of auxiliary aids and services covered from 1st September 2003. This Act, essentially an extension of the DDA as mentioned above, is particularly aimed at protecting disabled students in higher and further education within the UK, so university museums and other institutions providing material for learning support need to be compliant. An overview of what the Act means in practice, in a far more readable form than the Act itself, is available from the UK Centre for Legal Education (UKCLE) (www.ukcle.ac.uk/directions/issue4/senda.html).

There has been no court case involving website accessibility in the UK to date and it is unlikely that a museum would be sued, but it is obviously still incumbent on cultural institutions to act responsibly with respect to their website provision. The best point to act is the next time a major website redesign is planned, in which case the designers should be well aware of the legal issues of accessibility in the country concerned, as well as the technical and other solutions that are available to tackle the problems. For further information on and links to UK legislation, see recent work by Poole.[6] For more general information on legislation internationally, see Chapter 2 of Thatcher et al. (2002).[7] For US law, see Chapter 13 in the same book and Appendix C for the US Section 508 Guidelines on accessibility of electronic and information technology that apply to US Federal agencies. See also Appendix A of Clark (2003).[8]

Example Museum Websites

It is instructive to consider some museum sites where accessibility has been considered. This is now an aspect that is assessed in the Museums and the Web conference Best of the Web awards (www.archimuse.com/mw2003/best). As an example, the Natural History Museum of Los Angeles County in the US (www.nhm.org) was initially an exemplary website from the point of view of accessibility. This was largely because someone who is very knowledgeable of the issues involved designed and organized it in-house over a number of years. Perhaps the most interesting thing about this and other websites designed with accessibility in mind is that they need look no different on a modern graphical web browser from any other professionally designed website. This demonstrates that designing with accessibility in mind does not mean one has to compromise what is on offer for the able-bodied user with good web browsing facilities. Unfortunately the accessibility expert who used to be at this particular museum has since moved so the newly designed website is a retrograde step in regard to accessibility.

The British Museum COMPASS database, presenting a selection of the museum's best objects [www.thebritishmuseum.ac.uk/compass], includes a prominent 'Text Only' link at the top of its main page for disabled users to gain easy access to the available facilities. The information for the graphical and text-based information is served from the same database, thus ensuring that both are in step and up to date. The British Museum is also developing a general text-only link for its website, although this is still rather rudimentary (www.thebritishmuseum.ac.uk/text_only).

The Tate Gallery in London initiated the i-Map Project (www.tate.org.uk/imap) in association with a major exhibition on Matisse and Picasso in 2002.[9] This was designed to give access for visually impaired people via the Web using raised images, allowing these to be touched if printed on a special printer. Thus even art galleries that are obviously very visually oriented in general can make efforts to reach out to the blind.

The Imperial War Museum, also in London, has a text-only version of the 'Citizenship' area of its website under the auspices of its Education Services department (www.iwm.org.uk/education/citizenship). There is also a text-only page giving information for disabled visitors (www.iwm.org.uk/lambeth/disainfotxt.htm). However, finding these from the main homepage is difficult, if not impossible. It is always worth making it obvious that accessible material is available in a clearly labelled manner, both to make it easier for the disabled on-line visitor, and to demonstrate that the effort to make the material available has been made.

More generally, the UK Heritage Lottery Fund provides an exemplary text only version of the website, linked from the homepage (www.hlf.org.uk). This seems to be quite extensive, fast loading and easy to use, with a link back to the graphical version at the bottom of each page. The Virtual Library museums pages (VLmp) include an initial graphical hyperlink – with appropriate 'alternative' text for text readers – which links to a text-based version of the complete website, dynamically generated using the Betsie tool (see below) (icom.museum/vlmp).

The Disability History Museum (www.disabilitymuseum.org), a completely virtual 'museum', includes a text-only link and is approved by the Bobby tool that checks for website accessibility (see next section). Another example of a real museum with a text-only link is the Florida Museum of Natural History, USA (www.flmnh.ufl.edu). However, further links return to standard graphical pages, which is not ideal. The Neuberger Museum of Art at the State University of New York, USA, makes a better attempt with a whole set of text-only web pages available.

A museum with a good text version homepage, linked from the top of the main homepage, is the Smithsonian National Air and Space Museum in Washington DC (www.nasm.si.edu). However, again the links from this page lead to graphical pages on the rest of the site.

Positioning the text link as the first link on the homepage is the ideal position for it to be found by blind visitors, who must scan web pages sequentially using a text-to-audio conversion program such as JAWS (Job Access With Speech) for Windows from Freedom Scientific (www.freedomscientific.com). Note that the font size for the text-only link can be discreetly small if desired since the size does not affect the way the text is read. JAWS is available for evaluation free of charge (in a version that stops automatically 30 minutes after each reboot of the computer on which it is run). This is perfectly adequate for demonstration purposes. It is highly recommended that web designers and museum personnel listen to their web pages being read by such software to gain an idea of the difficulties encountered by blind users.

The Rural History Centre (including the associated Museum of English Rural Life) at the University of Reading is accessible in text-only form via the Betsie tool (access.museophile.net/www.ruralhistory.org). This software was originally developed by the BBC, who are exemplary in their website accessibility, despite having a graphically rich site (www.bbc.co.uk).

Betsie is now 'open source' software and is freely available to any organization that wishes to install it (betsie.sourceforge.net), although it requires a little expertise to do so. The software displays existing web pages by filtering their content to a version only displaying text in a uniform size, font and colour (see Figure 23.2). Betsie allows users to select text/background colour combinations, the font size and style on a special web page accessible via a link from the bottom of all web pages generated by the tool (see Figure 23.3). Thus it may be useful to partially sighted people requiring large-size text as well as colour-blind people and those who are completely blind. A further link is provided so the user can return to the standard version of pages displayed by Betsie at any time. An advantage of Betsie is that the text-only version of the website is dynamically generated from the normal web pages so there is no problem of ensuring that text-based pages are up to date. It can

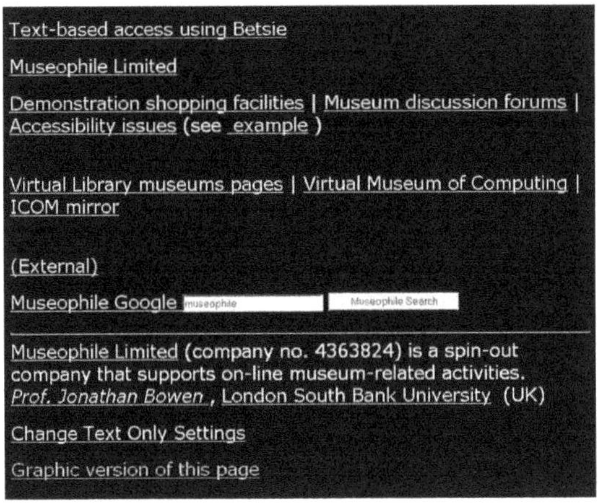

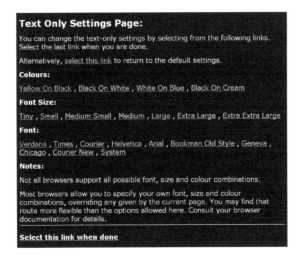

Figure 23.2   Example web page generated by the Betsie tool

Figure 23.3   Betsie options page

be very annoying to disabled users to be presented with inferior outdated information; so much so that they may actually prefer to attempt to access the main site anyway, even if it is less accessible.

Survey and Tools

The Bobby validator (bobby.watchfire.com), which can check for WAI compliance and also for US Government Section 508 compliance (www.section508.gov), has been used to evaluate the accessibility and usability of 25 UK and 25 international museum and related websites with respect to their disabled accessibility (and hence usability).[10-14] Bobby evaluates web pages for accessibility to users with disabilities. It checks for the presence or absence of particular features, or their characteristics, although it does not explicitly check HTML syntax. The W3C validator is recommended for checking HTML itself (validator.w3.org). The results of this survey can be found in Micheloni and Bowen (2002).

As well as the mechanical check using Bobby, a visual analysis was carried out manually using information provided by Bobby and also with textual browsing (for example, by using an audio browser) and partial sightedness in mind. Generally the sites fared quite badly with a significant number exhibiting some serious accessibility problems. The overall results for Bobby are shown in Figure 23.4, extracted from Micheloni and Bowen (2002). Priority 1 errors are most serious and must be corrected to meet the WAI guidelines already referred to. Priority 2 errors should be corrected if possible and Priority 3 errors may be corrected.

The Bobby tool is available for free use on individual web pages via an on-line

Bobby	UK		International	
Priority 1	No.	%	No.	%
No errors	10	40	7	28
1 error	12	48	16	64
2–5 errors	1	4	2	8
Triggered items	20	80	19	76
Non-triggered	25	100	25	100
Priority 2	No.	%	No.	%
No errors	1	4	5	20
1 error	5	20	5	20
2–5 errors	19	76	17	68
Triggered items	25	100	24	96
Non-triggered	25	100	25	100
Priority 3	No.	%	No.	%
No errors	2	8	2	8
1 error	5	20	8	32
2–5 errors	17	68	16	64
Triggered items	25	100	25	100
Non-triggered	25	100	25	100

Figure 23.4   Bobby validation results for museum websites
Source: Micheloni and Bowen (2002)

web interface (at a maximum rate of one page per minute to avoid misuse). A downloadable tool is also available at a charge for all major operating systems. An alternative, free (but more experimental) web accessibility verifier (for use under Windows) is available for download from the A-Prompt ('Accessibility Prompt') Project at the University of Toronto, Canada (www.aprompt.ca).

A useful tool for obtaining a text view of any web pages is the Lynx browser (lynx.browser.org), available for Windows and Unix. A Lynx viewer website exists on-line, which saves having to load the Lynx software on a local computer (www.delorie.com/web/lynxview.html). Any web page that is viewable satisfactorily using the Lynx browser is likely to be viewable by any web browser, so it is a useful check on the accessibility of web pages in practice. Just adhering to the accessibility standards is not enough to check all possible problems. As well as checks using Lynx and JAWS, for example, it is also highly recommended to try to have a disabled person access any new website, performing set tasks as well as undirected usage, ideally with the web designers present, and invite him or her give comments during and after the exercise.

Other Information Sources

An excellent guide with museums specifically in mind is the Ed-Resources.Net Universal Access website by Jim Angus (www.ed-resources.net/universalaccess). This includes an interesting comparison of the accessibility of three museum websites, as well as links to on-line web page validation services and further relevant resources.

In the UK, MAGDA, the Museums and Galleries Disability Association (www.magda.org.uk) is dedicated to improving access to UK museums and galleries in general for people with disabilities, as well as disseminating current best practice. It also provides an on-line forum for museum and gallery professionals to enable on-line discussion (groups.yahoo.com/group/magdamail).

The Jodi Mattes Access Award was launched in 2003 to encourage improved accessibility to museum websites by offering formal recognition to the most accessible site as judged by a panel of representatives from relevant institutions (www.museumscomputergroup.org.uk/index_award.htm). The award is endorsed by the UK Royal National Institute for the Blind (RNIB) (www.rnib.org.uk) as well as the UK Museums Computer Group (MCG) and MAGDA. It is named after Jodi Mattes (1973–2001) who was instrumental in the improved accessibility of the British Museum COMPASS resource (see earlier) amongst other projects. Hopefully this award will help to raise the awareness of on-line accessibility issues further in the cultural field by providing an incentive in the form of peer-reviewed recognition. The RNIB provide particularly good accessibility information on their website (www.rnib.org.uk/access), including good website design (www. rnib.org.uk/digital).

The number of books explicitly covering web accessibility has been very limited until recently, but at least four have been available since the mid-2003. *Web Accessibility for People with Disabilities* was the first book in the area known to the author. *Constructing Accessible Web Sites* is written by a range of experts, including legal aspects in some detail for example, and as such is perhaps the most authoritative book in this area to date. *Building Accessible Websites*, the most recent book, may be more approachable for some web designers, and *Maximum Accessibility: Making Your Web Site More Usable for Everyone* is also available.[15–18] It is hoped that more books in this important subject area will be produced in the future.

Conclusions

This chapter is intended to help raise awareness of the issues concerning disabled access on-line, especially in the context of cultural heritage organizations such as museums that are increasingly developing their on-line resources with ever-more sophisticated web technologies.

For people with learning disabilities, visual disabilities and reading impairments, print-based text can be completely inaccessible. While in recent years software developers have created electronic screen readers that convert text to speech, few of these programs offer effective control over how the text is displayed and read, nor do they provide flexible reading features. Therefore, for those with visual impairments, learning disabilities, reading disabilities or language proficiency problems, even electronic text can be difficult to decipher. The World Wide Web poses additional barriers; while the Web provides a great deal of useful, educational information, its reading levels, page design and emphasis on graphics can make it inaccessible or unusable for some.

There is much room for improvement in the reading and speaking qualities of screen readers. The museum website accessibility survey already mentioned has shown that in order to develop better accessibility the emphasis must be on improved web page coding practice.[19] The coding aspects of web pages are extremely important in ensuring wide accessibility of websites that will be useful to all, both able-bodied and disabled alike. This is possible with care and thought, but most web design professionals have yet to attain the skills to do this. It is hoped that this chapter will at least raise some awareness and interest in the issues involved, particularly for cultural institutions and other public bodies that pride themselves in their physical accessibility.

The Museophile initiative (www.museophile.com), a spinout from London South Bank University, aims to help museums on-line in areas such as accessibility, discussion forums and collaborative e-commerce. In particular, for on-line information on web accessibility relevant to museums, see http://access.museophile.net.

Acknowledgements

Giuseppe Micheloni undertook the survey reported here as a final-year project at London South Bank University. For full details, see Foonote 13.

Notes

There are two articles which are essential reading on this subject:

Bowen, J.P. (2001) 'Internet: A question of access', *New Heritage*, 04.01, 58
Bowen, J.P. (2001) 'Tackling web design and advice on accessible website design', *Museums Journal*, vol. 101, no. 9 (September 2001), pp. 41–3

1   W3C, *Web Accessibility Initiative (WAI)*, World Wide Web Consortium, 1994–2003; http://www.w3.org/WAI/.
2   Wooldridge, S. and London, K. (1973) *The Computer Survival Handbook: How to Talk Back to Your Computer*, David & Charles.
3   Nielsen, J. and Tahir, M. (2001) *Homepage Usability: 50 Websites Deconstructed*, New Riders Publishing.
4   Worthington, T. (2001) *Olympic Failure: A Case for Making the Web Accessible*; http://www.tomw.net.au/2001/bat2001.html.
5   Disability Rights Commission (2002), *Code of Practice (revised) – Rights of Access Goods, Facilities, Services and Premises*, UK Government; http://www.drc.gov.uk/law/codes.asp.
6   Poole, N. (2003) 'Web Accessibility and the Law', *Museums Computer Group Newsletter*, UK (April), pp. 9–10.
7   Thatcher, J. et al. (2002) *Constructing Accessible Web Sites*, Glasshaus.
8   Clark, J. (2003) *Building Accessible Websites*, New Riders, http://joeclark.org/book/
9   Howell, C. and Porter, D. (2003) 'Re-assessing practice: Visual art, visually impaired people and the Web', *Proceedings of MW2003: Museums and the Web Conference*, Charlotte, USA, 19th–22nd March 2003; http://www.archimuse.com/mw2003/papers/howell/howell.html.
10   W3C, as above.
11   Bowen, J.P. Disabled access for museum websites', *Proceedings of WWW2003: Twelfth International World Wide Web Conference*, Budapest, Hungary, 20th–24th May 2003; http://www.2003.org/cdrom/papers/poster/p335/p335-bowen.html
12   Bowen, J.P. and Micheloni, G. (2002) *Disabled Access for Museum Websites*, Technical Report, SCISM, South Bank University, London, UK, 2002. Presented at MCN 2002; http://www.museophile.lsbu.ac.uk/access/mcn2002/access.pdf
13   Micheloni, G. (2002) 'An accessible and usable art gallery for all', final year project, SCISM, South Bank University, London.
14   Micheloni, G. and Bowen, J.P. (2002) *Accessibility and Usability Survey on UK and International Art Gallery and Museum Websites*, Technical Report, SCISM, South Bank University, London; http://www.museophile.lsbu.ac.uk/access/men2002/surveypdf
15   Paciello, M.G. (2000) *Web Accessibility for People with Disabilities*, CMP Books.
16   Thatcher et al. (2002), as above.
17   Clark (2003), as above.
18   Slatin, J.M. and Rush, S. (2002) *Maximum Accessibility: Making Your Web Site More Usable for Everyone*, Addison-Wesley Professional.
19   Micheloni and Bowen (2002), as above.

Chapter 24

Accessible Internet Applications: Principles and Guidelines

Beate Schulte and Ulrike Peter

Abstract

Accessible Internet applications can only have an effect if all *parts of the system are accessible. For museums this means that when developing an Internet application one has not only to offer descriptions for pieces of art but also has to make sure that a person can reach these descriptions despite individual handicaps. Therefore it is necessary to follow the five principles of the Web Accessibility Initiative which can be found in the draft of the WCAG 2.0. We also would like to point to the fact that accessibility is not a new quality feature but has been part of DIN EN ISO 9241: this European standard has been used as a basis for usability for several years. If the two approaches go together this would create an effective and efficient way for implementing accessibility.*

Introduction

The fast technical developments in recent years have enabled museums, using multimedia applications and Internet offerings in numerous and imaginative ways, to bring art closer to interested people: either in introductory form over the Internet or in the museum itself, perhaps in the form of a kiosk system. This provides in particular a great opportunity for people with disabilities; to a certain extent disabilities can in part be compensated for, thanks to the technical possibilities and new access routes which can be created. Examples of this are model projects in which art works with creative image descriptions which are also understandable by blind people.

These technical possibilities can certainly only be used by disabled people if they are accessible: this means that the entire system must be designed in an accessible way. Therefore it is not sufficient just to describe paintings presented on the Internet in a richly expressive manner. It is also necessary to make sure that these descriptions can be reached.

A typical barrier which can block access to an on-line artwork, is, for example, the absence of the option that the Internet is reachable by the keyboard alone, without having to use the mouse. This is very important for visually disabled and blind people as well as (in particular) for people with motor deficiencies. Moreover, the standard interface to the keyboard is frequently used by assistive tools e.g. special keyboards or switches that are used for navigation and interaction.

Another frequently occurring barrier is an over-complex and confusing navigation system: users, especially if they are inexperienced or simply impatient, fail to reach their goal because they are defeated by the complexity of the site and they do not manage to see through its structure. This is particularly the case if the users are advised not to read the full navigation instructions.

In order to avoid these and many other barriers, guidelines have been developed internationally by various interest groups in recent years. A de facto international standard is provided by WCAG 1.0 (the Web Content Accessibility Guideline) which was developed by the Website Accessibility Initiative, a Working Group of the W3C (World Wide Web Consortium). The German translation of this has recently been adopted as an Appendix to the Decree on the Equal Opportunities for the Disabled Law.

In WCAG 1.0, developed in 1999, the emphasis is clearly on the design of systems with the help of HTML and CSS (cascading style sheets): this does not necessarily correspond to the current standard. Due to the rapid technological development and the consequential changes in the design of Internet systems, the WCAG 2.0 is still a draft. Experts say it will be finished in 2005. This involves simultaneously a higher level of abstraction. Developers who want to – or rather, must – build accessible applications cannot avoid understanding the following five principles and taking them into account in the selection of technologies and their application:

- Perceptibility – Can I take in the information, even if, for example, I cannot see or hear it?
- Operability – Is, for example, the application operable even without the mouse?
- Navigability – Is it clearly possible for me to properly use the navigation possibilities and easily orient myself inside the site?
- Understandability – Is the content provided as simply as possible and in a clearly presented form?
- Robustness – Is the Accessibility interface applied and can assistive tools be installed?

The Five Principles in Detail

Perceptibility

It is necessary to ensure that all intended functions and information are presented in such a form that they can be recognized by every user, with the exception of those aspects which cannot be expressed in words. It is important with regard to access to web content that information is presented to users in a recognizable form. The essence of this guideline and corresponding control points concern in particular those people with sensory impairments, so the information must be transformed and presented in such a form that it can be recognized by such people.

Example
Control Point 1.3   Preparation of all the content and structure independent of the presentation.

- Graphics displays of exhibits must be allocated to a corresponding text which reproduces both the content and also as necessary the function.
- Audio presentations must be available also in text form.

The interactive items in the content must be operable by every user. It is important that for this no special equipment should be used if possible. This guideline applies to blind or visually disabled people who have difficulties with eye–hand coordination of devices, people with motor disabilities who cannot manipulate a pointing instrument and for people with speech and learning impairments who wish to use speech input now or in the future.

Operability

Example
Control Point 2.1   All functionalities of the contents must be accessible using the keyboard.
Often only a part of a site can be reached by tab navigation. It must be ensured that the current window is always active in order that the keyboard or a special pushbutton is reachable.

Navigability

The key to effective use of web content is the possibility of navigating and moving quickly and simply inside a document or website. This guideline is useful for people who use a screen-reader so that they can quickly obtain an overview. People with cognitive and motor impairments are directed to a larger and more clearly arranged representation.

Examples
Control Point 3.2   Emphasizing the structure through presentation, positioning and labelling.
In order to guarantee a quick overview of the structure, simple design and use of multimedia can help; for example, support from colours, pictograms, sounds etc.
Control point 3.4   Application of consistent but not necessarily identical presentations.
In particular, if there are a number of developers working, inconsistencies easily occur in the navigational design, in error descriptions and marking of the buttons.

Understandability

Understanding the content and the control mechanisms must be as simple as possible. For people to understand the information provided, attention must be paid to the fact that people learn in different ways and that they have different backgrounds and experiences in using the application. The usage of language, illustrations and concepts which are probably known, hints regarding the similarities and differences between concepts and the provision of explanations for unusual expressions can help in understanding.

Examples
Control point 4.1   Write – tailored to the contents – as clearly and simply as possible.
In particular, when 'insiders' write a specialized text (for a particular discipline, profession or sector) it is common for special terms to be used without explanation.
Control Point 4.3   Annotation of complex information with summaries and definitions.
If the presentation of complex content cannot be avoided, because it is essential for the user, short summaries should be provided to give a rapid overview.
Control point 4.2   Supplementing the text with non-textual content.
In the museum field it should certainly be possible to increase the understandability of the content by the use of graphics etc.

Robustness of the Technology

Web techniques should be applied that make it possible to obtain the maximum access to the content using current and emerging access techniques and user agents.

Examples
Control Point 5.4   Ensuring an accessible user interface or provision of an accessible alternative.
Availability of technologies may mean that an application cannot be made accessible. In such cases the users must be informed so that they can select a simple, uncomplicated way through an alternative possibility.
Control point 5.3   Selection of technologies that support interoperability and compatibility.
Some technologies already provide accessibility features and interfaces.

Accessibility and Software Ergonomics

The requirement for accessible products is not new in the field of software ergonomics: general guidelines on software ergonomics require that software should be usable by everybody. So, if one follows the well known international standard DIN EN ISO 9241, user interests and capabilities have to be taken into account.
    The standard EN ISO 9241-10 describes seven 'dialogue principles':

- suitability for the task (the dialogue should be suitable for the user's task and skill level);
- self-descriptiveness (the dialogue should make it clear what the user should do next);
- controllability (the user should be able to control the pace and sequence of the interaction);
- conformity with user expectations (it should be consistent);
- error tolerance (the dialogue should be forgiving);
- suitability for individualization (the dialogue should be able customizable to suit the user);

● suitability for learning (the dialogue should support learning)

Especially the examples that illustrate the dialogue principle 'suitability for individualization' show that accessibility is an important issue within this standard: people should be able to choose colours and font and type size and influence time limits. With sensorimotor limitations one should be able to use individual input devices. The software should support people with different mental abilities.

Most of the broadly accepted test methods are based on this standard. The main reason that accessibility is not generally included in software tests may be found in a lack of awareness of the problems which people with disabilities have when using Internet applications. The standard gives examples but not a clear checklist.

We believe that test methods used today to check the quality of software products with a focus on software ergonomics can easily be upgraded so that not only lack of usability but also of accessibility are detected.

The key can be found in the principles of the WCAG 2.0: if one keeps the meaning of perceptibility, operability, navigability, understandability and robustness at the back of the mind than accessibility is a natural part of usability.

References

http://www.w3.org/WAI/

http://www.w3.org/WAI/GL/WCAG20/

DIN EN ISO 9241-10 (1995). *Ergonomic Requirements for Office Work with Screen Equipment, Part 10, Foundations for Dialogue Design.*

Chapter 25

Evaluating Websites for Accessibility

Brigitte Bornemann-Jeske

Abstract

A series of evaluation procedures is presented, designed to assist in the development and quality control of accessible websites. According to the German Disabilities Act, the authorities are obliged to make their information systems accessible to any user. The respective guidelines have been published in BITV (the Barrier-free Information Technologies Act). The paper will demonstrate some major rules for accessible web design, and point out some challenges for appropriate testing.

Available Guides

The rules for accessible web design are based on the Web Content Accessibility Guidelines, WCAG 1.0, published in May 1999, by the World Wide Web Consortium's Web Accessibility Initiative (W3C/WAI). The international guidelines were adopted with a few modifications by the German BITV which came into force in July 2002. There is an abundance of information and educational materials on the guidelines available worldwide as well as automatic test programmes. A manual for a test procedure was published first in August 2001 by the Education and Outreach Working Group of the W3C/WAI, and is being updated regularly. Despite all the available support, application of the manual shows that there is still a significant need for explanatory materials at the detailed level.

An Example: Text Alternatives for Graphics

The rules for accessible web design include both technical and content instructions, and so an automatic test can provide only limited results. The available test programs such as Bobby and the Wave test for conformance with the technical rules. They may be used as a tool in a testing procedure, but cannot replace professional judgement. Let us look at an example.

One of the most widely known requirements for accessible web design is text alternatives for graphics. Without this extra facility, graphical screen elements cannot be recognized by users such as those who read the Internet with text browsers or screen readers for the blind. In order to achieve its purpose, the alternative text must be functionally equivalent – that is, the text must reproduce the sense of the graphic's content or function. This is the requirement. Now for the verification: an alternative text is put into HTML code using the ALT attribute, which is a regular part of several code elements describing graphical objects. Automatic tools such as Bobby can determine if ALT attributes are missing. The Wave can also discover 'suspicious' alternative texts such as 'qxdark56.gif'. Essentially however, human judgement is necessary to judge whether or not an alternative text is equivalent. Navigation elements such as buttons and 'hotspots' need an alternative text which gives the objective of the link. Alternative texts for graphical writing should reproduce the written form. Photographs, diagrams and technical drawings should be briefly pointed out in the ALT attribute and need also a detailed description if one is not already provided in the text of the web site (this can be added in the LONGDESC attribute). Even graphical elements without informative functions need an ALT attribute – examples are decorations, coloured lines or transparent graphics inserted as distance separators. For such purely decorative graphics one puts ALT="", an empty ALT attribute, and thus gets the text browser to fade out the element and not provide the file name so that reading is not affected.

These detailed requirements are not defined in the guidelines, but instead on practical knowledge which is documented in a scattered manner. A checklist, which systematically puts questions on all these requirements, would be a rational supplement to the currently available guidelines and test programs.

The BIK Test Procedure

Practical knowledge regarding the guidelines is currently being collected and evaluated. A structured test procedure is being developed, to which the author has contributed. The BIK project, Barrierefrei Informieren und Kommunizieren (Inform and Communicate without Barriers /for Accessibility), is a joint initiative of two German societies for the blind, DBSV and DVBS, as well as the Hamburg company, DIAS, supported by the Ministry for Employment and Social Welfare. Advisory points are being established across the entire country which will provide assistance for the design of accessible Internet development. A Competence Centre is collecting specialist knowledge and developing tools for consultancy work.

The BIK test procedure is conceived as a tool for manual evaluation of websites. Like a script it leads one through the requirements criteria, explains the background, shows the application of automatic tools and provides the questions, which must be answered using individual judgement.

Test Procedures as Instruments for Software Development

Standardized tests are a well recognized instrument in the development and quality control of software. They are applied in order to optimize desired product characteristics, to evaluate the conformance to legal requirements, and to compare products in market analyses. Different methods are applied, from benchmarking to large-scale test series with a representative set of sample users. The latter procedure is widely known under the term of usability testing, although it is only actually necessary when the requirements of users are not known. Due to its high cost, systematic testing against user requirements has, until now, been restricted to the major brands, such as Microsoft, Apple and SAP, or to the academic field.

The guidelines for accessible Web content now offer a broader approach to implement user requirements in the process of software development. The guidelines and their affiliated technical documents represent a requirements catalogue which has been collected from a large community of Internet users. The test procedures which are now under development can focus on finding the respective product characteristics, which can be detected and judged by a professional testing team. A test catalogue on the basis of product characteristics provides a compact control instrument, which already can be efficiently applied in the development phase of Web applications.

Another rationale for a compact and efficient test procedure is the need for a quality mark which could certify the conformance to BITV. As a pre-condition, the procedure should be recognized by an authorized body and executed by trained staff. A recognized quality mark would offer website providers the security of investment which they feel they need for their engagement in accessible design.

Design Principles

In order that a test procedure can efficiently support website development processes, it should be built in a modular manner. A very interesting approach for this is the organization following design principles, which is provided by WCAG Version 2.0, publicly available at the time of writing in a draft version. In WCAG 2.0, the requirements denoted in WCAG 1.0 have been restructured following five design principles for accessible websites: perceptibility, operability, navigability, understandability and robustness.

The principles make it clear that accessibility is concerned not with special needs but with generally valid ergonomic principles, which are applied here to restricted usage conditions. Not only 90% of the population should be reached, as is the goal in general ergonomics, but also the fringe groups. Fulfilling this demand makes the Internet appropriate as a general information and communication medium which connects people of the most diverse capabilities and usage situations with each other.

Organization along generally valid principles enables the matching of experiences from disability-centred design with those from general ergonomics, and the integration of both approaches in a single system. The standards for ergonomic design of computer workplaces (ISO 9241) hold a lot of specifications which may illustrate the principles of accessible web design; that is perceivability, operability and understandability etc. Ergonomic knowledge can be used to refine some of the still somewhat abstract checkpoints in the rules for accessible design, especially the requirements for elderly people with multiple low-level impairments. On the other hand, principles such as 'learnability' and 'suitability to task' which currently have a central place in usability research, can be added to the catalogue. The result will be an instrument to support the various aspects of 'Design for All'.

Short Test

A short test is needed to arrive quickly at relevant practical results, whereas the development of the full test procedures represents a demanding and protracted programme. The short or preliminary test should tackle the most frequent contraventions against accessible design which are at the same time easy to detect. The checkpoints, which come into question for such a development step, are currently being discussed in the BIK project. Candidates include alternative texts for graphics, frame titles, scalable lay-outs and alternatives for JavaScript and Flash. If these requirements are not fulfilled, the basic knowledge of accessible design is lacking, which must be compensated for by training. If the short test is passed, it is justifiable to move onto a comprehensive conformance test. The instrument should also enable editors and web designers to carry out a first evaluation of their websites.

References

BITV or Accessible Information Technology Decree – Annotated version at www.wob11.de/gesetze/a_bitv/index.html.

W3C Web Accessibility Initiative, *Web Content Accessibility Guidelines 1.0*: can be seen at www.w3.org/TR/WCAG10.

W3C Web Accessibility Initiative, *Web Content Accessibility Guidelines 2.0 Working Draft*: www.w3.org/TR/WCAG20.

W3C Web Accessibility Initiative, *Evaluating Web Sites for Accessibility*: www.w3.org/WAI/eval

Bornemann-Jeske, B. (2002) 'Employing universal design in an Internet city guide – Case study of an evaluation and retrofitting process', *WWDU 2002 Proceedings*: can be downloaded from www.bit-informationsdesign.de/download/wwdu_bj.pdf.

Model Project BIK Inform and Communicate Accessibly: can be accessed at www.bik-online.info.

Chapter 26

Breaking Down Barriers: Electronic Aids for Non-Speaking People

Jochen Scherer

Abstract

There are inevitably major communication barriers for people lacking the ability to speak. The task for the educational specialist is to take care of these people by helping them, if possible, to communicate and interact effectively. This is the role of Kommhelp (Come Help), a registered charitable association, which is described in this paper, especially as regards the significance of its work and the type of work undertaken. The work goes back over a decade and has created a community of interest, whose development has been extended with Kommhelp's Word Wide Web fora. A specific case is described in depth as regards its aims and conduct: this case concerns Nur Abide A, a young mute woman living in Berlin in a bilingual environment of German and Turkish. The paper describes the means of communication before and after the intervention, which used a German and Turkish speaking computer. The Communica program is described and semiotic aspects of language and sign are discussed. Bliss, the symbol language used by the young woman, is described, as is also a web-based database for miniority languages and symbol languages such as Bliss an Word Strategy.

Introduction

The barriers to communication by non-speaking or mute people are substantial due to the many blockages and difficulties. The consequences and limitations for the quality of life are thus very significant. The task for social educators working in the field of communication is therefore a challenging one. In response to the challenges, they have made steady efforts to find new ways to enable people who apparently have such blockages to communicate with others. The aim has been to use personal computers for this purpose and to develop suitable software and models. This task in this field is concerned with the boundaries, or rather with the extension of the term 'communication', which can be revolutionized by the technical possibilities of the computer. Talking computers can replace missing voices and picture tables (such as Bliss and Word Strategy) can be reproduced to enable non-verbal interaction.

The paper firstly describes the conceptual approach developed over a decade and then the community-based approach to provide background and context for the main part of the paper. The case study is of a young mute woman in Berlin who faces a particularly difficult situation: she lives in a dual language environment where both German and Turkish are used. The paper then discusses the scientific issues involved using the semiotics approach and gives information on Bliss and useful web resources.

The Concept

'Communication' (Kommunikation) and 'help' are the two words which together form 'Kommhelp' and they represent a programme for the work in which we have been engaged for more than a decade. As a charitable organization we support people in the usage of electronic technical aids for communication. Software program development for this has formed part of the Kommhelp Institute's work since its beginning; for example, Schreibschnell (Write Quickly) and the Communica Bliss project, 2002. Projects regarding speech in its spoken form or speech control in the sense of capturing text have had a special role at Kommhelp since 1991; for example, Handihawk, Lesen (Read) and the Dragon Dictate project.

The skills of our members and associates in web technologies are shown by their work with databases on various websites. Paintings on the computer for exhibitions and books on Buddhism as well as for Christmas cards have established Kommhelp at the centre of a network for reciprocal help, the content of which is determined by the activities of its members. The charity is dependent on income from contributions and donations to carry out its work.

The Community

In the Kommhelp communities, the intention is to facilitate experience exchange

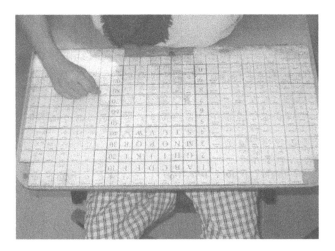

Figure 26.1   Bliss panel in use

between people appealing for help on different topics (for example, the Bliss project, people unable to read print, jokes). Services range from members' computer services to (in official charity terminology), the so-called 'target businesses', but our main activity is carrying out public sector projects to help non-speaking children. The scope of these activities includes school and help-groups. Focal points are maintenance and technical instructions, also related personal issues, the acquisition of configuration aids for system application and, as necessary, the development of applications and support for the training of disabled people during the installation of technical communication aids. This includes assisting in 'acquiring by doing' of high levels of handling competence; for example, for the control of equipment such as PCs or electronic wheelchairs. These above-mentioned social therapeutic measures represent a particularly technically qualified way of carrying out individual aid cases. Under favourable circumstances, such a process may taken place over two years.

The Case Study

Nur Abide A. was born in Berlin in 1978, yet her living circumstances are not characteristically German. She comes from a Turkish family in which her mother language is also nurtured. However, she was never able to speak due to cerebral palsy. She attended a school for physically disabled people in Berlin. Her teacher was convinced that she could read. Her alert and lively eyes signalled that she could grasp and understand everything around her but, imprisoned in her injured body, she was incapable of self-articulation using the usual conventions. To request the assistance of a helper she pointed to the desired Bliss sign from the range which was provided on the panel in front of her (see Figure 26.1) on the wheelchair for every expression of her needs. Due to her condition her pointing movements were often not clear. As a consequence a high degree of attention and concentration was always necessary and in particular untrained helpers were overtaxed. It was often necessary to work by excluding squares in order to find the correct Bliss sign. She had learned the signs at school and the ergonomic therapists had worked through this basic knowledge with her.

We proposed the application of a speech computer employing extended use of the Bliss signs (see below for the technical explanation) using the Communica program, a development of a closely related research project of the Free University of Berlin (AAC or Augmented and Alternative Communication) led by Professor Dr Martin Hildebrand-Nilshon, who was engaged in communication initiation and the development of communication for non-speaking children and young people. The idea for this program came from the needs and difficulties in the development of alternative and extended forms of communication. We used Communica version 4.0 in specific cases. Communication tables are, like gestures, often used as means of extending and supplementing audible spoken communication.

Communica carries over the principle of the communication table to the computer and extends it by the multimedia possibilities of modern technology. In Communica the computer screen may be divided as required into a number of fields according to the skills of the user. Thus it corresponds to the individual pages in a communications folder. As many as desired of these Communica pages, which are ordered like the pages of a book and which may be scrolled forwards and backwards like turning the pages, then form the communications map. In addition, there is the possibility of placing a completely new communications map behind each field. Thus, hierarchies of any desired number of levels may be created, which expands enormously the traditional communications map concept. The individual pages or communication maps can be ordered by different main themes. Photographs, pictures and self-designed or off-the-shelf symbols can be inserted into the individual fields. The activity of selecting a field produces a result that consists of a combination of symbols, images, sounds, text, video sequences and synthetic speech as required. Other programs can similarly be opened as required. Through the option of split-screen control thousands of signs, words, phrases, images and even video sequences may be controlled by a few mouse clicks or touch-screen movements. Selection of fields is employed for communication purposes. The entire contents which can lie behind a field are freely configurable. Communica then leads to the use of pictures and symbols and also to image and symbol recognition. The connection of symbols with their meaning and matching of writing and symbols, tuning of precise motor movements as well as working with the computer, can be (re)learnt. Entire texts can be written, stored, printed or spoken as a whole with the help of synthetic speech output.

Selection of the input medium is particularly important, since it must fit the specific cognitive and physical characteristics of the user in order to provide non-tiring and quick access to all fields. In the case of Nur, who is motor-impaired, she uses only a button which she moves with her right knee. She can use just one button for the field frame by pressing the key to move from field to field: as required the movement can be carried out automatically by a time control. Various scanning modes are correspondingly integrated into the program. After a year Nur can use the system by herself and for the first time express herself verbally. Thus, she is also able to express herself on complex subjects. She will soon join a work group and it is beneficial for her to have this equipment.

Scientific Issues

Language is a sign-based communication system between people. Semiotics is the scientific field which is concerned with the systematic study of signs. A sign is something which stands for something else and is a corresponding representation. In the research field of semiotics both verbal and non-verbal sign systems are included as well as both human and animal communications. Signs (Fr. 'signe') consist of the form of the sign (sound picture) and the concept. The sign forms are, in 'Saussures' terminology, both the signified object (Fr. 'signifiant') and the concept of the signified object (Fr. 'signifie'). These two aspects of the sign are purely conceptual in nature and are inseparably related with each other, like the two sides of a coin.

One of the most important characteristics of signs, the relationship between sound picture and concept, is not innately determined but is arbitrary and is dependent upon the conventions of the language region. So one cannot separate the sound picture from the concept and the concept from the sound picture. This thesis is underpinned by the different sound pictures in various languages for one concept; for example, for the concept of 'tree', one can use the German 'Baum' or the French 'arbre'.

Bliss

Bliss is an assistive language consisting of graphical signs with strong symbolism, which possesses the characteristics and criteria of a language including syntax. Thus, just as our language combines letters to form words and sentences, in Bliss individual graphical segments are combined with each other. There are 26 basic segments which can be combined with each other between the lower and upper boundary lines according to the rules. Some signs are very pictographic whereas others are more ideographic. Pictographic symbols play a special role, since generally they can be learnt by young children in a short time and in part without instruction. With relatively simple connections the Bliss user can produce personal signs or, independently from the official version, define his or her own signs.

Indicators are small specific signs which take the role of grammatical functions. All indicators are located on a conceptual help line, the indicator line, which lies above the upper line.

Related Signs

In the Bliss Institute in Toronto there are about 2,400 words deposited and registered. Language versions are available for the most important languages: US English, UK English, Spanish, German, French, Russian, Italian and Brazilian Portuguese. But there are some 230 living languages in Europe alone, without counting the different dialects. Above all, for the lesser languages there is no suitable solution. Just to provide something for Nur Abide we translated all the words in her knowledge bank into Turkish and produced the corresponding sound files.

On our website we have placed the following fields in a data bank (signs as graphics, meaning, male and female sound-files) and prepared them for downloading. Currently we want to record all the data records of this table for all the lesser languages in Europe. As well as Bliss signs, picture systems can be recorded such as Word Strategy, which deaf people like to use, or reference words with the phonemes in this project.

Reference

www.kommhelp.de

PART 7
INTERACTIVE REALITIES
AND FUTURE POSSIBILITIES

Chapter 27

New Media Art and the Contemporary Museum Environment: A Case Study Based on the NMPFT's Award-Winning Gallery

Malcolm Ferris

Abstract

This paper describes the award-winning National Museum of Photography, Film and Television's (NMPFT) 'Wired Worlds' digital media gallery which was part of a £16 million museum refit and took almost 2.5 years to develop. The gallery consists of 500 square metres of primary 'black box' space situated in the heart of the NMPFT's main building in Bradford. The gallery is highly unusual in that it dispenses with the traditional museum approach built around static object displays, and adopts an expository schema based around a series of highly participatory digital interactive installations. Furthermore, the majority of these installations are by media art practitioners whose work is largely unknown by the general public in the UK. As such the project marks a significant milestone in the use of digital media art in public cultural spaces. The paper takes this leading-edge development as a case study and examines key issues surrounding the project.

Media Art and Museums – A Productive Relationship?

In 1997 the National Museum of Photography Film and Television (NMPFT) embarked upon a £16 million redevelopment programme entitled 'Imaging Frontiers'. A primary aspect of the programme was to systematically extend the NMPFT's remit to digital technologies and to create an agenda whereby the NMPFT might evolve as a leading centre for digital media exhibition, research and practice in the next decade. The public centrepiece underpinning this new orientation was to be a prestigious new permanent gallery exclusively devoted to digital media.

For someone with a background in both the media arts and museology, like the author, the NMPFT project presented a marvellous opportunity. Curating is about discovering and developing new relationships and perceptions, and the project gave the chance to explore an agenda whereby the interests of both the arts and the museum might fruitfully meet.

Certainly there were good reasons why the NMPFT and the digital media arts might wish to engage one another. To begin, the museum was acutely aware that its audience expectations were changing. Digital technologies are diffused across most sectors of society and people are regularly using IT at work, school and home. Young adults, particularly, are also increasingly exposed to, or at least aware of, the innovative kinds of digital VJ-ing and (sometimes interactive) video installation to be seen on the club scene and in the art world. Along with wider changes in the ways in which media and society interact, these factors are changing the ways that museum displays are thought about and understood. Digital media interfaces are not intrinsically threatening to visitors.

Moreover, the NMPFT, as with most museums, was increasingly looking to improve visitor access and participation through new interpretive strategies. This, along with its existing interests in the history of image media, meant that there was a predisposition towards experimentation with the deployment of digital interactive technologies that might enhance the visitor experience.

Last, and most important from the curatorial perspective, was the way in which the NMPFT, as part of the National Museums of Science and Industry, reflexively approached the social and cultural spheres through the technology of the image. This resonated with the way that the digital media arts tend to foreground technology both as medium and rhetorically as subject (as opposed to mainstream contemporary arts practice which is predominately 'low-tech' and has recently tended to foreground strategies of irony, cultural quoting and critical references to art and media history). Indeed, a debate exists as to whether the term 'art' is helpful to describe digital media activities which, whilst creative, are frequently concerned more with the aesthetics of formal coding, interface and interaction theory, information mapping and network architectures, than with – say – working inside, or with reference to, the canon of late 20th century visual art.

Framing a Curatorial Agenda

The digital media field is extremely diverse and evolving rapidly. Since the late 1960s the digital arts scene alone has seen the development of algorithmic art, generative art, multimedia art, interactive art, and net.art, to name but a few of the headline typologies. To make sense of this territory – one which has often been shrouded by the mists of commercial hype or (sometimes absurd) techno-theory – it is necessary to be aware of working practices and ongoing debates across a range of disciplines. The curatorial issue (in other words, the need to do justice to this complexity) becomes one of developing a curatorial 'script', or agenda, that might successfully generate a number of representations and place the subject simultaneously in several discursive spaces.

Therefore, the first thing to set about on the NMPFT project was to formulate a proposition that could serve as the reference point of such a curatorial agenda. Like a simple program that generates complex end-user effects, this 'philosophical nucleus' had to be capable of admitting multiple expressions or views of the field, articulated within the specific museological context. This context was, of course, crucial to the development of the whole enterprise: the collections within the

NMPFT reveal a media history moving from still image, to image combined with time to generate movement within the pictorial frame. The continuation of this vector, located in computer-based audio-visual media, is the extension of time and movement beyond the frame into the real world of user interaction. In a very real sense the user becomes part of the system – part 'machinic' – and is impelled to work within the normally quite explicit rules that the system must impose for it to be able to function and therefore have value. Thus, although digital tools can expand human communication and creativity, it is often forgotten that specific digital tools and interfaces embody certain modus operandi.

This did not, however, mean that we wanted to focus exclusively on digital media production tools and processes for photography, film and television. Rather, we wanted to extend the enquiry into the way audio-visual experience is evolving through a broader set of digital interactive mechanisms that include telematic networks, computer games as sophisticated graphic interfaces, machine vision systems, virtual and augmented reality systems, artificial intelligence and artificial life and so on.

Moreover, this project was not to be like a traditional museological gallery, describing and revealing a past. As much as anything, its purpose was to encourage an understanding of the present and emerging possible futures. We took the view that we had to ask what it might mean to live, work and play in a culture increasingly shaped by the weaving of these virtual mechanisms into the fabric of everyday life: in short, *'to explore how digital media are altering and extending common notions of narrative, representation, location and identity'*. This beguilingly simple statement supported a flexible, questioning and investigative stance that was nonetheless explicit enough to generate a powerful set of connective relationships across a wide range of activities in the field.

Again, a congruence of thinking was identified within the 'artist/developer' community. Here was a sector pursuing an imaginative, research-oriented and, by and large, commercially independent position in relation to the subject, which, in the work of its most accomplished representatives, promoted reflective engagement with the cultural implications of digital systems and networks.

Developing the Subject Space

From this 'philosophy' or position statement, the discursive space of the gallery was orchestrated as a sequence of inter-textual relationships between the physical and the electronic media space. On a practical level, these relationships were framed as a series of step changes between (a) the individual installations, (b) the 'domains' of related exhibits, and (c) the gallery in its entirety – leading from, and out to, the wider museum collections.

At the domain level, five modular spaces were modelled, each composed of a cluster of closely related issues and content. In agreement with our earlier decision to explore a broad set of digital interactive mechanisms, these five discursive spaces were: (1) Seeing the World (computer based 'vision' systems that interacted with the real world beyond the machine); (2) Synthetic Worlds (discrete worlds that existed wholly within the confines of the machine and included VR and artificial life systems); (3) Connected Worlds, (the Internet and telematics); (4) Pleasure Worlds (focused upon the film, broadcast and animation industries); and (5) Interactive Worlds (especially focused upon the nature of the interactive game-spaces found in video games). Together, this domain system would frame the discourse concerning the ways we view ourselves in a digitally mediated world.

Each of the domains was intended to feature at least one major installation by an artist/developer, which in turn would be supported by a number of smaller didactic displays (some of which would also contain additional examples of important works by artists, animators and experimental filmmakers). In the final iteration, each domain contained between three and five interactive displays, making a total of eighteen interactive exhibits across the gallery. Ten of these could be considered large-scale placements; and six were major set-piece installations created by the artist/developers.

The Rhetorics of Display

It was crucial that the spatial layout and physical architecture of the gallery should also support the discursive connections we wished to generate, yet not detract from the experience of the installations. It was clear that the gallery should be utterly different from that of the traditional museum container of static displayed objects, and that the time- and process-based nature of digital media pointed towards some form of fluid information environment. We also wanted to avoid the use of the tired 'touch-screen' kiosk and standard video loop in public spaces. Rather, we wanted to elevate the screen to the scale of the architectural, eliciting an immersive experience, where translucent materials and large-scale projections might create a 'virtual information architecture'.

Following these thoughts, the design and display of the gallery was developed as a reading of the process-based re-programmable nature of computational media and the way in which visitor behaviours relate to notions of immersion and interactivity, performance and participation in 'interactive' media spaces. On an experiential level, we imagined a space formed by light and imagery, where light does more than simply illuminate, but carries information – a space that might be as manipulable and re-programmable as the digital material it contained. 'Information as Light' became the rhetorical concept articulating these ideas. It also provided a conceptual link to other NMPFT areas where lens-based photographic, cinematographic and electronic televisual forms of image making are explored.

In the end it was indeed a rhetorical position because in the context of the pre-existing space and our budget limitations, the vision was not executable – at least to the level we would have hoped for. Nonetheless, the vision did heavily influence all interior design, rigging and fitting out and, to judge by the design awards the gallery has subsequently received, can be considered successful.

The Rhetorics of Interactivity

The next step was to develop a series of criteria for these major set-piece installations. Primarily, we wanted installation displays that might blur the boundary between art, information and entertainment. We sought displays that, while retaining a critical cognitive and aesthetic dimension, might also engage physical, pleasure-experiencing and emotional faculties, and offer a point of access to almost all ages and levels of understanding, and both genders. Thus there would be very little in the way of pointing and clicking on these major works; but rather, the scope to move bodily and freely in and around space. Consequently our criteria were essentially (although not exclusively) centred on the use of unencumbered and intuitive interfaces that would interweave virtual media space with real gallery space to create the so called 'hybrid spaces' of 'mixed reality architectures'. Mostly these interfaces depend upon commonplace methods of communication such as movement and gestures, sound, speech and touch; and many have a distinct 'performance' edge to them. Whilst we considered all these possibilities, we finally opted for works essentially employing video and magnetic position detection, as the specific characteristics of the commissioned pieces particularly suited our curatorial and interface requirements.

It was also important to extend the notion of the interactive interface beyond direct human–machine interaction to include innovative forms of collaboration and participation whereby visitors might be required (or wish) to communicate with each other to further their understanding of the work.

Again, a correspondence of thinking was recognized within the 'artist/developer' community; these kinds of innovative interface are exactly the areas in which installation-based media artists are active. The major commissioned artists we selected included Nigel Johnson (UK); Toshio Iwai (Japan); Art+Com (Germany); Paul Sermon (UK); Jeffrey Shaw (Australia); and Jane Prophet (UK). Brief descriptions of these installations and their role in the gallery schema, along with a selection of images, now follow. However, it is important to realize that these are presented as a representative selection and not as the full set of gallery projects.

'Digital Portal' by Nigel Johnson

Visitors are introduced to Wired Worlds (Figure 27.1) by passing through an interactive 'Digital Portal', with its associations of passage from one state to another – the physical analogue world into the digital domain of the gallery. The 'Portal' imparts the idea that in the digital domain, all representation is founded on the basic but powerful principle of logic states represented by the ones and zeros of binary notation. As visitors pass between its walls, their shapes, size, position and movements are sensed and their forms interpreted as moving, 'pixelated' blocks and points of light.

The installation is approximately 3 m x 2.5 m x 3 m and consists of two opposing vertical walls comprising 6,912 red light-emitting diodes (LEDs) sandwiched between plate glass. Each wall houses 54 autonomous but linked display modules, each containing 128 LEDs, a Scorpion K4s microcontroller and infrared sensors, arranged as a 6-column by 9-row matrix.

'Another Time, Another Space' by Toshio Iwai

The installation exploits computer-manipulated real-time video technology to create

Figure 27.1   Nigel Johnson's *Digital Portal*

strange and beautiful distortions of the time and spatial dimensions. The work consists of four video cameras capturing live video of visitors that are manipulated in different ways by computers and then displayed upon a rig of viewing monitors (Figure 27.2). These manipulations alter time and spatial references by, for example, shuffling a frame stack to create time-lapse delays, slow-motion effects and time compressions. Individual horizontal pixel lines within frame stacks are scanned and these are combined as output to create spatial distortions.

All of these processes could, theoretically, be achieved using traditional film editing techniques, but not in real time.

'Ride-the-Byte' by Art+Com

This is a 'visible web' project designed to convey graphically a sense of the global network of servers routing information data packets.

The exhibit consists of a large 3D representation of the earth composed of satellite imagery and projected onto the gallery wall at resolutions of up to 1 kilometre per pixel. From a touch-screen terminal visitors can surf approximately 100 bookmarked sites from locations around the world. When a site is selected, a zoom-out is initiated on the wall projection from the museum until the virtual camera is looking down on the earth from space (Figure 27.3). The communications trace is then drawn across the globe as the data packet travels through various servers to its destination, whereupon the 'homepage' opens. Past traces remain on the globe to indicate the 'traffic' of previous surfers and give a sense of the distribution and layout of the Internet.

Figure 27.2   Toshio Iwai's *Another Time, Another Space*

Figure 27.3   Art+Com's *Ride-the-Byte*

'Telematic Dreaming' by Paul Sermon

The work consists of two double beds in different locations; one is within a blue screen environment, the other in the gallery space. Both have cameras above them and are surrounded by monitors. The gallery bed also has a digital projector above it placing live video of the person on the blue screen on the bed (Figure 27.4). A further surreal twist is added by pre-recorded video mixed into the live projections so that the bed surface may become, for example, water in a swimming pool.

The installation extends tele-presence beyond the screen to spatialize the site of interaction and transforms it into a live theatrical event in which members of the public are key performers. With all its connotations of intimacy and dream states, the work allows visitors to explore presence, absence and the psychology of human interaction within technologically mediated communications.

'Games Area – Battlezone'

This exhibition domain is focused upon the interactive spaces to be found in video games and is divided into four sub-themes. These are (1) Historical Traces, which

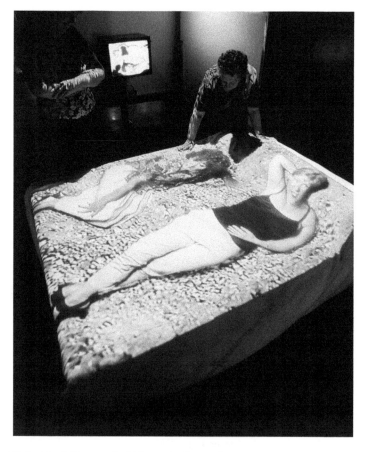

Figure 27.4 Paul Sermon's *Telematic Dreaming*

plots the history of computer games and presents a selection of iconic titles; (2) Gaming Genres, which reviews and presents the main typologies dominating the current single-player experience; (3) On-Line Games, which presents the evolving multi-user paradigm in gaming through an installation in which up to three visitors participate in a networked world; and (4) Games and Society, which examines issues revolving around violence and games (including the phenomenon of the military-infotainment industry) and gender politics. As in all the gallery domains, as seen in Figure 27.5, the emphasis is firmly upon allowing the visitor to participate in the interactive experience in order to be able to understand the gaming phenomena at first hand.

'The Golden Calf' by Jeffrey Shaw

In this work, both the real and the virtual depend upon each other to complete the meaning of the piece. An object in real space – an empty plinth – becomes the location and ground for a synthetic sculptural object in electronic space – the Golden Calf. The virtual sculpture is viewed on a hand-held LCD. As it is manipulated in front of the plinth, the virtual perspectives correlate with the real depth and distance cues the viewer has of the plinth. Moreover the 'Calf' has a reflective surface in which viewers can see the gallery space around the installation. The installation used application software by Gideon May and was produced at ZKM, Karlsruhe, Germany.

'TechnoSphere III' by Jane Prophet and Gordon Selley, 1999

This installation consists of a 3D real-time world populated by artificial life forms.

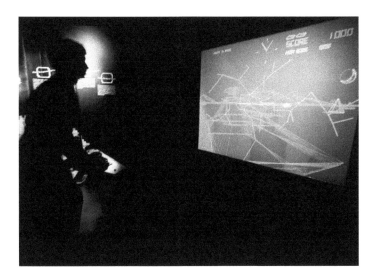

Figure 27.5   *Games Area – Battlezone*

The world consists of 16 square kilometres of terrain capable of supporting approximately 4,000 creatures who chase, eat, grow, mate and produce offspring that – as digital DNA – are variants of the parents. Each creature's 'fitness for survival' is influenced by the interactions between its attributes and the environment. Visitors create creatures via touch-screen terminals. Once 'ported' into the TechnoSphere they can be observed within the world on a series of large projection screens.

The project raises issues to do with virtual life and competitive 'Darwinian machines'. Although each creature behaves slightly differently, certain patterns spontaneously emerge. For example, although there is no explicit flocking algorithm, creatures often organize themselves into groups, impelled by mating and feeding attractors.

What were the Rewards for the Artists?

The project did not present an easy brief for the artists. Their work had to uphold its claim as a critical exercise within the context of a museological space whose function was to inform in a discriminating yet entertaining and accessible manner. It was crucial that a high level of trust existed between both artists and museum and that the curatorial vision was one that was shared by all. An important part of the author's role as the lead curator was to alleviate any worries that the gallery schema would subsume or trivialize the artists' work under the demands of 'infotainment'.

Beyond this the rewards of participation for the artists were high and varied. To begin, they included proper payment and contractual agreements respecting the artists' rights – factors that are, unfortunately, not necessarily a common feature in the digital media field. Digital media artists often do not have a fixed and unique commodity to sell such as those making 'traditional' object-based art, and the commercial models that might support digital media arts – especially net.art – are still evolving. The artists also had the satisfaction and status of knowing that their work was being collected, displayed and preserved by an institution with an international standing. Moreover, and importantly, the NMPFT was a museological institution whose collections situated this new work within a broad history of media forms and, as well as bringing new perspectives to its understanding, legitimized the crossover between art, technology and entertainment.

Finally, and perhaps most importantly, the NMPFT delivered radically new audiences to these works. As a free museum within the demographic of West Yorkshire, its audience is particularly diverse. It includes many who perhaps would not typically visit an 'art' show; through to a professional audience segment that is phenomenally well-versed in interactive media practice and theory. Nonetheless, none of the artists flinched from the challenge this range of audience presented, nor from the many technical and practical hurdles that we had to surmount in the course of the exhibition's development. Indeed, it is worth saying that their attitude to the inevitable problems that arose was exemplary and almost invariably consisted of 'let's see if we can solve this', rather than 'no, that's not possible'. It says a great deal about their professionalism and commitment to the project.

Was the Project a Success for the NMPFT?

From the museum's perspective, there was no guarantee that an experiential approach based on artists' works would be equal to, let alone supersede, a traditional object-based descriptive approach. Moreover, many institutions would be intimidated by the thought of putting so much interactive technology into a permanent gallery with its eight-hours-a-day, almost 365-days-a-year performance requirement. What with the issues of acquisitioning and maintaining these collections, many would simply shy away. Fortunately the NMPFT was not like this. It has a history of dealing with time-based media technologies and an appreciation of the value of multiple and non-object-based artefacts.

This act of confidence has been rewarded. The digital media gallery project is generally regarded as being an overwhelming success. Since reopening two years previously, annual visitor attendance figures have steadily grown from below 700,000 before the re-launch to an estimated 1 million at the time of writing. The gallery appears to have been instrumental in supporting this increase – the annual independent Visitor Survey records it being consistently voted the top permanent attraction at the museum.

The project has also received an excellent critical reception from the press and professional bodies. It has won two major design awards, scooping both 'Best Show' and 'Best Permanent Exhibition' categories in the Design Week Year 2000 Awards, as well as winning the 'Exhibitions' category in the Design Business Association's Year 2000 'Design Effectiveness' Awards. All in all, it is fair to say that the NMPFT has been seen as making a pioneering contribution to the use of 'new media' in public cultural spaces. Not least is the way it has demonstrated that interactive media installations can work within gallery spaces to engender new forms of participation and engagement in the museum experience.

However, beyond these relatively crude facts and figures, any detailed and objective understanding of the visitor experience and reaction is unfortunately not available. The museum Visitor Survey does not seek to capture this level of detail and, as far as the author is aware, the NMPFT does not conduct systematic audience evaluation at the level of individual exhibits. This is not an uncommon position in that formal analysis of visitor interaction in museum interaction design generally remains thin on the ground. (This is perhaps about to change. For example, at the time of writing, I note that a large UK-based ESRC-PACCIT-funded video-based ethnographic field study into museum interaction technologies and audience participation is soon to begin under the auspices of the interaction research group at King's College, London.) However, informal observation of visitor behaviours and gallery exit discussions suggest that the NMPFT's new digital media gallery is generating a wide range of experiences and reactions – mostly positive – across a range of experiential levels. These include the intellectual pleasures of 'reading' (both literally and through imaginative inference) the inter-textual discourses generated within and between the individual installations and the domains. However, it also includes the delight of discovery, of 'performing' oneself; the pleasures in participating in concert with others; the vicarious enjoyment to be had in watching others perform; and the overall aesthetic and 'spectacle' of the entire gallery space. All these levels, and probably more, can be experienced during a visit.

In short, the gallery becomes a kind of game world in which rule-based systems, at one level or another, work to support informally negotiated relationships in which users experience aspects of commitment, reciprocity, verbal and non-verbal communication, as well as the emotional, reflective and cognitive inputs derived from these processes.

Concluding Points

1. Given the scientific and technological orientation of the digital media arts, there are good incentives for museological institutions – especially those of a scientific or technological disposition – to explore the idea of collaborative projects with artists.
2. Audiences are moving fast in their understanding and acceptance of digital media interfaces. A well-designed interface can be informative, playful and reflective – and based in dialogue and exchange rather than in the passive reading of a single authorial (curatorial) voice.
3. Digital media are inherently 'open-ended' and processes-orientated, and facilitate endless content updates. Beware the (software/hardware) obsolescence and upgrade cycle. Remember that good 'content' is not only often expensive to produce; it will also cost you to move it to new platforms. On the other hand, a well-designed gallery system can facilitate the upgrading of content and supporting information in a way that would be difficult to achieve regularly under traditional gallery display conditions.
4. The field is extremely diverse and changing rapidly and there is a lot of hype and theory surrounding it. When curating in this field, it is important to have a clear perspective, or curatorial agenda, of the position you are taking up and to do the regular 'reality' check. Your position should nonetheless be flexible enough to generate multiple readings of the field and capable of accommodating change – both conceptually and at a pragmatic systems level.
5. Media artists – both installation and web-based – are working at the edge of innovative interface and interaction design. Some of these interaction methods are likely to become mainstream practices within museum galleries in the next five years or so.
6. It is important to think 'real space' as much as 'virtual'. All digital media systems, including the Internet, are 'embodied' in real-world situations and this is, of course, especially true of gallery-based installations.
7. Finally, always remember we are limited more by our imagination than the technology. It is a challenging area in which to work, but well worth the effort.

Reference

http://www.nmpft.org.uk/guide/galleries/wiredworlds.asp

Chapter 28

MuseumNet: Reactivity – A New Application Metaphor

Alessandro Mecocci

Abstract

An approach to designing museum visitor systems using a combination of pressure and vision-based social interfaces is described in this paper. It represents an advanced version of the 'New Archaeological Museum' of Bolzano, containing the Mummy of Similaun. The approach includes representing the museum as a set of virtual rooms consisting of a 'forest of trees' or a 'VirtualMuseumGraph'. The system design and technical methods with both vision and pressure sensors are described and then its implementation in a museum of ancient theatrical arts in Monticchiello, near Siena. The system thus provides a unique experience resulting from the behaviour of each visitor group and there is a variety of different interactive devices (for example, videos and 3D sound effects). Future plans include a role for 'emotional agents' to provide artificial psychological approaches.

Introduction

Realism and interactivity are important aspects in communicating and understanding cultural heritage; in this context, multimedia techniques show important features that can offer many new opportunities. In particular, two technologies appear to play a dominant role in this scenario: 3D representations (virtual environments or VEs), and wireless appliances (WAs). VEs help in building up 3D documentation of complex cultural heritage structures. Moreover, VEs facilitate hypothesis and testing, by making it possible to simulate different scenarios and reconstructions (different lighting conditions, different assemblies of fragments belonging to cultural items, simulated temporal evolution of cultural assets from past, to today, to forecasted future). On the other hand, WAs give flexible responses to the needs that generally arise during visits to museums or archaeological and nature areas. WAs improve the comfort and the interactivity between the user and the support infrastructure, thus granting a greater freedom of movement while assuring high levels of both safety and satisfaction.

In this paper we introduce another important idea: museum reactivity. This interaction metaphor is strongly related to the concept of multi-sensor social interfaces (MSIs) which enable a new class of multi-user man–machine interfaces.[1] Museum reactivity is a completely new metaphor that will be the basis for a new generation of museum fruition systems.

Museum Reactivity

Computing resources in public spaces (for example, inside museums) represent a paradigm that differs from the conventional desktop environment and requires user-interface metaphors quite unlike the traditional mouse, pointer, icons and windows. In particular, an MSI (an interface between multiple persons and multiple computers in relatively large spaces) must be capable of autonomously initiating, and terminating interactions on the basis of multiple people behaviour. Moreover, it must be capable of handling multiple interaction devices in parallel, and allocating, dividing and de-allocating resources among multiple customers in a conclusive and equitable way. This approach represents a significant departure from current practices, but it will become increasingly important as computing resources migrate from desktops into public open spaces. It is important to note that there is a forthcoming change from single-user structured interactions (typical of desktop systems), towards unstructured interactions with multiple customers freely moving in open spaces.

MSIs enable museum reactivity: it is no longer necessary for visitors to press buttons or touch screens to start multimedia interactions or presentations. The museum 'sees' the behaviour of visitors through multi-sensor social interfaces (such as vision-based or pressure-based sensors) and then autonomously reacts by affecting the environment (perhaps starting a sound, activating a video or enacting visual events). Because the museum knows something about what is going on, it can act and react appropriately. From the active participation point of view, the role of the visitor is greatly enhanced with respect to previous approaches; people actually build up the visit and they do this in a social way. In other words, multiple parallel interactions by multiple visitors at the same time, determine how the museum reacts, causing the dynamic evolution of what is presented and how it is presented.

This paper describes the integration of pressure-based and vision-based social interfaces in the framework of MuseumNet©, a product for the creation and management of clusters of museums distributed over the territory. MuseumNet© is an advanced modular system developed by Etruria Innovazione S.C.p.A. (a society of the Tuscany Region for the technological transfer towards small and medium-sized enterprises or SMEs), in cooperation with the University of Siena (which developed the innovative parts).[2] The system evolved from an earlier architecture (devoted to multimedia museum fruition) that has been designed by the author for the 'Nuovo Museo Archeologico' of Bolzano (currently hosting the Mummy of Similaun, claimed to be the oldest mummy in the world). The museum, with its distributed multimedia fruition system, was opened to the public on 28th March 1998. It was reviewed by the *New York Times* as one of the top ten museums recently opened in Europe at that time.

System Architecture

The integration of MSIs inside the MuseumNet© architecture has been implemented by considering a layered approach comprising three main parts: (1) control subsystem; (2) sensor subsystem; and (3) actuation subsystem. This approach allows breaking the description of social interfaces (that could be a complex task), into simpler sub-problems, and also permits separating the logical and semantic aspects from the physical implementation.

The control subsystem is the principal part, which starts from an abstract description (see below) of the whole set of MSIs that are present in the museum and supervises all the events that arise in the different physical areas. It dispatches internal messages, starts, stops or kills threads, initializes the physical devices and implements the changes in the environment through suitable output devices.

The sensor subsystem takes care of suitably initializing and handling the hardware and the software running on peripheral input devices. Due to the fact that MSIs generally require some processing to be done at the input-signal level to extract useful information (for example, in the case of vision-based sensing of human behaviour), this subsystem must take care of the proper loading of the set-up data for each physical device, to schedule appropriate logging and data reporting, and to monitor the proper execution of the different subtasks. Moreover, the sensors are described through suitable abstractions that encapsulate device-specific details behind a generic interface and enable a separation between physical and virtual worlds. Each abstract sensor provides generic methods for accessing the input values in a uniform way independent from the real physical device. The physical devices are interfaced through low-level special purpose routines. This is very similar to the approach taken in the Java 3D APIs.[3]

The actuation subsystem takes care of acting on the environment; that is, it implements the reactions of each social interface inside the museum. This subsystem is very similar to the sensor subsystem mainly differing in its efferent role.

The VirtualMuseumGraph

Each museum generally comprises more than one MSI, and each MSI is located in a different physical area. To appropriately interact with users, each MSI must be aware of its own environment; that is, it needs a model of the environment itself. The global description of the museum uses a metaphor based on 'virtual rooms'. Each virtual room contains the environment model (the physical space related to that room) and the model of each MSI that relates to that room. Each MSI is described by specifying the sensors, and the related 'stages'. A stage is the description of a subpart of the room environment where an interaction takes place. A Stage contains the information about the kind of interaction, about the conditions that must be met to start/stop the interaction, about the actuators that are used to implement the interaction, and about the exact location of the physical subpart of the environment with respect to the whole local environment (the whole local environment is described in the virtual room). By specifying the relative position of each stage with respect to the virtual room environment, it is possible to fuse properly information coming from different sensors to obtain higher-level descriptions. For example, it is possible to extract the 2D position of people by means of suitable computer vision algorithms applied to the images acquired by a camera. Thereafter the data can be fused with those of other similar cameras to extract the 3D location of people with respect to the virtual room environment. The transformations are contained in the respective stages (or in a single stage comprising multiple sensors). The description of the whole museum is given by using a 'forest of trees' that has been called a VirtualMuseumGraph. The VirtualMuseumGraph is an abstract representation that comprises one or more virtual rooms that in turn comprise one or more stagegraphs. Each stagegraph comprises sub-trees of attributed nodes. Each node can be a group or a leaf and represents an entity in a stagegraph. Leaf nodes can be abstract sensors or sounds or actuators (actually a sound is a special kind of actuator). Groups are used to assemble multiple actuators or sounds or abstract sensors in a single coordinated unit. For example, a group of lights that must be switched on in sequence can be described as a single logic unit by means of a group node whose children are leaves, each representing the single light of the light-set. Each node or group can have an associated behaviour. A behaviour can do anything; for example it can perform computations, update its internal state, modify the stagegraph, start a thread, send a message or activate an interaction. Multiple behaviours can be composed so that independent behaviours can run in parallel to obtain special interactive effects or complex presentations (such as starting multiple sounds while playing video presentation at the same time as opening boxes or acting mechanical analogical models). Normally a behaviour must be enabled only when a visitor is nearby; this condition is specified by enabling bounds – a volume delimited by a sphere, a box, a generic polyhedron, or their Boolean combination. Obviously a behaviour can be permanently enabled by making its enabling bounds greater than the environment associated to the virtual room to which it belongs. Even if enabled, a behaviour can be fired only if some predetermined conditions are met. In particular, 'firing criteria' and 'firing conditions' are connected to each behaviour.

The VirtualMuseumGraph is created by means of a special editor that is used:

● to give the actual conformation and dimension of the physical spaces where each MSI operates
● to give the description of the sensors and of the actuators
● to specify the interactions by setting up the appropriate behaviours and by binding them to the corresponding stages
● to specify the exact position of each stage with respect to the environment of the virtual room which it belongs to.

The VirtualMuseumGraph structure is used by the control subsystem, by the sensor subsystem and by the actuation subsystem to obtain the information and data needed for the correct functioning of the whole museum.

Vision-Based MSI

To enable reactivity in museums, some form of perceptual intelligence is needed so that the system becomes capable of classifying the current situation and appraising the important variables in order to react in an appropriate and socially acceptable way. This can be obtained, for example, through suitable computer vision algorithms capable of detecting and tracking the position of multiple visitors inside a specific area of the environment. In the proposed system, a vision-based MSI has been implemented that is capable of detecting the presence of visitors. Thereafter it tracks them by means of multiple TV cameras. For each camera an adaptive multi-class temporal median filter is used, coupled with a colour and shape statistical model. According to the model, visitors are segmented from complex textured backgrounds under variable viewing and illumination conditions. People are modelled by means of blobs whose colour statistic is continuously updated. A multi-valued Gaussian mixture is used to account for background spatio-temporal variability.[4] Colour histogram indexing and normalized colour descriptors are used for tracking multiple visitors in real time (see Figure 28.1).

The detected 2D blobs are back-projected to obtain 3D position estimation; when more than one camera is available homographic-based multiple-image-fusion is used to improve position estimates. In the actual implementation the flat ground hypothesis is assumed to hold (which is almost always true in museum applications). It is important to note that the visitors' detection is done in parallel enabling, following the social interface principle. A computer can now evaluate which kind of interaction to start and how to react. This evaluation can be done by grouping the visitors and by matching them with the interaction resources that are available in the room (described by the stagegraphs that belong to the virtual room). Multiple interactions can be started in parallel, targeted at different visitor sub-groups.

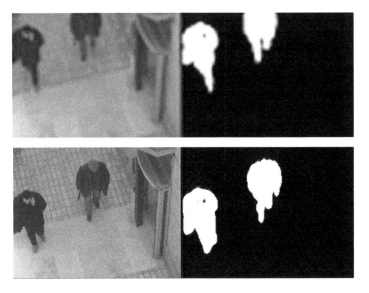

Figure 28.1   Example of tracking museum visitors in real time

Pressure-Based MSI

Another important sensing and tracking strategy is based on arrays of pressure sensors. This is particularly true in those applications where illumination conditions or the spatial conformation are too severe to apply vision-based people sensing (for example, if it is needed to implement dark rooms where special purpose interactions can be enacted). In particular it is possible to implement floating floors tessellated by means of suitable tiles over a bed of pressure sensors. One typical configuration uses four pressure sensors for each squared tile used to pave the ground. In such a way, by reading the pressure values on the four vertices of each tile and by considering the neighbouring tiles (the neighbour dimension depends on the tile dimension), it is possible to estimate the position and the number of persons on the floating floor with sub-tile accuracy (see Figure 28.2).

The Control Subsystem

At start-up, the control subsystem loads the VirtualMuseumGraph and extracts the whole description of the various virtual rooms inside the museum. Each virtual room in turn contains the description of the physical environment related to the MSIs and of the corresponding sensors, sounds, actuators and behaviours. These data and information are used to initialize the social interfaces and all the physical devices needed to enable museum reactivity. After the initial housekeeping, all the global behaviours are started. These behaviours can vary from virtual room to virtual room, so that different tracking and interaction strategies can run in different areas of a single museum. For example, in a certain area there can be a pressure-based MSI, while in another zone a vision-based MSI. The area that uses pressure sensing is described by the corresponding virtual room abstract structure; it also specifies which are the areas where interactions can be started by the reactive museum. The stagegraph contained in the virtual room structure describes the areas. When the global behaviour of the virtual room detects some visitors inside a behaviour enabling bound, it starts the behaviour that corresponds to that bound and looks for its firing criteria and conditions. If both of them are met, the behaviour is

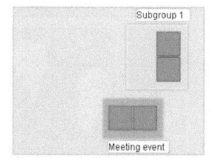

Figure 28.2   Events detected by pressure-based MSI

fired and the corresponding stage is activated. The stage contains the description of the actuators and sounds that the fired behaviour uses to interact with the visitors. Needless to say, the multiple enabling bounds can be activated by the same or by different sub-groups of visitors, so multiple behaviours can be running at the same time. In the same way a specific behaviour can affect multiple stages so that multiple parallel modifications of the environment can be obtained (for example it is possible to start a presentation sound or a background sound in a specific place while switching on lights or videos in another location). This is how the museum can react in parallel to multiple solicitations by multiple contemporaneous users.

The Museum of Monticchiello

The previously described system is fully integrated into the MuseumNet© architecture as a specialized module for museum reactivity. This architecture is currently used inside the Museum of Monticchiello (a little village near by Siena, Italy) devoted to old theatrical arts. The museum hosts two different MSIs; one is pressure-based and the other is vision-based. At the entrance, visitors go inside a dark room where some ancient objects, sounds and videos are presented. Special illumination effects at the corners allow visitors to progressively discover the environment and to see ancient things. At the same time projections over the walls and from the floor (some tiles are semitransparent) at different locations are used to illustrate various aspects of the ancient theatrical art. It is important to note that the presentation does not follow a predetermined path: it is the museum that reacts to the visitors, depending on their movements as detected through the array of pressure sensors. In this way each visit is a unique experience developing from the social behaviour of the current visitor group (see Figure 28.3).

From the dark room, visitors go into a tunnel which leads them to a vision-based MSI. The room has four cameras at the ceiling corners that are continuously looking for visitors. At the centre of the room a very ancient sink has been equipped with hidden interactive presentation devices. In particular, videos can be shown at the

Figure 28.3   Pressure-based MSI during implementation

bottom of the well, while sounds can be played through multiple rings of speakers hidden all around the sink border. These devices are used to show images, descriptive narrations and videos, and to create 3D sound effects. The cameras are used to track the visitors' position in real time so that the control system constantly knows their spatial distribution on the floor. The positional information is used to enable reactive events during the visit. For example, when a predetermined number of persons enter the room, a background appealing sound is enabled to attract their attention towards the sink that is in the middle of the room. When a suitable number of persons are near the sink (the MSI uses vision to verify that there are sufficient people), video presentations start and are projected on the well bottom. The video presentations depend on the number of visitors around the sink (that is, the museum reacts in different way depending on people behaviour). If another group of visitors concentrates in another position while the remainder are around the sink, the museum reacts by starting a video presentation over the nearby wall, while the presentation at the sink continues. If, after some time, the people around the sink still remain there, the museum reacts by stopping the video on the well bottom and starting a sound while opening a little hidden vane on the opposite part of the room. Again the interactions are not predetermined: they basically depend on people's behaviour; moreover multiple interactive presentations can go on in parallel targeted at different sub-groups of visitors.

Conclusions

In this paper we have presented an innovative module that has been integrated in the MuseumNet© architecture. The module enables the use of multi-sensor social Interfaces inside museums. Social interfaces are new interaction metaphors that allow multiple visitors to interact in parallel with multiple computers; moreover, the interactions can be autonomously initiated by the system, so enabling interaction mechanisms completely different from traditional approaches. The system has been implemented in practice at the Museum of Monticchiello, near Siena, devoted to ancient theatrical arts. In the near future a support subsystem for emotional agents will be added to the proposed architecture. The MSIs will have their artificial psychology. This fact will allow more effective interaction activities by enabling 'motivational behaviours' based on the MSIs' own internal state.

Notes

1   Pentland, A.P. (1998) 'Smart Rooms: Machine Understanding of Human Behaviour', in *Computer Vision for Human-Machine Interaction*, R. Cipolla and A. Pentland (eds), Cambridge University Press, 1998.
2   Mecocci, A. (2001) 'MuseumNet: 3D virtual environments and wireless appliances for improved cultural experiences', EVA 2001 Electronic Imaging and the Visual Arts, Florence, *Conference Proceedings*, pp.137–42, Pitagora Editrice, Bologna, 2001.
3   Sowizral, H., Rushforth, K. and Deering, M. (2000) *Java 3D API Specification*, 2nd edition, Addison Wesley.

4   Moschetti, F., Mecocci, A. and Sorci, M. (2001) 'Motion estimation for digital video coding based on a statistical approach', *Proceedings of IEEE-ICICS2001*, Information, Communications & Signal Processing, Singapore, 2001.

Chapter 29

Design of a Hand-Held Interactive Support for Museum Visitors

C. Ciavarella and F. Paternò

Abstract

The growing availability of small devices has raised an interesting discussion on how to exploit them to support users in various contexts of use. We propose a solution that can be easily adopted for museum visitors. The basic elements are the use of a multimedia PDA (Personal Digital Assistant) whose main purpose is to support a user who can move freely about within a museum. The structure of the user interface allows users to easily orient themselves through appropriate visual representations and then sees to providing the information that would be of be interest to them by exploiting the multimedia capabilities of the device.

Introduction

The growing availability of small devices whose computational and interactive resources are continuously increasing in terms of power and capacity has raised an interesting discussion on how to exploit them to support users in various contexts of use. In this work we consider users who freely move about a building (in particular, in a museum). In these environments the most effective support is currently provided through either interactive multimedia kiosks or interactive audio recorders. In the former case the main limitation is that the kiosk does not allow the user to move while receiving information, whereas the latter allow the user only to hear predefined texts associated with each work.

In the meantime, at a research level an increasing interest in location-aware systems has arisen with the goal of better assisting users. However, systems based on automatic generation of location-aware information suffer from the limitations of adaptive systems, in which often users interact with an interface that changes in the attempt to better support them, but which in doing so actually causes disorientation. For example, one typical problem with location-aware, indoor systems is that they can automatically generate information regarding the closest work of art while the user is actually looking at one that is located farther away. In addition, location-aware systems often require technology that is either expensive or difficult to install in a widespread manner or they do not work perfectly in all circumstances. For example, infrareds need to be installed for each work of art and require that the emitters and the receivers are lined up in order to communicate.

In our work we have designed an application that aims to overcome such limitations. We propose a solution that can be easily adopted by many museums without requiring difficult-to-install technology. The basic elements are the use of a multimedia PDA (without the support of location-aware technology) whose main purpose is to support a user who can move freely about within a museum. The user interface is structured in such a way as to allow users to easily orient themselves and then provides the information that can be interesting for them. In this paper we discuss and report on our initial design and the improved design based on the user feedback.

Our Initial Design

In our approach the design is driven by three main elements: the context of use that includes both the device used for the interaction and the environment where such interaction occurs, the tasks users wish to perform and the objects they need to manipulate in their performance (both interface and domain objects).

Context of Use

For the context of use, we consider both the interaction resources used and the environment where the user performs the tasks.

The application has been developed on a Compaq Ipaq 3660, with Windows CE and additional 64 MB (megabytes) Flash Memory Card. We have used Embedded Visual C++ 3.0 as programming language and the Microsoft Foundation Class toolkit for the user interface development. We decided to use text-to-speech synthesis for supporting audio comments. Unfortunately, the possibility of dynamic text-to-speech generation is not supported in these environments because the necessary libraries are lacking for Windows CE. In addition, the synthesized Italian voice was considered too unpleasant and was replaced with audio-recorded comments.

At the time of writing, the application contains description of about 130 works of art, each of them with an associated JPEG picture (dimensions are about 140 x 140 pixels). The audio files are in MP3 format. For the English version we have used text-to-speech provided by Text Aloud MP3. Overall the application requires about 30 MB of memory.

The application has been developed for the Marble Museum at Carrara. The managers of the museum decided to provide their visitors with information additional to that contained in traditional labels. They often had the problem of finding guides able to provide such information and in some cases the guides were not able to communicate with foreign people. The structure of the museum forces to some extent the order of visit among the rooms. Such rooms contain many types of objects, from works by the ancient Romans to pieces of quarrying technology of the past century. Thus, visitors need support to interactively select those more interesting for them and to receive related information.

Tasks

In the design of the user interface we considered three types of tasks that users can perform in the context considered:

Orientation within the museum   For this purpose three levels of spatial information are provided: a museum map, a section map and, for each physical environment composing the section, a map with icons indicating the main pieces of work available in the room and their location. By selecting such icons the picture of the related element is displayed along with some basic information and the corresponding audio description is activated. The purpose of the picture is not to show the details of the work of art (that is supposed to be in front of the user), but to allow users to check that the information they are receiving relates to the work that they are viewing.

Control of the user interface   For example, it should allow visitors to change the volume of the audio comments, to stop and start them, and to move through the various levels of detail of the museum description.

Access to museum information   Also this is provided at different abstraction levels (museum, section, physical environment, single work).

At any time the application was able to highlight where the users were in the museum area, assuming they were in the same room as the works last selected. The orientation information was triggered by selecting the 'i' button on the bottom menu-bar that appears when the map of a physical environment is displayed.

Objects

The information regarding the museum and the works that it contains is provided using both the audio and the visual channels. The visual information is mainly used to allow users to orient themselves and receive some supplementary information. It provides information at different logical levels:

- The museum: it displays a map that shows the logical organization and the physical structure of the museum
- Sections: the map of each thematic section of the museum is provided; when it covers multiple physical environments it is possible to select each of them to get more detailed related information
- Environments: they are either rooms or separate environments partitioned with various techniques; the system provides a map with icons indicating where the main objects of interest are located
- Works of art: in this case a picture and basic information are provided.

Since the museum considered is an interdisciplinary museum that contains various types of works, different icons are used to represent each type, as shown in Figure 29.1.

for showcases containing historical artefacts, models or reproductions

     for pictures or photos hung on the museum walls

     for capitals

     for representing sculptures

     for the marble exposition

     for the reading-desks

Figure 29.1   Icons for various types of works of art

An alternative solution would have been to use pictures of the works considered in the room map instead of icons. However, the resolution of the PDA (240 x 320) would have made it difficult to interpret such images. Figure 29.2 shows an example of a room map annotated with icons highlighting the main works of interest. The doors represented in the map are interactive and allow the user to change the room representation in the PDA (while physically moving in the new room).

Presentation of Information and Navigation

The audio part has been implemented, reflecting the logical structure of the necessary information. There are comments introducing the museum, its sections, each environment and each work located in them. They are provided in two languages: the first is English, using text-to-speech synthesis. The resulting audio message is somewhat metallic, but clearly understandable even by non-native English speakers. The other language is Italian, for which a pre-recorded female voice was used for the comments because the synthesized speech was considered unpleasant.

The resulting navigation was based on the museum map. The user starts the visit from the museum map. Then, they select the section of interest. Lastly, in the section map they can select the physical environment of interest and at any time they can go to the museum map to select another area. Figure 29.2 shows an example of a sequence of accesses.

Figure 29.2   Levels of navigation in the first version of the guide

The Improved Version

The initial version of the application was made available to museum visitors at the beginning of the summer, 2001. This allowed us to perform a usability evaluation involving many users. The test took place in the Marble Museum of Carrara during the summer, when the number of visitors is highest, and it involved 95 users, 34 of whom were Italian. More details regarding how the test was performed and its results are provided in our report.[1]

The test highlighted the need for:

- a different way to navigate that would allow users to orient themselves better
- better highlighting of how to get into and out of the rooms
- different ways to provide help information
- supporting use of videos played through the PDA to enrich the user experience.

Taking into account the results of the user tests we developed a new version. We decided to present information about user location differently. We took into account that users always start their visit from a given point and that the structure of the museum imposes a linear path to the visit. Although visitors can at any time go up and down along this path and get disoriented, they cannot take a different route. Thus, we decided to have the PDA displaying where they are at the outset of the visit. Next, after having shown some basic information on how to use the application (such as the meaning of the icons), the application displays a map of the first museum section while providing audio information about it. Sections are made up of one or more rooms with a common theme. Then, they can select a room and receive indications as to where it is, followed by its map with the possibility of selecting specific works of art and receiving related information. In the new user interface we used arrowheads on each door in the map of the room to clearly highlight the suggested order of access. In this version, when users move to the next room they can just select the related door in the map and the new room map will appear. If a new section is encountered, then a general map with related information is first provided and subsequently a map of the selected room is displayed.

One of the main differences with respect to the previous version of the application is that the museum map no longer drives user access to information. However, the overall museum map is still available on request in the event that visitors do not want to follow the path suggested by the physical museum structure.

Conclusions and Future Work

The new version is now available to the museum visitors. We are planning a new evaluation study with revised questionnaires and automatic analysis of logs of user interactions.

Technology for location detection is improving in terms of both cost and accuracy. Its introduction will be investigated in the near future, at least to automatically identify the room where the user is.

Future work will be dedicated to identifying adaptive features of the application that can increase the users' interest without disorienting them.

Acknowledgments

We gratefully thank Assessorato alla Cultura, Comune di Carrara for their support.

Note

1   Ciavarella, C. and Paternò, F. (2001) *Design of a Handheld Interactive Support*, CNUCE Internal Report 2001-012, November 2001.

Chapter 30

The Impact of Haptic 'Touching' Technology on Cultural Applications

Stephen Brewster

Abstract

New technologies from the area of virtual reality (VR) now allow computer users to use their sense of touch to feel virtual objects. Touch is a very powerful sense but it has so far been neglected in computing. State-of-the-art haptic (or force-feedback) devices allow users to feel and touch virtual objects with a high degree of realism. An artefact's surface properties can be modelled so that someone using a haptic device could feel it as a solid, three-dimensional object with different textures, hardness or softness. These haptic devices could have a large impact on museums; for example, making very fragile objects available to scholars; allowing visitors who live far from museums to feel objects at a distance; letting visually impaired and blind people feel exhibits that are normally behind glass; and allowing museums to show off a range of artefacts that are currently in storage due to a lack of space. This paper describes the background to haptics, some of the possibilities of haptic technology and how they might be applied to cultural applications.

Introduction

Haptic technology provides the possibility of widening access to information and artefacts held in museums. Haptic, or force-feedback, devices allow people to use their sense of touch in computer-based applications. Until recently, most computer-based simulations of objects were visual. The user might don a headset that presented a three-dimensional image or look at a computer screen to see an object. There might also be some sound to improve the display. One key element that is missing is the ability to feel the object – to get a sense of how heavy it is, what it is made of, or its surface texture. Haptic technologies try to solve this problem. An artefact's surface properties can be modelled so that someone using a haptic device can feel it as a solid, three-dimensional object with different textures, hardness or softness.

There are many applications for this new technology. In this paper potential uses in cultural applications will be discussed, along with some examples of how the technology is being used in research projects at Glasgow to give some idea of what its capabilities are. To begin, some of the main terms used in the study of haptics and our sense of touch are described, followed by an overview of the main technologies currently available.

Haptic Perception

Haptics is a general term relating to the sense of touch. This is very broad and there are many component parts to the global sense of touch.[1] Not all of these parts are well understood as there has been much less psychological research into touch than into the senses of hearing or vision.[2] This section outlines some of the key aspects of touch.

The word 'haptic' has grown in popularity with the advent of touch in computing. The human haptic system consists of the entire sensory, motor and cognitive components of the body–brain system. It is therefore closest to the understood meaning of 'proprioceptive' (see Figure 30.1).[3] Under this umbrella term, however, fall several significant distinctions. Most important of these is the division between cutaneous and kinesthetic information[4] (Figure 30.1). There is some overlap between these two categories; critically both can convey the sensation of contact with an object. The distinction becomes important, however, when we attempt to describe the technology. In brief, a haptic device provides position input like a mouse but also stimulates the sense of touch by applying output to the user in the form of forces. Tactile devices affect the skin surface by stretching it or pulling it, for example. Force feedback devices affect the finger, hand, or body position and movement. Using these definitions (summarized in Figure 30.1), devices can be categorized and understood by the sensory system that they primarily affect.

Term	Definition
Haptic	Relating to the sense of touch.
Proprioceptive	Relating to sensory information about the state of the body (including cutaneous, kinesthetic and vestibular sensations).
Vestibular	Pertaining to the perception of head position, acceleration and deceleration.
Kinesthetic	Meaning the feeling of motion. Relating to sensations originating in muscles, tendons and joints.
Cutaneous	Pertaining to the skin itself or the skin as a sense organ. Includes sensation of pressure, temperature and pain.
Tactile	Pertaining to the cutaneous sense but more specifically the sensation of pressure rather than temperature or pain.
Force Feedback	Relating to the mechanical production of information sensed by the human kinesthetic system.

Figure 30.1   Definitions of main terms used when describing haptics and the sense of touch
Source: Oakley et al. (2000)

Haptic Technology

Haptic devices allow users to feel virtual objects.[5] Minsky et al. (in Blattner and Dannenburg[6]) describe the technology thus:

> Force display technology works by using mechanical actuators to apply forces to the user. By simulating the physics of the user's virtual world, we can compute these forces in real-time, and then send them to the actuators so that the user feels them.

What this really means is that a person using a haptic device can feel a simulation of a solid object as if it was really in front of them.[7,8]

Basic haptic devices have been used in research laboratories for some time (going back to the 1960s for some robotic tele-operator systems).[9] However, as Stone also suggests

> ... it is only quite recently that haptic technologies have appeared that are capable of delivering believable sensory stimuli at a reasonable cost, using human interface devices of a practical size.

It is more recently still that these devices have become commercially available and robust enough to be used by the general public. Burdea[10] provides a good review of haptic technology with details of the mechanics of most of the major devices.

The main haptic device used in research is the PHANToM from SensAble Technologies (see Figure 30.2).[11] This is a very high-resolution, six-degrees-of-freedom (DOF) device in which the user holds the end of a motor-controlled, jointed arm. (With respect to haptic devices, degrees-of-freedom refers to the number of dimensions of movement: for the PHANToM these are x,y and z dimensions plus

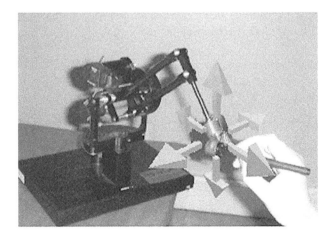

Figure 30.2   PHANToM 1.0 haptic device (from SensAble Technologies, www.sensable.com)

pitch, roll and yaw.) It provides a programmable sense of touch that allows users to feel textures and shapes of virtual objects and modulate and deform objects with a very high degree of realism. In Figure 30.2, overlaid arrows show possible movements. The device is shown with the user holding a stylus: a thimble attachment (into which the user inserts a finger) is also available. One of the key (and most compelling) features of the PHANToM is that it can model free-floating three-dimensional objects – for example, a user of the PHANToM could feel an object such as a Roman helmet from all sides – front, back, top, bottom – just as if holding it in his/her own hand. In our classification from Figure 30.1, it (and the Wingman device described below) is a force-feedback device, as it applies forces to the user and can resist his/her movements or even move the user around.

There are several alternative devices available. For example, the Wingman force-feedback mouse from Logitech is a simpler alternative to the PHANToM.[12] It only provides 2 DOF (*x* and *y* dimensions, like a normal desktop mouse) but is much smaller and can be used as a replacement to a standard PC mouse (see Figure 30.3). This does not allow the exploration of free-floating objects in 3D but can allow the representation of flat surfaces and edges (as might be found on a coin, for example). The mouse is attached to a base that replaces the mouse mat and contains the motors used to provide forces back to the user.

Cost of Haptic Devices

The most sophisticated devices can cost a large amount of money. The PHANToM in Figure 30.2 is generally considered one of the highest fidelity and most flexible devices on the market but currently costs over £20,000. This is clearly impractical for many individuals and museums to buy. On the other hand the Logitech Wingman force-feedback mouse currently costs only £60 and will run on a standard PC, making it a much more practical solution. There are some devices that are cheaper still: for example, the 'rumble packs' that can be added to computer games consoles provide only limited (1 DOF) feedback but can cost as little as £15.

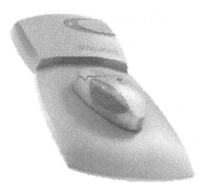

Figure 30.3   Logitech Wingman force-feedback mouse (www.logitech.com)

The prices of devices will fall in the future. There is a large demand for force-feedback controllers for games (a range of joysticks and steering wheels are currently available that allow users to feel when a gun is fired or when a car crashes). This is increasing demand and thus lowering cost. This also means that many devices are built to be robust to withstand harsh treatment in games, making them good for public displays of the type that might be found in a museum.

Some Limitations of Current Haptic Technology

Even the best haptic devices are limited in some respects. One of the main limitations is that all contact is through a single point (like a single finger or a probe). There are no whole-hand devices that yet provide high-fidelity force-feedback. This limits the range of applications that haptic devices are currently good for.

A further problem is that cutaneous feedback (see Figure 30.1) is very limited in most haptic devices as they stimulate the sense of touch by applying output to the user in the form of forces and movement. Subtle surface textures are normally perceived cutaneously as tiny deformations in the surface of the skin. This is very difficult to do mechanically and most haptic devices do not do it at all. This limits the range of surface textures that can be displayed. However, it is still possible to model some surprisingly subtle things. For example, Dillon et al.[13] are modelling textiles using the Wingman mouse and Crossan et al.[14] are using the PHANToM to train students in medical examinations (see below). McGee et al. are trying to solve the problem by using other senses – they are investigating the use of sound to add in some of the cutaneous feedback missing from the PHANToM by substituting another sense.[15]

The Use of Haptic Technology for Cultural Applications

Haptic technology is already being used in museums, but on a small scale in very specialized situations. One such is the University of Southern California's Interactive Art Museum (digimuse.usc.edu). This museum has begun to look at the use of the PHANToM device within the museum to allow visitors to feel artefacts. As McLaughlin et al.[16] say:

> Our team believes that the 'hands-off' policies that museums must impose limit appreciation of three-dimensional objects, where full comprehension and understanding rely on the sense of touch as well as vision. Haptic interfaces will allow fuller appreciation of three-dimensional objects without jeopardizing conservation standards.[17]

This is one of the key reasons for using haptic technology – to improve the experience of objects and artefacts that visitors have. Just looking at exhibits, even as 3D graphical models, is limiting. If allowed, most visitors would immediately pick up an object, feel it, trace its shape and surface texture, feel its weight.[18] Just having a visual presentation misses out on much important information that can be gained by touch. Haptics allows the visual displays to be extended to make them more realistic, useful and engaging for visitors.

Four main benefits might come from the use of haptics. A number of these extend the use of graphics and 3D graphical models already used in some museums; others provide new experiences that are currently not available.

Allowing Rare, Fragile or Dangerous Objects to be Handled

Objects which are very fragile, rare or dangerous may not be handled by museum visitors or scholars. Visual models can be created but there are many aspects of the object that this does not capture – for example, how heavy does it feel? How rough is its surface? To solve this problem objects could be haptically modelled and then visitors or researchers could feel them using a haptic device. This means that these objects can be made available to large numbers of people.

Allowing Long-Distance Visitors

There are many potential visitors to a museum who cannot get to visit. They might live far away or be immobile, for example. If objects are haptically modelled and then made available on a museum's website, then other access methods become possible. A school could buy a haptic device so that children can continue to feel and manipulate objects after they have been for a visit. A scholar could examine the haptic aspects of an object from a university across the world. With a haptic device at home a visitor could feel and manipulate the object via the Internet.

Improving Access for Visually Disabled People

Visually impaired and blind people often lose out when going to museums because objects are behind glass. There are over 1 million people in the UK who are blind or partially sighted.[19] The UK's Disability Discrimination Act legally requires museums to provide access for people with visual disabilities but this can be very difficult to do.[20] Some museums provide special exhibits that blind people can feel. However, these exhibits are usually small and may not contain the objects that the blind visitor is interested in (there is also the problem of fragility from the point above). With haptic technologies such visitors could feel and interact with a much wider range of objects, enriching their experiences in a museum. Many normally sighted users would also enjoy the opportunity to touch museum exhibits.

Increasing the Number of Artefacts on Display

With limited amounts of space, museums can only show a limited range of artefacts from their collections. If other objects that are not on show are modelled graphically and haptically then visitors could experience these on computer, without taking up museum space. With several haptic devices a museum could allow many people to feel objects at the same time, sharing the experience.

Potential Problems with Haptic Devices in Museums

One of the main problems with devices such as the PHANToM is cost. As they are so expensive it is impractical to use them on a large scale. As discussed above, prices are falling so this may not be a problem in the future. It is therefore important to investigate the use of such devices now.

Another problem is reliability and robustness. Most of the devices are fairly reliable and robust because they have been built for games or other demanding environments. We have used our PHANToM devices at university open days and careers fairs many times with lots of people using them over long periods of time, and have had few problems. However, they are always supervised by an attendant. This will be costly to do in a museum for a long period of time.

Projects at Glasgow

To give an indication of some of the possibilities of haptics for cultural applications, some of the research being undertaken at Glasgow will be outlined. Not all of these applications are cultural ones but they do show the capabilities of haptic devices and some of the different types of things for which they can be used.

'Senses in Touch II'

The Computing Science Department and Hunterian Museum at Glasgow University recently completed a haptic museum exhibit. This built on a previous exhibition held in the museum in 1998, called *Senses in Touch*, which allowed blind people to feel real objects from the museum. The *Senses in Touch II* exhibit was designed to allow blind and partially sighted museum visitors to feel virtual objects in the collection via a PC and Wingman haptic mouse (see Figure 30.3).[21] It was particularly aimed at blind and partially sighted school children visiting the museum. Figure 30.4 shows some screen shots from the exhibit (it also contained synthesized speech to give information to blind users). The top left image shows the menu of objects that are available to feel. The right and bottom images show the details of two particular objects (an adze[22] and some Egyptian hieroglyphics).

Objects were chosen for the exhibit based on the nature of the Wingman mouse – it can only present objects in two dimensions. Objects such as coins, engraved Egyptian hieroglyphics and the cast of a dinosaur footprint were used as they had strong edges that could be felt, but were two-dimensional. Each object was modelled by using a greyscale image, with the different levels of grey in the image representing areas of different heights (white = high, black = low). Crossing an edge in which the grey level increased corresponded to moving over a raised edge, and an oppositional force was applied (to the user this felt like moving over an edge). Conversely, moving between two areas in which the grey level decreased caused a force to be applied towards the lower area. This gave a good sense of a range of different heights using the mouse. This method was simplistic but worked well for certain types of objects:

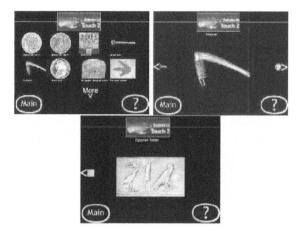

Figure 30.4   Screenshots from the *Senses in Touch II* museum exhibit

- Objects with many varied textures: for example, the rope work in the adze provided an interesting contrast in texture compared to the wooden handle. Likewise, a William Hunter coin provided a smooth coin background in contrast to ridged hair.
- Objects with strong, simple edges: for example, the outside of the coins or the edges of an individual hieroglyphic symbol.

The exhibit was designed iteratively, with input from experts and users at each stage to make sure that it was effective and usable by our target user group. In particular, there was detailed input from the Glasgow and West of Scotland Society for the Blind (GWSSB). The exhibit was put into the museum for testing for a period of several weeks and the designers conducted walkthroughs and questionnaires with visitors to assess its effectiveness. Fifty people evaluated the system and 26 questionnaires were returned. Unfortunately, over the time the evaluations took place no blind school children came to the museum, so the evaluations were conducted on sighted people (although evaluations were done with blind people at the GWSSB). The results from the evaluations showed that people in general liked the exhibit and could use it easily.[23] Children in particular found it very engaging. An interesting observation from the museum was the use of the virtual exhibits in conjunction with the real ones. The computer running the exhibit was located near a tablet of Egyptian hieroglyphics, which visitors were not allowed to touch. However, the hieroglyphics were modelled in the *Senses in Touch II* exhibit. The result of this was that children would look at the real hieroglyphics, go to the computer to feel the virtual version, go back to the hieroglyphics to have another look, and so on. In that situation the proximity meant that the real and virtual exhibits worked very well together. The children really wanted to know what the hieroglyphics felt like and the virtual exhibit allowed them to find out.

MultiVis – Presenting Graphical Information in Haptics

An area of research interest at Glasgow is making information accessible to blind and partially sighted people. *Senses in Touch II* was part of this, as is the MultiVis project. Here the aim is to provide access to visualization techniques (such as graphs, tables and 3D plots) that are currently very hard for blind people to use. These occur in many areas of everyday life and could range, for example, from a graph showing the value of the pound against the dollar to technical information used in the fields of mathematics, science and engineering. There are currently only limited methods for presenting information non-visually to blind people (mainly Braille and synthetic speech) and these do not provide an equivalent speed and ease of use to their graphical counterparts.[24]

As part of the MultiVis project we have developed a system to allow line graphs and bar charts to be presented via a haptic device (in this case both the PHANToM and Wingman mouse are being used). The lines are grooves cut into a virtual haptic surface and users can run their fingers along these to feel the shape of the line (see Figure 30.5). Subjects in experimental evaluations of the graphs have used them very successfully. They were easily able to find maximum, minimum and intersection points. For tables the value in each cell is mapped to height so that a surface is created. Users can then move over the surface, easily finding high and low points.

Haptic devices used in this way allow users to interact directly with their data – to get an overview of a graph users could just run their fingers along it. This has many advantages over raised paper graphs that are used by blind people.[25] For example, our system is dynamic so that we can render a haptic scene in real-time, rather than having to wait for a raised paper graph to be printed. Our scenes can be fully three-dimensional rather than just raised lines. Users can also change the graphs themselves; for example, by changing the value of X in the graph and seeing what effect it has, just as a sighted person might do with pen and paper. For a museum these techniques would allow information about exhibits to be presented to blind visitors more effectively. For example, a graph of geological era, showing how landscapes change over time, is easily understood by a sighted person but presenting this graphical information to a blind person is very difficult. The techniques

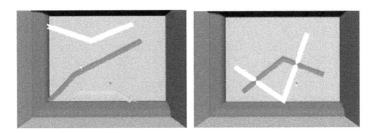

Figure 30.5   Screenshots from the MultiVis system showing two line graphs with multiple lines

developed for MultiVis would allow it to be presented to a blind person in an effective way.

Veterinary Training Applications

The Department of Computing Science is working in collaboration with the School of Veterinary Medicine at Glasgow to provide a training system for veterinary students using haptics.[26] Medicine (in particular surgical training) was one of the first areas to adopt haptic technology,[27] especially in the area of minimally invasive surgery training. Learning how to examine and operate on humans and animals is difficult and potentially dangerous for the patients. For the Veterinary School, using a simulator:

- improves safety for the animals
- reduces cost as fewer animals need to be kept at the School
- allows the students more time to practice examinations
- provides access to rare or unusual cases that the student might not encounter during normal study.

The Horse Ovary Palpation Simulator (HOPS, see Figure 30.6) allows veterinary students to learn how to perform ovarian palpation to assess the stage of ovulation. This is an important but difficult technique to learn. The student must learn to discriminate between the different surface features on an ovary, to size them and how hard to press. With a simulator all of this can be done without danger to an animal. The system uses the PHANToM (Figure 30.2) and the ovaries are modelled as free-floating objects. In Figure 30.6, the bright dot in the centre is the cursor.

The HOPS system shows the subtlety that is available via haptic devices. The ovaries are soft, the surface features small and they move whilst being examined, but they can be modelled effectively so that students can learn how to perform examinations. For a museum a haptic simulator (along with a visual display) might allow visitors to try out activities that would normally be too dangerous or difficult to do, expanding the range of experiences offered.

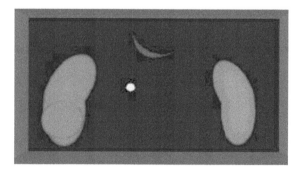

Figure 30.6   Screenshot from the HOPS system showing two ovaries being examined

Conclusions

Touch plays a key role when examining objects in the real world but until recently it was not possible to use this realistically in virtual environments and computer-based displays. This has meant that some of these displays lacked realism and usefulness. Now haptic technologies are available that let museums add this missing aspect back into their computer-based exhibits. They allow the visual displays to be extended to make them more realistic, useful and engaging for visitors and scholars. This has many potential benefits for museums; for example in allowing greater access to rare and fragile objects, allowing access for people who live far away and cannot easily get to the museum, improving the opportunities for blind and visually impaired people and increasing the number of artefacts on display. Haptic devices have a lot to offer museums and are likely to have a big impact on the quality and usefulness of computer-based exhibits.

Acknowledgements

Part of this work was supported by EPSRC grant GR/M44866. Thanks to Virtual Presence for their support. The work on *Senses in Touch II* was done by Emma Gibson, Jehane Penfold-Ward, Stuart Tasker, John Williamson and Colin Wood and was run in collaboration with Jim Devine from the Hunterian Museum.

Notes

1 Lederman, S.J. and Klatzky, R.L. (1987) 'Hand movements: a window into haptic object recognition', *Cognitive Psychology*, vol. 19, pp. 342–68.
2 Goldstein, B.E. (1999) *Sensation and Perception*, 5th edn., Brookes Cole Publishing Co., Belmont, CA.
3 Reber, A.S. (1985) *The Penguin Dictionary of Psychology*, Penguin Books, London.
4 Oakley, I., McGee, M., Brewster, S.A. and Gray, P.D. (2000) 'Putting the feel in look and feel', in *Proceedings of ACM CHI 2000*, The Hague, Netherlands, ACM Press, Addison-Wesley, pp. 415–22.
5 Massie, T. and Salisbury, K. (1994) 'The PHANToM Haptic Interface: A Device for Probing Virtual Objects', in *Proceedings of the ASME Winter Annual Meeting*, Symposium on Haptic Interfaces for Virtual Environments and Teleoperator Systems, Chicago, IL.
6 Blattner, M. and Dannenberg, R.B. (eds) (1992) *Multimedia Interface Design*, ACM Press, Addison-Wesley, New York.
7 Ramstein, C. and Hayward, V. (1994) 'The Pantograph: A large workspace haptic device for multi-modal human-computer interaction', in *Proceedings of ACM CHI 1994*, Boston, MA, ACM Press, Addison-Wesley, pp. 57–8.
8 Vince, J. (1995) *Virtual Reality Systems*, Addison-Wesley, Wokingham, UK.
9 Stone, R. (2000) 'Haptic feedback: A potted history, from telepresence to virtual reality', in *The First International Workshop on Haptic Human–Computer Interaction*, Glasgow, UK, *Springer-Verlag Lecture Notes in Computer Science*, pp. 1–7.
10 Burdea, G. (1996) *Force and Touch Feedback for Virtual Reality*, Wiley Interscience, New York.

11   Massie and Salisbury (1994), as above.
12   Latest information is that the Wingman mouse is reportedly no longer in production. It has been replaced by the iFeel mouse which is actually a different and apparently improved product (and currently only US$39.95).
13   Dillon, P., Moody, W., Bartlett, R., Scully, P. and Morgan, R. (2000) 'Simulation of tactile sensation through sensory evaluation of textiles when viewed as a digital image', *The First International Workshop on Haptic Human–Computer Interaction*, Glasgow, UK, *Springer-Verlag Lecture Notes in Computer Science*, pp. 63–8.
14   Crossan, A., Brewster, S.A. and Glendye, A. (2000) 'A horse ovary palpation simulator for veterinary training', in *Proceedings of PURS2000*, Zurich, Switzerland, pp. 79–86.
15   McGee, M.R., Gray, P.D. and Brewster, S.A. (2001) 'Haptic perception of virtual roughness', in *Extended Abstracts of ACM CHI 2001*, Seattle, WA, ACM Press, pp. 155–6.
16   McLaughlin, M., Sukhatme, G., Shahabi, C. and Hespanha, J. *Use of Haptics for the Enhanced Musuem Website-USC Interactive Art Museum*, University of Southern California Interactive Art Museum, last accessed May 2001. http://digimuse.usc.edu/MuseumRelatedResearch1.htm.
17   See also Margaret McLaughlin paper from the EVA 2000 Edinburgh Conference Proceedings.
18   Lederman and Klatzky (1987), as above.
19   RNIB, website of the Royal National Institute for the Blind, last accessed May 2001, http://www.rnib.co.uk.
20   HMSO, *Disability Discrimination Act*, website of Her Majesty's Stationery Office, last accessed May 2001, http://www.hmso.gov.uk/acts/acts1995/1995050.htm.
21   Gibson, E., Penfold-Ward, J., Tasker, S., Williamson, J. and Wood, C. (2001) *Senses in Touch II*. University of Glasgow, Third-year project report.
22   A carpenter's tool similar to an axe.
23   Gibson et al. (2001), as above.
24   Edwards, A.D.N. (1995) (ed.) *Extra-Ordinary Human–Computer Interaction*, Cambridge University Press, Cambridge, UK.
25   Kurtz, M. (1997) 'Rendering drawings for interactive haptic perception', in *Proceedings of ACM CHI 1997*, Atlanta, GA, ACM Press, Addison-Wesley, pp. 423–30.
26   Crossan et al. (2000), as above.
27   Bro-Nielsen, M., Tasto, J.L., Cunningham, R. and Merril, G.L. (1999) 'Preop endoscopic simulator: A PC-based immersive training system for bronchoscopy', in *Proceedings of Medicine meets VR*.

For details of our work see http://www.dcs.gla.ac.uk/~stephen

Chapter 31

The Gulliver Project: Performers and Visitors

Anton Nijholt

Abstract

This paper discusses two projects in our research environment. The first is the Gulliver project, an ambitious project conceived by some artists connected to our research efforts. The second is the Aveiro project, also ambitious, but with goals that can be achieved because of technological developments, rather than being dependent on artistic and 'political' (for which read 'financial') sources. Both projects are on virtual and augmented reality. The main goal is to design inhabited environments, where 'inhabited' refers to autonomous agents and agents that represent humans, real-time or off-line, visiting the virtual environment and interacting with other agents. The Gulliver environment has been designed by two artists, Matjaž Štuk and Alena Hudcovicová. The Aveiro project is a research effort of a group of researchers trying to design models of intelligence and interaction underlying the behaviour of (groups of) agents inhabiting virtual worlds. In this paper we survey the current state of both projects and we discuss current and future attempts to have music performances by virtual and real performers in these environments.

Introduction

There are many ways to have (real-time) art and music performances in virtual worlds. Here we use 'virtual' to stand for distributed 2D or 3D environments where visualization of environment and activities is an important issue. Many examples of these environments exist. They have developed from chat or game worlds, from computer-supported cooperative work environments, teleconferencing environments etc. In these environments human-like objects have been introduced, sometimes standing for a visitor and controlled by the visitor but also sometimes standing for a virtual person, who has been introduced in the environment to perform and visualize a certain task, in interaction with one or more visitors.

We have developed several virtual worlds. One of them is the virtual theatre, as part of our Agents in Virtual Environments (Aveiro) project. The theatre is a virtual 3D VRML copy of an existing theatre. Visitors can walk around, explore the building and the information that is offered. It includes a 3D embodied agent called Karin, who can answer questions about actual performances and their performers. Since she is accessible on WWW, people can use this system in order to get up-to-date information.

The second virtual world is the Gulliver environment. While the theatre environment has the aim of modelling multi-modal human–agent and agent–agent interaction in the context of non-entertainment situations (information services and transaction, teaching, collaborated work etc), the Gulliver project aims at creating an environment where visitors can get involved in performances and where the distinction between performers and audience disappears. While the theatre project has already investigated different kinds of interactions and serves the role of a laboratory for research, the Gulliver environment has only been modelled in virtual reality in a rudimentary way and now waits for performers and visitors to interact. For that reason many of our current activities are devoted to issues that deal with generating behaviour in virtual reality, with modelling of musicians based on music scores, and with modelling autonomous behaviour of embodied agents that have to interact with other virtual agents and human interactors.

The next section explains more about the origins of the Gulliver project. We discuss the theatre environment in the third section. The fourth section is on the state of the art of performances by virtual actors. Interesting issues are the possibility of having an actor's behaviour influenced by the behaviour of other players, the reaction of an audience (virtual or real) or, for example, a conductor trying to lead the performance. The last section presents some conclusions.

The Gulliver Project

The Gulliver project, by the artists Matjaž Štuk and Alena Hudcovicová, aims at building a variety of virtual and real objects that are connected through the Internet and that can be visited by the audience, both in reality and in virtual reality environments, preferably by using the World Wide Web. The project, as perceived by the artists, includes the realization of 'Gulliver's Travelling Museum of Living Art', an example of migrating architecture. It is a transportable building made out of light construction material, with transparent walls and designed as a human body that represents Gulliver, the hero of Swift's *Gulliver's Travels*, lying on his back

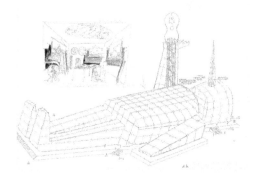

Figure 31.1   Design of the Travelling Gulliver

(Figure 31.1). It is a large construction; visitors can enter Gulliver, see expositions, go to a museum shop or a restaurant, interact with art installations etc. Gulliver's right arm is meant to be a panorama tower. The arm contains an elevator and stairs. On the hand's palm is a clockwork device with a carillon and with colours that change according to the time of the day.

Part of the museum is 'Gulliver's Kitchen' (Figure 31.2). This kitchen is meant to allow visitors to the museum to change the environment using multi-modal interaction. Visitors can use their own gestures or speech to change colour patterns on Gulliver's skin or to orchestrate the carillon in the palm of his right hand. It is assumed that the travelling museum has some counterparts. The main counterpart is a virtual Gulliver (Figure 31.3) that is accessible through the World Wide Web. Wherever the physical Gulliver appears it should draw the audience's attention to the virtual Gulliver. Moreover, the audience should be able to connect to the virtual Gulliver and experience what is going on there through the 'Kitchen'. In this paper the emphasis is on how we can use this environment, building on research in the

Figure 31.2   Design of the Kitchen

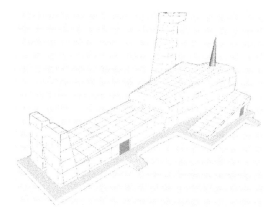

Figure 31.3   View of virtual Gulliver

Aveiro project and on projects performed by other research groups, to create performances by interacting autonomous agents and visitors.

The Aveiro Project

As mentioned, in our Aveiro project we work on interacting embodied agents in virtual environments. For that reason we built a laboratory-like environment representing a theatre in our hometown. In this virtual theatre we can find the usual locations: entrance hall, information desk, coffee stands, performance halls, stairs, lounges, stage etc. Users who access the WWW-page of the virtual theatre can visit the locations, explore the building etc. The environment contains books, posters, paintings etc., on which visitors can click to obtain more information, to hear music or to activate certain events. For example, clicking a poster will give more information about the performance displayed; clicking a TV screen activates a video preview of a performance. Using the mouse, simple melodies can be played on a virtual keyboard. In the environment a seating map is available on which a user can click to get transported to the corresponding chair in the main performance hall. On stage is a simply animated piano player and a slightly more advanced dancer that can perform baroque dances corresponding to music that is played. Standing behind an information desk is Karin, a 3D animated avatar that can enter into a dialogue with the visitors about performances and performers. Karin is in fact the interface between the visitor and a database containing information for the current season. Questions can be asked in natural language and Karin uses visual speech to articulate her answers. See Nijholt and Hulstijn for a survey of the virtual environment.[1]

In recent years various versions of this environment have been investigated. These versions included the introduction of other agents, such as a navigation agent, the introduction of speech access, the introduction of an agent platform and allowing multiple users to enter the environment using the Deep Matrix system.[2] Figure 31.4 displays a situation where a visitor represented by an embodied agent approaches the information desk. Experiments are going on in which Karin also displays natural gaze behaviour during her interaction with a visitor.

Figure 31.4   Embodied visitor meets domain agent Karin

Virtual and Augmented Reality Performances

In sophisticated systems that have become known as interactive theatre, interactive cinema or interactive story telling, multiple players connected by a network can take part in a performance as actors. The performers are represented as avatars in a virtual environment and, with motion-capture systems (cameras or sensors), avatar movements can be made to reflect player movements. Gestures, touch and facial expressions of the players can be tracked and given as input to the avatar's animation algorithms. With the help of speech technology the player's emotion and utterances can be interpreted. Plays can have branch points and due to the interactions particular branches can be chosen. The virtual stage may have actors that are provided by the theatre and that show some autonomous behaviour according to some action patterns. They have a role, but the way they perform this role is determined by interactions with the human player and his or her alter ego avatar. See Takahashi et al.[3] for a recent example of interactive theatre.

There are also several examples where the actors are musicians. In its most primitive form we have a band of virtual musicians just playing along. There is no variation and there is no interaction between the musicians or between the musicians and a possible audience. See Figure 31.5 for an example. More interesting are examples where we can provide the musicians with different scores and there is an automatic mapping from these scores to audio and corresponding animations. For example, see Figure 31.6, where a virtual drummer is displayed, animated from a midi-score that is provided as input.[4] In this project, performed at our research group, we are also experimenting with the possibility that drum movements of a human player are detected by sensors and transformed to animations of the virtual drummer. In September 2001 a concert was organized where we asked two student bands to replace their real drummer with the virtual drummer (see Figure 31.7). The audience was asked to wear 3D glasses (Figure 31.8).

There are several other projects worth mentioning. The Diva project allows a visitor, wearing a data dress suite, data gloves and a sensor-mounted baton, to conduct an ensemble of animated players holding different musical instruments.[5]

Figure 31.5   VRML band (by Dennis McKenzie, Geometrek)

Figure 31.6   Virtual drummer

Figure 31.7   Virtual drummer in concert

Figure 31.8   Audience during concert

The conductor can lead the tempo and direct the playing of particular instruments. Clearly, animations of musicians and instruments have to be done in real time, reading the movements from an animation file and synchronized with the music.

In the VirJa (Virtual Jazz Session System) project a virtual jazz piano trio is modelled (see Figure 31.9).[6] The aim of the project is to simulate the interaction between human players (using musical sounds and visual cues). The system enables virtual musicians to listen to other virtual and human players and to see each other's

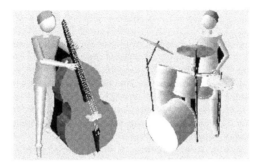

Figure 31.9   Jazz musicians in the VirJa project

bodies and gestures. Midi-data of each player's performance is received by the other players to react upon. The gestures of the human players are recognized by a real camera, those of the virtual players by a virtual camera. In Walker's study,[7] a model for musical improvisation is developed, based on conversational turn-taking, that allows the collaboration of different players using a shared platform.

Two other projects are the virtual piano player,[8] a project aimed at modelling the interaction between a virtual piano player and the virtual piano, and some projects on computer-animated opera singers or jazz musicians.[9]

Conclusions

In this paper we surveyed the developments in our projects on the design of virtual interest communities, the way people can represent themselves in these communities and how they can explore and interact, not only with each other, but also with community agents with task and domain knowledge. In particular we looked at the possibility of collaboration between visitors and domain agents. In particular we looked at the possibility of having joint performances of real and virtual musicians. Modelling autonomy in virtual actors is one of our main concerns in the near future.

Acknowledgments

Many people helped to design and realize the Gulliver and Aveiro projects and the (performing) agents that inhabit these worlds. Particular thanks go to Martijn Kragtwijk for his work on the virtual drummer, Eelco Herder and Wytze Hoogkamp who worked on the virtual Gulliver, and Job Zwiers for his attempts to coax everyone working on these projects to agree upon agent communication, agent modelling and (VRML and Java 3D) programming standards.

Notes

1   Nijholt, A. and Hulstijn, J., (2000) 'Multimodal interactions with agents in virtual worlds', in *Future Directions for Intelligent Information Systems and Information Science*, N. Kasabov (ed.), Physica-Verlag: *Studies in Fuzziness and Soft Computing*.

2   Reitmayr, G., et al. (1999) 'Deep matrix: An open technology-based virtual environment system', *The Visual Computer Journal*, vol. 15, pp. 395–412.

3   Takahashi, K., Kurumisawa, J. and Yotsukura, T. (2000) 'Networked theatre', *Proceedings of the First IEEE Pacific-Rim Conference on Multimedia*, December 2000, University of Sydney, Australia.

4   Kragtwijk, M., Nijholt, A. and Zwiers, J. (2001) 'Implementation of a 3D virtual drummer', in *Proceedings of CAS2001, Eurographics Workshop on Animation and Simulation 2001*, Manchester, UK, Springer, New York, M. Magnenat-Thalmann and D. Thalmann (eds), pp. 15–26.

5   Lokki, T., Savioja, L., Huopaniemi, J., Hänninen, R., Ilmonen, T., Hiipakka, J., Pulkki, V., Väänänen, R. and Takala, T. (1999) 'Virtual concerts in virtual spaces – in real time', Invited paper, Joint ASA/EAA Meeting, Berlin, Germany, 14th–19th March.

6   Goto, M., Hidaka, I., Matsumoto, H., KurodaY. and Muraoka, Y. (1996) 'A jazz system for interplay among all players', *Proceedings of the International Computer Music Conference 1996*, pp. 346–9.

7   Walker, W.F. (1994) 'A conversation-based framework for musical improvisation', Ph.D. thesis, University of Illinois at Urbana-Champaign.

8   Esmerado, J. (2001) 'A model of interaction between virtual humans and objects: Application to virtual musicians', Ph.D. thesis, EPFL-LIG, Lausanne.

9   Rowe, R., Singer, E.L. and Vila, D. (1996) 'A flock of words: Real-time animation and video controlled by algorithmic music analysis', in *Visual Proceedings, ACM SIGGRAPH 96*, New York.

PART 8
CONCLUSIONS AND
FUTURE TRENDS

Chapter 32

Conclusions and Future Trends

James Hemsley, Vito Cappellini and Gerd Stanke

Conclusions

In the early years of the new century the efforts of the previous twenty years in the culture and technology field may seem a bewildering set of diverse and unrelated initiatives. Nonetheless, from the collection of papers in this volume and from elsewhere, it is possible to discern a number of common threads in this colourful tapestry, many of which originated in the pioneering years in the 1980s which have been pursued and developed, despite setbacks. It is also possible to develop some conclusions regarding significant achievements and pointers to the future including both positive and negative ones. In general they complement and/or reinforce those from the DigiCULT roadmap.

We consider firstly some positive conclusions:

1. An increasingly firm and widely held belief – tempered by greater realism – in the medium to long-term potential, especially for users, of culture and technology as indicated in the paper by Mulrenin. The ready availability now of massive cultural databases on the Web is but one example.
2. The emphasis on the benefits for the scientific and technology R&D community itself from engagement with the cultural sector as regards helping to drive technology – not just in the application of technology developed in response to other drivers such as the military sector.
3. The increasing proportion of the cultural world engaging with new imaging and other technologies, having moved from an almost exclusive focus on 'flat art' in the 1980s to a wide view across almost the whole cultural spectrum – from the visual to the performing arts and from archaeology and architecture to history and societal issues such as 'virtual worlds', including socio-cultural issues.[1]
4. The number and balance of senses being used, with touch now emerging in a significant manner (as shown in Brewster's paper) and multi-sensor systems being employed in museum system design (as reported by Mecocchi). Although the image-processing part of the brain is the largest and most powerful, increasing attention now being given to the other senses in more complete 'multimedia' systems than those of the 1980s and 1990s.
5. The remarkable international spread of activities of the global 'culture and technology' community, as indicated but certainly not fully reflected in this work. The example of Russia, as reported by Brakker and Kujbyshev, shows

how this important country has made significant relative progress in the 1990s, as also shown for other countries such as Italy and Scotland. This offers substantial grounds for optimism as regards those countries and regions still lagging in the field.

6.   The growing realization that organizational size is no insurmountable barrier to use of ICT: across most of Europe, North America, Russia, Japan and other parts of the world this is now well recognized. For example, in the ORION study on archaeology museums and 3D a surprising survey finding was that a high proportion of small museums are using IT for research.[2] Thanks to the Web in particular, research is no longer the prerogative of the large museums and libraries.

7.   A growing emphasis on the needs of the disabled – as an integrated element in 'Design for All' – which received an extra push in the European Union in 2003, the 'European Year of the Disabled'. This is clearly shown by the authors of the papers in this section of the book, reflecting the general movement towards raising the quality of life for the disabled. This places the use of technology to improve access to and enjoyment of cultural heritage as an important step up the Maslow triangle towards self-actualization.

However, before we indulge in too much congratulatory text on the achievements in this relatively short time-span of less than twenty years, it is also important to consider some of the false dawns and dashed hopes during this initial period, due to 'rose-coloured spectacles' and excessive optimism, as well as the challenges ahead. Some of the less than satisfactory aspects compared with optimistic expectations in the early 1990s – and in certain cases raised to absurd heights during the 'dotcom bubble' – may be seen as follows:

1.   There has been no vast revenue stream flowing to the cultural sector from the digitization of its assets and, as Mulrenin in the book's first paper points out, this is unlikely to happen even in the medium term in Europe.

2.   There have similarly been no great financial rewards to businesses trying to capitalize on these assets. There is also a lack of successful business models.

3.   Take-up and application in certain areas expected initially to be prime candidates for successful cultural technology use (such as university art history departments) have been well below early expectations, the barriers not being primarily technological but rather organizational, human factors, copyright and of course financial ones. At the time of writing the more recent initiatives such as Prometheus offer hope that the early expectations are coming closer to achievement. Also there is at the time of writing a great surge of interest in e-learning and progress now is once again hoped to be significant and rapid, building on major digitization and system investments; for example, the Curriculum On Line programme of £500 million for England and Wales and many other major programmes across Europe and internationally. However, judging from the past, there are grounds for caution.

4.   The 'cultural technology' industry itself is still greatly fragmented and restricted mainly to national markets, with some exceptions, mainly large US and Japanese companies. Lamentably, major pan-European commercial activities have not yet proved successful, but the efforts will doubtless continue.

5. Multilingual access problems are still a major problem area, and it is here that Europe in particular could take a leading role, impelled by the challenges of the increasing size and linguistic variety of the expanded multilingual European Union, although with only a small part of the world's 6,000 languages. Language learning could also be helped more by using the combination of culture and technology.
6. Sizeable areas of the world are still not benefiting sufficiently from 'culture and technology' to a significant extent, including even parts of the 'developed world'. This is particularly so for disadvantaged sectors of the community, including the disabled (despite the efforts reported in this book which need multiplication, not just addition), minorities and the aged.
7. There is still a gap between the 'creative artists' and the 'cultural heritage' communities as regards the use of the new technologies.

This list could easily be extended and there is therefore no justification for complacency by activists in 'culture and technology' and certainly there are many challenges, which also constitute opportunities to 'push' technology R&D from a user-oriented point of view, for example in the 3D field.

Future Trends

The only forecasts which may be regarded as 'safe' are generally held to be limited to the following types:

●   demographics – barring 'doomsday' developments
●   the continuation of change, in technology, tastes, markets etc, but without being able to predict the precise changes.

In trying to look ahead twenty years and beyond, it is nonetheless helpful to consider the perspective of the changes in the last twenty years and before, including as regards technology progress.

Firstly as regards demographics, it is increasingly well recognized – with the caveat that major natural disasters, war, mass epidemic disease and other catastrophes, or a totally unexpected dramatic rise in birth-rates are excluded – that most of the industrial world (including also much of China) will continue to move even further along the 'ageing society' curve, so noticeable already in Japan and parts of Europe, due to a combination of low birth-rates and increasing longevity. By 2020, those born in the 1980s, the children of the 'First Culture and Technology Age', will be in key positions and have grown up familiar with computer technologies. Many of the future 'Silver Generation' of the over-50s in much of the world also will have enjoyed the trials and tribulations of technology-dominated life: they will also have enjoyed the benefits, including (we hope) untrammelled access to cultural heritage by and of the entire world reflecting the shift away from the view of the last century in particular that focused almost exclusively on Europe and North America. The new 'Silver Generation' will be by then the most numerous segment of the population and the young will thus be even more precious than now.

The whole nature of society and work will be continue to change dramatically, with pension rights after 30–35 years of work just a distant memory – except for the very old – the 'pension time bomb' having exploded by then. In particular, even a greatly expanded European Union, including countries such as Ukraine, may well account for a smaller proportion than now of the world's population, with countries such as Germany, Italy and Spain currently expected to experience particularly dramatic population downsizing unless there is massive immigration. There will correspondingly be a much more important role for China, India, Latin America and Africa – if this latter area can emerge victorious from the battle with AIDS in particular. These demographics-driven changes plus other societal factors, such as the continuing rise of the role of women in society, are likely to be the dominating features in the 2020s. Looking back on the remarkable changes just in the last twenty years, against a backdrop of the whole of the 20th century and before, it is reasonable to expect significant such changes – and even greater ones if 'disaster scenarios' unfortunately occur.

The second key factor we consider here is technology change. There is a strong view that technological changes tend to occur in long 'Kondratieff Waves' of some 50 years or so in duration,[3] based on consideration of the history of major technology waves such as those associated with the industrial revolution and subsequently. According to this theory the current electronics-based wave of technology development and consequent economic expansion is now in its final phases. In this view the hopes for renewed vitality from the biological sciences or other drivers is unfortunately not to be realized for some time and that, in any case, the hopes for continuing dramatic changes in the next twenty years in information and communications technologies (ICT) will prove unfounded. As regards 'cultural technology' and its siblings such as learning technology, the implications of this view for users are not necessarily all negative, since for example the difficulties and costs of rapid systems obsolescence will be much reduced. Moreover, the ICT R&D community will be anxious to use additional drivers (including the cultural sector) to squeeze out the remaining opportunities for further progress. Delivery of actual operational results in a more cost-effective, stable and sustainable manner will be an increasing priority. However, even in this view there will not be an absence of technological change in the next two decades, with such innovations as ubiquitous and personalized systems as well as 'real 3D' systems for computers and digital television. The latter are confidently expected to appear in a major way as the remaining technical problems are solved and costs are driven down from the current (mid-2003) $10,000 for a 'real 3D screen' to a targeted few $100 before 2010. Such an emphasis on cost targeting is also noticeable in the cultural sector for which the European Commission Cultural Heritage Unit set targets in early 2003 for its future funded projects in the Sixth Framework Information Society Technology (IST) Programme to help in reducing digitization costs by 50% over the following five years.[4]

Contrasted with this view, based on 'Kondratieff's Law' (which is an empirical hypothesis rather than a well-demonstrated law of physics), is that of the technology optimists. Their approach is sometimes presented as one of 'an accelerating pace of change'; for example, by picturing the last 3,000 years in an hour on a clock face, so that each minute represents fifty years and each second just over a year.[5] This would then suggest the durations of each medium as shown in Figure 32.1.

Medium	Time
Writing	1 hour
Printing press	9 minutes
Radio	80 seconds
Television	60 seconds
Audio and videocassettes	22 seconds
PC	18 seconds
Games consoles	12 seconds
Internet	7 seconds

Figure 32.1　Duration (to date) of various media

This form of representation is used to demonstrate an inexorable speeding up of the rate of technological change, the eventual projected result however being somewhat unlikely if one considers the mathematics.

It may well be that the 2020s will be in an intermediate position between innovation slow-down and acceleration – time will tell, of course. In the closer future within the timescale of the next ten years (that is, the Sixth and Seventh EC Framework Programmes, 2003–2006 and 2006–2010, it seems more than likely that there will be a reasonably strong continued flow of ICT innovation, despite regular expressions of concern that Moore's law is about to be no longer valid.[6]

In any case, whether the pace of technological change continues to speed up, slows down somewhat or stays at its present high level, the set of papers in this book indicate that there will be an exciting time ahead in both the application of technology to the cultural sector – and the use of culture-centred problems by scientists and technology R&D specialists to push the technology – with benefits for the whole of human society. Future historians of science, technology and culture will, we hope, judge this period of the late 20th and early 21st centuries to be of interest for the type of efforts reported on in this book.

Ask not only what Technology can do for Culture, but also what Culture can do for Technology.

Dominique Gonthier, European Commission, circa 1995

If we knew what we were doing, it wouldn't be called research – Albert Einstein
Notice in Institute of Archaeology, University College London, 2003

Notes

1　de Bruin, J. (2003) 'Virtual worlds and an inhabited virtual worlds movement', *EVA 2003 London Proceedings*, ECI, London.
2　Clarke, D., Hemsley, J., Kaayk, M. and Spearman, M. (2003) 'Archaeology museums and 3D in the 21st century', *EVA 2003 Florence Proceedings*, Pitagora Editrice, Bologna.

3   Kondatrieff, N. D. (1926) 'Die langen Wellen der Konjunktur', *Archiv für Sozialwissenschaft und Sozialpolitik*, vol. 56, pp. 573–609. There are considerable materials available on the Web (including on the next upturn) which are readily available via Google.

4   Smith, Bernard (2003) 'Activities and research for cultural heritage in the European Union', *EVA 2003 Moscow, Proceedings*, see http://evarussia.ru/eva2003/english/index.html.

5   Little, R. (2003) 'E-learning earns its wings', *E.learning Age*, September, Bizmedia, Reading, UK.

6   Schaller, R. 'The origin, nature, and implications of Moore's Law: The benchmark of progress in semiconductor electronics' can be accessed at http://mason.gmu.edu/~rschalle/moorelaw.html.

Index

Milton Keynes UK
Ingram Content Group UK Ltd.
UKHW031128141024
449569UK00006B/362